Pennsylvania

Douglas Root
Photography by Jerry Irwin

COMPASS AMERICAN GUIDES
An imprint of Fodor's Travel Publications

Compass American Guides: Pennsylvania

Editors: Chris Culwell, Kristin Moehlmann
Compass Editorial Director: Daniel Mangin
Designer: Tina Malaney
Photo Editor: Jolie Novak
Archival Research: Melanie Marin
Editorial Production: Tom Holton
Map Design: Mark Stroud, Moon Street Cartography

Cover photo, Jerry Irwin: Country road near Sugar Grove

Second Edition
Copyright © 2003 Fodors LLC
Maps copyright © 2003 Fodors LLC

ISBN 0-676-90141-7
ISSN 1543–1665

The content of this book is based on information supplied to us at press time, but changes occur all the time, and the publisher cannot accept responsibility for facts that become outdated or for inadvertent errors or omissions.

Compass American Guides, 1745 Broadway, New York, NY 10019
PRINTED IN SINGAPORE

10 9 8 7 6 5 4 3 2 1

To my two grandmothers, Helen and Esther, who dearly loved their husbands and children but dreamed of traveling the world.

C O N T E N T S

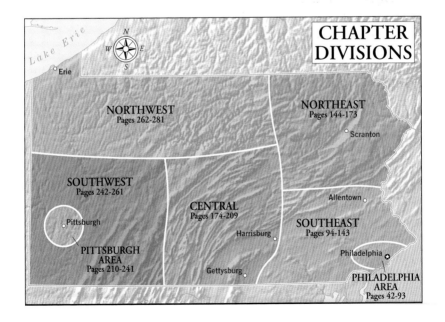

CHAPTER DIVISIONS

Lake Erie

Erie

NORTHWEST
Pages 262-281

NORTHEAST
Pages 144-173

Scranton

SOUTHWEST
Pages 242-261

Pittsburgh

CENTRAL
Pages 174-209

Allentown

SOUTHEAST
Pages 94-143

Harrisburg

PITTSBURGH
AREA
Pages 210-241

Gettysburg

Philadelphia

PHILADELPHIA
AREA
Pages 42-93

Topical Essays and Sidebars

Literary Extracts

Maps

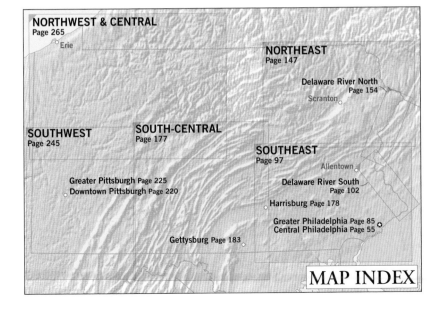

MAP INDEX

AVERAGE JANUARY TEMPERATURES

Celsius	Fahrenheit
-1.1	30
-2.2	28
-3.3	26
-4.4	24

AVERAGE JULY TEMPERATURES

Celsius	Fahrenheit
23.3	74
22.2	72
21.1	70
20.0	68

NEW YORK

Lake Erie

North East

Erie

Avonia

Lake City

Jamestown

Olean

Waterford

Albion

Union City

Warren

Pittsfield

Bradford

Allegheny Reservoir

Smethport

Port Allegany

Coudersp

Cambridge Springs

Sheffield

Kane

Lantz Corners

Pymatuning Reservoir

Conneaut Lake

Meadville

Titusville

Tidioute

Emporium

Kettle Creek State Park

Jamestown

Greenville

Oil City

Franklin

Tionesta

Ridgeway

St Marys

Driftwood

Shenango River Lake

Mercer

Shippenville

Clarion

Brockway

OHIO

Slippery Rock

Brookville

Mayport

Reynoldsville

Du Bois

Clearfield

Bellefonte

New Castle

New Bethlehem

Philipsburg

Butler

Punxsutawney

Port Matilda

State College

Kittanning

Rochester

Home

Freeport

Tarentum

Indiana

Barnesboro

Ambridge

Pittsburgh

Murrysville

Blairsville

Edensburg

Altoona

Huntingdon

Carnegie

Paris

Greendburg

Latrobe

Johnstown

Mt

Washington

Scenery Hill

Ligonier

Jennerstown

Kanter

Bedford

Shad

Brownsville

Youghiogheny

Chamber

Waynesburg

Uniontown

Berlin

Farmington

Mt Davis 3,213
(highest point in Pennsylvania)

Garrett

Meyersdale

Mercersburg

WEST VIRGINIA

MARYLAND

WV

N W E S

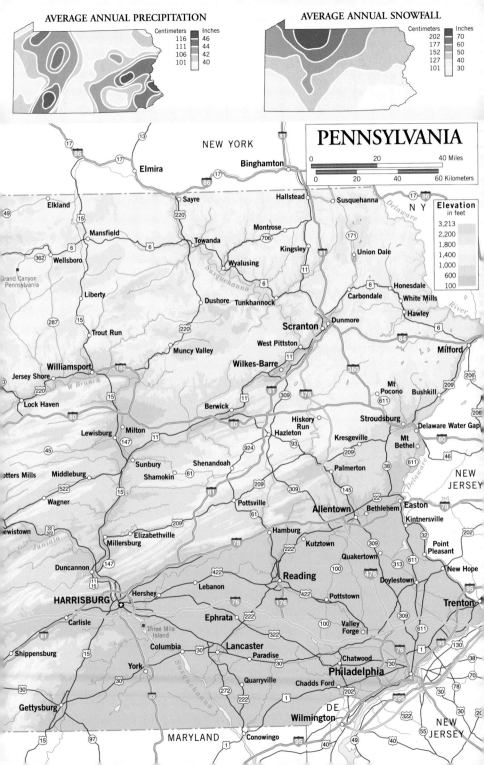

AVERAGE ANNUAL PRECIPITATION

Centimeters	Inches
116	46
111	44
106	42
101	40

AVERAGE ANNUAL SNOWFALL

Centimeters	Inches
202	70
177	60
152	50
127	40
101	30

PENNSYLVANIA

0   20   40 Miles
0   20   40   60 Kilometers

Elevation in feet

| 3,213 |
| 2,200 |
| 1,800 |
| 1,400 |
| 1,000 |
| 600 |
| 100 |

NEW YORK

Binghamton
Elmira
Elkland
Sayre
Hallstead
Susquehanna
N Y
Mansfield
Towanda
Montrose
Kingsley
Union Dale
Wellsboro
Wyalusing
Honesdale
Liberty
Dushore
Tunkhannock
Carbondale
White Mills
Hawley
Trout Run
Muncy Valley
Scranton
Dunmore
Milford
Grand Canyon Pennsylvania
Williamsport
West Pittston
Wilkes-Barre
Mt Pocono
Bushkill
Jersey Shore
W Branch
Lock Haven
Berwick
Stroudsburg
Delaware Water Gap
Lewisburg
Milton
Hiskory Run
Hazleton
Kresgeville
Mt Bethel
NEW JERSEY
Middleburg
Sunbury
Shenandoah
Palmerton
Wagner
Shamokin
Pottsville
Easton
Kintnersville
Elizabethville
Millersburg
Hamburg
Allentown
Bethlehem
Duncannon
Kutztown
Point Pleasant
Quakertown
New Hope
Reading
Doylestown
HARRISBURG
Hershey
Lebanon
Pottstown
Trenton
Carlisle
Valley Forge
Ephrata
Shippensburg
Columbia
Lancaster
Paradise
Chatwood
Philadelphia
York
Quarryville
Chadds Ford
Gettysburg
DE
Wilmington
NEW JERSEY
MARYLAND
Conowingo

PENNSYLVANIA FACTS

THE KEYSTONE STATE

Capital: Harrisburg

State motto: Virtue, liberty, and independence

State flower: Mountain laurel

State tree: Eastern hemlock

State bird: Ruffed grouse

State song: "Pennsylvania," lyrics by Eddie Khoury, music by Ronnie Bonner

Entered Union: December 12, 1787 (second state to do so). The state is named after Admiral William Penn, the father of William Penn, the state's founder.

Counties: 67

Bridges: 57,000

State Highways: 44,000 miles

■ POPULATION: 12,281,054 (2000)

FIVE LARGEST CITIES

Philadelphia:	1,517,550
Pittsburgh:	334,563
Erie:	103,717
Allentown:	106,632
Scranton:	73,345

■ GEOGRAPHY AND CLIMATE

Area: 45,888 square miles

Highest Point: Mount Davis, 3,213 feet above sea level

Lowest Point: Delaware River, at sea level

Highest recorded temperature: 111 degrees on July 10, 1936, at Phoenixville

Lowest recorded temperature: –42 degrees on January 5, 1904, at Smethport

■ INTERESTING FACTS

- The Port of Pittsburgh is the largest inland port in the United States.

- The median age in Pennsylvania is 35.

- Pennsylvania has the 17th-largest economy in the world, just after Mexico and before Switzerland.

- In 2001, more than 187,000 Pennsylvania workers had high-tech jobs.

A Hershey's Kiss streetlight.

- Pennsylvania was the first state to establish a library, zoo, or a pharmacy, build a turnpike, or broadcast a radio or television program.

- About one-third of the state's residents live in rural areas.

- Pennsylvania has more covered bridges and pretzel bakeries than any other state and is home to Hershey Foods, the nation's largest candymaker.

■ FAMOUS PENNSYLVANIANS

Louisa May Alcott, author ■ John James Audubon, naturalist ■ Samuel Barber, composer ■ Daniel Boone, frontiersman ■ James Buchanan, U.S. president ■ Alexander Calder, sculptor ■ Rachel Carson, author ■ Mary Cassatt, painter ■ Bill Cosby, actor ■ W.C. Fields, comedian ■ Milton Hershey, chocolatier ■ Lee Iacocca, auto executive ■ Robinson Jeffers, poet ■ Gene Kelly, dancer, actor ■ Grace Kelly, actress and princess ■ George C. Marshall, World War II general ■ Margaret Mead, anthropologist ■ George Meade, Civil War general ■ Andrew Mellon, financier ■ James Michener, author ■ Joe Montana, athlete ■ Arnold Palmer, golfer ■ Robert Peary, explorer ■ Man Ray, photographer ■ Fred Rogers, TV host ■ Jimmy Stewart, actor ■ Jim Thorpe, athlete ■ John Updike, author ■ Andy Warhol, artist ■ August Wilson, playwright ■ Andrew Wyeth, painter.

CULTURE & HISTORY

[Pennsylvania] is a clear and just thing, and my God that has given it me through many difficulties, will, I believe, bless and make it the seed of a nation. I shall have a tender care for the government, that it be well laid at first…. I purpose that which is extraordinary and to leave myself and successors no power of doing mischief, that the will of one man may not hinder the good of an whole country.

—William Penn's letter to a friend in 1681

■ LANDSCAPE AND EARLY HISTORY

Long before the King of England bequeathed Pennsylvania to the good-hearted English aristocrat William Penn, its lands had been home to tribal nations that reaped the bounty of its forested mountains, rushing rivers, and fine valleys. When the first European explorers arrived in Pennsylvania in the early 17th century, they found the peaceful Lenni Lenape tribe, the Susquehannocks, and the Eries. These tribes were by that time vassals to the powerful and warlike Five Nations of Iroquois, which had expanded from what is now New York during the previous century. Weakened by war, Pennsylvania's tribes had lost most of their population to measles and smallpox, diseases that had made their way inland from European coastal settlements during the previous half-century. Despite the terrible difficulties of the Indian, writes Sylvester Stevens in *Pennsylvania, Birthplace of a Nation*:

> He was living in an advanced Stone Age culture, which included settled life in villages and farming. He was making pottery vessels for his cooking and for the storage of food…even decorating his pottery in the later years of this era….He was growing corn, along with tobacco. He lived in semipermanent bark houses and they were grouped into villages…Penn described those [native people] he saw as "generally tall, straight, well built, and of singular proportion; they tread strong and clever, and mostly walk with a lofty chin."…In councils he found them very well able to conceal their true feelings in a certain impassive attitude…. He noted their "Liberality" and that "Nothing is too good for their friend."

Performers reenact the first reading of the Declaration of Independence.

Swedish and Finnish explorers began a fur and tobacco trade with the Indians and by the middle of the 17th century had established a few scattered forts—near New Castle in the southwest and around Wilmington, Chester, and Philadelphia in the southeast. However, Dutch settlers in New Amsterdam (now New York City), who feared their lucrative trade with the Iroquois would be siphoned off at the source, weren't pleased. Their soldiers marched on the settlements and, with little resistance, won control.

The Dutch made a half-hearted effort to colonize the territory, changing the name of the Scandinavian fort near New Castle to New Amstel, and resettling other areas. But in 1664, the Dutch were driven out when the English dispatched hundreds of troops to claim the territory.

Native American Man of the Northeast Woodlands *(ca. 1820),* artist unknown. *(Philadelphia Museum of Art)*

■ ENGLISH SETTLEMENT

By the 1680s, British control had thrown the territory wide open to European colonists—ragtaggers of every sort, some from Great Britain, some from Germany fleeing wars in the Rhineland. Most newcomers favored the lower Delaware River area and its nearby countryside, but there was no plan to the settlements and the territory was sorely in need of a strong governor.

Into this unsettled landscape came the aristocratic English idealist William Penn, granted title to Pennsylvania by Charles II of England. Penn was a Quaker, a follower of theologian and Society of Friends founder George Fox, who preached that individuals have a direct relationship with God and did not need the priests or ministers of religious institutions to mediate their faith. Civil hierarchies were similarly discredited: Fox's followers did not recognize titles, to the consternation of the titled British, nor would they take oaths. Religious persecution took the form of civil prosecution: William Penn himself was imprisoned four times, once for refusing to swear allegiance to the crown.

Charles II's gift to William Penn can be seen as a brilliant solution to an intractable problem. Penn's beliefs, along with his status, eloquence, and charm, made him a disruptive force in England. His father, Admiral William Penn, had been a distinguished naval officer, the holder of various government posts, a wealthy landowner, and, most importantly, the king's friend and creditor. After Admiral Penn died, his son requested and accepted the land in payment of the king's debt.

The only land available to Penn was territory inland from the coveted North American seacoast, though what England's rulers considered undesirable hinterland would quickly turn out to be one of the richest and the most strategically located of all the new American colonies. The difficult young aristocrat, who arrived in his new territory in 1682, stayed only two years before he sailed home again.

■ TOLERANT, WELL-GOVERNED SOCIETY

Penn's Quaker faith informed his new passion, the planning of government and the laying out of cities in the new colony. When Penn arrived to enact his vision of a free and tolerant society, about a thousand Europeans were living near the Delaware River, many of whom had risked everything for an opportunity to make their fortunes unfettered by government interference. They awaited the first address of their new lord with apprehension. Penn's public proclamation to these people, written in Quaker style, began as follows:

Dear Friends,
You are now fixed at the mercy of no governor who comes to make
his fortune great. You shall be governed by laws of your own making,
and live a free, and if you will, a sober and industrious people.

For the populace, it was as if the King of England himself had removed his crown and thrown it into the crowd. Penn's beliefs pleased the people of his new colony, although it wouldn't be long before some of his "citizen friends" took advantage of their governor's haphazard way of surveying land.

Although William Penn lacked business acumen, he made up for it in his promotion of his colony to immigrants and investors and in his "urban planning." He took advantage of some of the progressive thinking of the time, including the

In the 1840s, sign painter Edward Hicks painted several idealized versions of Penn's treaty with the Indians, including the one shown here. (Shelburne Museum)

notion that cities and towns be located to serve as trading and supply centers for farming areas. For Philadelphia, the capital of the new colony and, eventually, the de facto capital of all the American colonies, Penn envisioned a "greene Countrie Towne" of straight, wide streets, with orchards and gardens interspersed with buildings. Although the vision only partly materialized, it served to inspire the planning of hundreds of other cities in the new nation.

By the time of his death in 1718, the most important legacy Penn had left to his province was a genuinely tolerant and self-governing democracy—an extraordinary legacy in a world ruled by autocrats.

Penn's sons, less idealistic than their father, hoped to profit from the sale of land he had promised to the Indians, and they promoted Philadelphia in European newspapers and journals as the best place to set up a business in the colonies. Penn's middle son, Thomas, even advertised in the *English Bristol Journal* that any craftsman willing to "go over to the most flourishing city of Philadelphia" would be given a new suit of clothes.

■ PROSPERITY AND TAXES: RECIPE FOR A REVOLUTION

In 1700, Philadelphia's population was about 6,000 and that of the outlying territory totaled 20,000. By the beginning of the Revolutionary War, 75 years later, Pennsylvania's population was estimated at 300,000. Most of the new settlers came as indentured workers, obliged to work off their ship passage and supply costs to businessmen in Great Britain and other parts of Europe. Promotional advertising by the Penn family and letters from settlers back to family and friends were well timed. Opportunity abounded in the brisk trade with the West Indies, especially in the grain, meat, and lumber that Pennsylvania possessed in abundance. As treaties with the Indians were broken and settlements spread inland, the city became a point of internal transshipment for produce and animal furs.

A powerful, literate, and worldly merchant class—most of them Quaker—soon emerged in Philadelphia. It was the taxes these wealthy men paid that made possible the military adventures of the British Empire, such as the French and Indian War. The merchant classes were furious at the taxes levied upon them to support these campaigns, and eventually they would use their wealth to finance the Continental Army in the War of Independence.

One of the most prosperous of these early businessmen was Robert Morris, in whose house on High (Market) Street, below Sixth Street, George Washington

WILLIAM PENN: THE FOUNDER

William Penn (1644–1718) had made every effort to correct England's ills before he decided to start from scratch in the New World. He had preached and protested. He had railed against the excess and luxury of the church. He had refused to take off his hat or swear allegiance to the crown, and he had championed human rights. He had written tracts with titles like "No Cross, No Crown" and "The Great Case of Liberty of Conscience." He had defended not only his right to practice his Quaker faith, but also the right of all citizens to follow their own beliefs. But in England, he had not been persuasive enough to bring about the changes he sought.

Penn had another reason for founding his colony. His father died in 1670, leaving him an uncollectible debt from King Charles II. The Crown was land-rich and cash-poor, a condition Penn himself would one day know all too well. He took Pennsylvania in payment.

The new colony was vast, making Penn the largest landholder in the kingdom aside from the king. Penn owned the lands outright with "free, full and absolute power." Remarkably, he did not take advantage of his power but instead wrote liberal charters, allowing more and more representative government. He and his Council proposed laws that were then approved by the Assembly.

He did not grow rich. The people who ran the colony were far more conscientious about billing him for their salaries than they were about collecting rents for him. His land did not bring him wealth but cost him an estimated 75,000 pounds. His trusted Quaker agent in London defrauded him, and a debt owed to the agent's widow landed Penn in prison for several months. Finally, insolvent and in despair, Penn made plans to return the colony to the Crown, but he suffered a stroke before he could sign the transfer documents.

Penn wrote prolifically on religious, philosophical, and political subjects. In Pennsylvania, he thought he could put some of his most cherished ideas to the test. That they did not entirely succeed is not the fault of his plan of government. As he himself wrote, "Governments, like clocks, go from the motion men give them; and as governments are made and moved by men, so by them are they ruined too."

Penn made only two visits to his colony, the first from 1682 to 1684, and the second from 1699 to 1701. One of Penn's unrealized dreams was that colonists and Indians would live side by side in harmony. In the words of one historian, "He seems to have been one of the few genuine Christians Christianity has ever produced."

Pennsylvania's founder, the idealist-aristocrat William Penn, at the age of 22.
(Atwater Kent Museum, Historical Society of Pennsylvania Collection)

would live as president from 1790 to 1797. At the time of the American Revolution, Robert Morris was reluctant to break with England, but he finally gave in and raised the money necessary for George Washington to move his army to Yorktown in 1781.

The most famous of Philadelphia's businessman-politicians was Benjamin Franklin, who at age 17 had arrived from Boston and, at 23, had established his own newspaper, the *Pennsylvania Gazette*. He pursued elective and appointive offices, including that of deputy postmaster general of Philadelphia. In his role as postmaster, Franklin introduced the novel idea that the postal service pay for mail too long delayed. And, like Robert Morris, he believed that disagreements with England over taxes could be resolved, and as a colonial agent in London, he attempted to negotiate solutions.

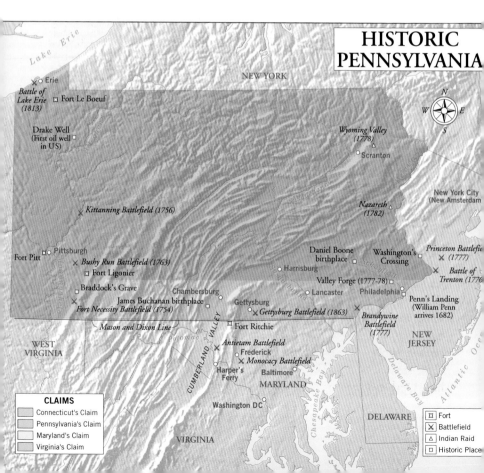

HISTORIC PENNSYLVANIA

Lake Erie

NEW YORK

Erie
Battle of Lake Erie (1813) □ Fort Le Boeuf

Drake Well (First oil well □ in US)

Wyoming Valley (1778) △
○ Scranton

New York City (New Amsterdam)

Kittanning Battlefield (1756)

Nazareth △ (1782)

Fort Pitt □○ Pittsburgh
× Bushy Run Battlefield (1763)
□ Fort Ligonier
Braddock's Grave
× Fort Necessity Battlefield (1754)

Daniel Boone birthplace □
○ Harrisburg
Valley Forge (1777-78) □
Chambersburg
James Buchanan birthplace □
Gettysburg
× Gettysburg Battlefield (1863) ×
○ Lancaster
Philadelphia □
Washington's Crossing □
Princeton Battlefield × (1777)
× Battle of Trenton (1776)
Penn's Landing (William Penn arrives 1682)
Brandywine Battlefield (1777)

NEW JERSEY

Mason and Dixon Line
Potomac
CUMBERLAND VALLEY
Fort Ritchie
× Antietam Battlefield
○ Frederick
× Monocacy Battlefield
Harper's Ferry
Baltimore ○
MARYLAND

WEST VIRGINIA

Washington DC ○

VIRGINIA

Chesapeake Bay

DELAWARE

Delaware Bay

Atlantic Ocean

CLAIMS
☐ Connecticut's Claim
☐ Pennsylvania's Claim
☐ Maryland's Claim
☐ Virginia's Claim

□ Fort
× Battlefield
△ Indian Raid
□ Historic Place

Second Street North from Market *(ca. 1799), by William Birch. Christ Church is visible in the center of Birch's painting, which depicts a bustling and orderly Philadelphia. (Free Library of Philadelphia)*

■ DISSENTERS, SEEKERS, AND PLAIN PEOPLE

The liberal and tolerant principles of William Penn's government did not go unnoticed in Europe, with the result that Pennsylvania attracted a steady flow of immigrants. Some were dissenters desiring religious freedom; some were from the lower classes wanting economic opportunity. In Pennsylvania, they had heard, a person might easily accumulate enough land to be able to vote and even become an elected official. There was no compulsory military service, and civil liberties were guaranteed, even to native peoples.

Between 1680 and 1710, most settlers who followed William Penn were, like him, Quakers from England, Wales, and Germany. Their numbers and wealth

PATCHWORK OF FAITHS

William Penn's Quaker faith persuaded him to form a colony where all could worship freely, not just the Quakers. He succeeded. A visitor to Penn's colony reported finding "Lutherans, Reformed, Catholics, Quakers, Menninists or Anabaptists, Herrnhuters or Moravian Brethren, Pietists, Seventh-Day Baptists, Dunkers.... In one house and one family four, five and even six sects may be found. . . ."

Quakers

In England, these followers of the theologian George Fox had been persecuted because they believed in neither churches nor creeds but in the "inward light" by which they could sense God's presence. At meetings they meditated silently or testified to their faith. To this day, they practice tolerance and pacifism and demonstrate simplicity and honesty by adopting plain dress and manners.

Mennonites

Mennonites, who emerged in Europe well before the Society of Friends was founded by George Fox in 1650, first reached Pennsylvania in 1683. Mennonites were Anabaptists, believers in baptism only for those who have chosen the faith. They sought to live separately from the rest of society, but in time showed a willingness to mingle in the non-Mennonite world, where their social concerns have led them into the helping professions and even politics.

Amish

Jakob Ammann was a Mennonite leader who preached that church members who had left the fold should be shunned. After he and his followers broke away from the Mennonites in 1693, they became known as the Amish. Like the Mennonites, the Amish are Anabaptists and pacifists, but they have remained more strictly apart from the world, true to their chief tenet: "Be ye not conformed to the world." Whether to enforce their separation from society or to demonstrate it, they maintain an archaic style of dress and speech and avoid the use of cars, telephones, and electric lights.

Moravians

Predating the Reformation, the Moravian Church is an outgrowth of the teachings of John Hus, a heretical Catholic priest from Prague burned at the stake in 1415. The church was founded in Bohemia in 1457 and claims to be the oldest organized Protestant church. It was nearly wiped out after the Thirty Years War and was renewed by Count Nicholas Von Zinzendorf of Saxony in 1722. The influence of German Pietism, which sought a more personal, less intellectual faith than that prevailing at the time, shows in the Moravian love feast and in the church's strong missionary tradition.

*Mennonite girls
waiting to enter
school in Hinkletown,
1942.
(Library of Congress)*

made them the dominant force in the Pennsylvania Assembly until 1756, when their pacifism lost them the support of frontier settlers who wanted armed protection against Indians.

Along with the Quakers came the first of the Germans from the Rhineland, beginning with Francis Daniel Pastorius, the Mennonite founder of Germantown, now a part of Philadelphia. The early German settlers were mostly members of smaller religious sects who settled as groups—Mennonites, Amish, Dunkers (German Baptists), German Quakers, and Moravians—though sometimes the immigrants converted from one religion to another after their arrival. Pastorius, for instance, left Germany as a Mennonite but converted to Quakerism after meeting William Penn.

After 1727, German immigrants were mostly members of the larger Lutheran and Reformed churches. With their farming methods, they transformed the region they settled into a rich agricultural area. By the time of the American Revolution, the Germans numbered about 100,000, more than a third of Pennsylvania's population. German farmers provided food for the Revolutionary Army and German craftsmen made the legendary "Pennsylvania long rifle," used by George

This 1757 engraving depicts Bethlehem, a communal religious settlement about 50 miles north-west of Philadelphia that eventually became an industrial city. (New York Public Library)

Washington's soldiers in many battles. The Germans' skill in the decorative arts added to the beauty of the area, now known as "Dutch" country, a derivation of the German word *Deutsch* ("German").

Between 1717 and 1776, about 250,000 Scots-Irish emigrated from Ulster to America. These were Presbyterians whom the English had moved into northern Ireland to thwart the Catholic Irish, but the economic hardship they faced was so severe that many signed on as indentured servants to pay their way to Pennsylvania. At first they settled in the Dutch country, farming without much success. From 1730 on, they led the movement west and north, to the frontiers. The Scots-Irish were a stern and self-sufficient group, too independent to settle into the agrarian communities envisioned by Penn but devoted to education and to the founding of schools. Eventually they became leaders in the revolutionary movement.

■ WESTWARD EXPANSION

Settlement was far from orderly. William Penn had envisioned a land of townships of 5,000 acres, each consisting of farms and a central village. Lands were offered to "first purchasers" in England at a uniform price, to be resold as farms, with 10 percent retained by the proprietors as manors. That plan was undermined after a decade or two by speculation on the part of the proprietors, by additional purchases from Indian tribes, and by the refusal of settlers to live in villages.

Until 1730, most expansion beyond Philadelphia followed the Schuylkill and Delaware Rivers. But the landlocked farm region to the west of Penn's original three counties had a population sufficient to justify the creation of Lancaster County in 1729. By the middle of the 18th century, new waves of immigrants, border disputes with other colonies, and the colonial government's consequent encouragement of settlers pushed the boundaries beyond the Susquehanna into southwestern Pennsylvania. As Stevens describes in *Pennsylvania, Birthplace of a Nation:*

> The first stage in the growth of the farming frontier was the true
> wilderness of the typical frontiersman. He usually squatted upon the
> land for a time and lived in a crude cabin or lean-to. He was the man
> with the leather jacket and breeches, the fur cap, and the long
> Pennsylvania rifle with which he shot game, or Indians. He came on
> foot, or at best with a pack horse or mule. He was not apt to own
> any livestock and lived from hunting, fishing, and crude cultivation
> of the soil in a small clearing on which he raised corn and vegetables.
> This type of pioneer was restless and did not wish to be crowded.

As settlement continued, towns were laid out, and some emerged as cities in the wilderness. Between 1768 and 1788, two-thirds of the total area of Pennsylvania was wrested from Indians.

■ REVOLUTIONARY ERA

In Boston in 1773, a group of anti-tax demonstrators disguised as "Indians" threw a shipload of tea into Boston Harbor. In Philadelphia, protesters invited the captain of a British tea ship to their own more polite protest, and in London Benjamin Franklin put up his finger and detected ill winds blowing toward Britain from the colonies. As all this was happening, new ideas were coursing through the land. Quakers and

*A drawing of John Nixon reading the Declaration of Independence on July 8, 1776.
(Library of Congress)*

other Protestant sects had long stressed the importance of individual conscience, free of the dictates of traditional institutions and guided by a sense of civic responsibility. One aspect of this notion was the Protestant belief that all people should be able to read the Bible, and the high concentration of Protestants living in the northern colonies created one of the highest literacy rates in the world. The spirit of freedom of individual expression encouraged the writing of ideas and opinions, especially in the fields of religion and politics. Philadelphia, the publishing center of the colonies, was the place where many of the books and pamphlets by political thinkers such as Thomas Paine were published and distributed.

These literate, forward-thinking individuals were 4,000 miles from Great Britain, a distance sufficient to encourage rebellion against the monarchy. Democratic government did not lack precedent—models came from the ancient world, from Athens and early republican Rome. But though many of the colonists were willing to take the bold step into self-government, some knew there would be more than a few bumps in the road. The institution of slavery tarnished America's democratic idealism, and more than a few free thinkers in the colonies had said so,

Paine among them. At the time of the Revolution, this injustice seemed beyond remedy and at any rate secondary to maintaining a united front against Britain. Moreover, though Jefferson himself owned slaves, apologists for slavery were a source of frustration to him. The original draft of the Declaration of Independence included condemnation of the slave trade, but Southerners and some New England politicians insisted on its deletion.

■ GREAT MEN CORRESPOND

By 1774, the men who would become the patriots of the American Revolution and the founders of the United States were in correspondence. In Philadelphia, City Tavern was the center of social, business, and political activities. Informal debates held there laid the groundwork for the Declaration of Independence and later for the Revolution.

The Philadelphia Committee of Observation, Inspection, and Correspondence, operating out of its tavern headquarters, proposed that a Congress of the Thirteen Colonies convene in September 1774 to discuss grievances with Britain. This first meeting of the Congress in Philadelphia adjourned without a demand for independence, but after the British marched on Lexington and Concord the following April, the voices of those advocating rebellion grew louder. By May, Paul Revere was galloping toward Philadelphia. When he arrived, he made straight for City Tavern seeking support for the city of Boston. A second Continental Congress convened, and the few Pennsylvania conservatives in attendance were no match for the fiery oratory of Philadelphians like Thomas Paine.

Virginian Richard Henry Lee offered a resolution declaring "That these United Colonies are, and of right ought to be, free and independent States," and that a plan of confederation be created. A committee that included Thomas Jefferson, John Adams, Benjamin Franklin, Roger Sherman, and Robert R. Livingston was formed to draft a declaration "setting forth the causes which impelled us to this mighty resolution." Working at a desk in the home of a young bricklayer and drawing on the political thought of the Enlightenment, Jefferson wrote the Declaration of Independence in two weeks. On July 2, 1776, Lee's resolution was adopted after a heated debate, and two days later the Congress formalized this act by adopting the Declaration of Independence.

The course of armed struggle for independence was set. When the Congress met in July 1776, at what is now known as Independence Hall, to adopt the document,

Washington reviews his troops at Valley Forge in this 1883 painting by William B. T. Trego.
(National Center for the American Revolution/Valley Forge Historical Society)

the few remaining Pennsylvania conservatives reluctantly added their signatures. The English monarch, King George III, was not amused. From his point of view, the insurgents were traitors and deserved a traitor's punishment. The British army consulted with colonial representatives, after which war was declared.

■ REVOLUTIONARY WAR

The early years of the war did not go well for the Americans. The circumspect and soft-spoken general from Virginia, George Washington, led an inexperienced and poorly supplied army. The government that was to support him barely existed and had almost no money. Having lost several early campaigns in New York, he was forced to retreat across New Jersey to Pennsylvania.

The tide turned—and popular support for Washington rallied—the day after Christmas 1776, when he ordered a successful surprise attack on a garrison of German mercenaries camped on the east bank of the Delaware River, in Trenton. A month later, he captured another contingent of British soldiers at Princeton.

The British commander who had taken New York City, Major Gen. William Howe, struck back, defeating the forces of the Continental Army at Brandywine Creek in Pennsylvania in September 1777. Howe then settled into Philadelphia, forcing the Congress into exile. George Washington and his farmer-soldiers did not give up. Digging in at nearby Valley Forge through what turned out to be a brutal winter, they suffered disease, hunger, and cruel cold.

More than 2,000 of the 12,000 soldiers perished during the encampment. But the Continental Congress, still on the run, had taken heart in Washington's resistance, especially after the Battle of Saratoga in October 1777, which resulted in the surrender of British forces in New York.

■ FRENCH ASSISTANCE

The fledgling United States government, lacking funds and allies, looked to France for help against Britain, their common antagonist. In late 1776, Benjamin Franklin sailed to France for a meeting with King Louis XVI. Self-interest had already prompted the king to offer help, but Franklin's enormous popularity in France may have increased the king's generosity. Louis immediately ordered secret

Benjamin Franklin meets Marie Antoinette (shown seated, in a yellow gown) at Versailles in 1776. Franklin had been sent to Paris to seek aid from the French government for the Revolutionary War effort. (Library of Congress)

assistance to the revolutionaries, and in 1778, after treaties had been signed promising favorable trade status, the French declared war on Britain and sent their fleet of warships in open support. Howe raced out of Philadelphia to reinforce his troops in New York.

In 1781, the highest-ranking British commander, Lord Cornwallis, settled in the Virginia seaport town of Yorktown after failing to capture Thomas Jefferson in a chase through the Piedmont region of the colony. George Washington saw another opportunity for surprise attack and forced the Continental Army—16,000 strong—on a horrendous march south from New York. Aided by French soldiers, Washington's forces cornered the British troops, who waited in vain for reinforcements to come by sea. After a three-week standoff, the vastly outnumbered Cornwallis surrendered.

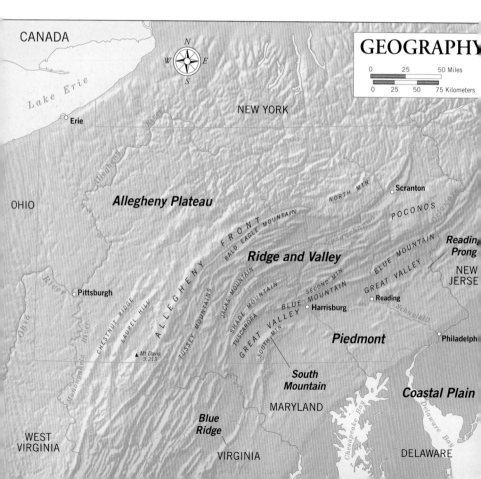

Though several battles continued in New York during the next 18 months, General Washington's stunning defeat of the British at Yorktown had secured victory for the American forces. The captured British colors were sent to Philadelphia by Washington and presented to the Continental Congress in a formal ceremony in Independence Hall. Philadelphia, and Pennsylvania with it, had been the staging ground for a revolution. When the Constitutional Convention met at Independence Hall after a few years of an unsatisfactory confederation, Philadelphia further fulfilled William Penn's dream of "planting the seed of a nation." In December 1787, Pennsylvania became the second state, after Delaware, to ratify the United States Constitution.

■ PROGRESS IN PENNSYLVANIA

Pennsylvania was in the vanguard of states that took advantage of the economic freedoms guaranteed by the new central government. In the decade after independence, both Philadelphia and Pittsburgh began developing the infrastructure required for an economy with the capacity to trade with the world.

From the 1780s through the 1820s, the state experienced an expansion of roads, bridges, and canals. The federal government had moved to Washington by the early 1800s, but Philadelphia still held special status: because of its financial commitment in the war, the city enjoyed a brief period as the financial center of the new United States. Pennsylvania was primed to lead the way in a second economic expansion, from the mid-1820s through the 1850s, that would bring the state to the level of many of Europe's economic powerhouses.

The key was the state's abundant natural resources—among them the largest anthracite coal deposits in the world, lumber to meet the building demands of an expanding nation, and waterways to transport these products.

■ CAN SUCH A UNION LONG ENDURE?

If Pennsylvania was central to the founding of the nation, it was also intensely involved in the moral and emotional debates that preceded the Civil War. Quaker-dominated Pennsylvania had abolished slavery in 1780, the first state to do so, and it had long been a stop on the Underground Railroad, which directed escaped slaves north. Its people were sympathetic to the abolitionist cause. Yet as the place where the union of the states had first begun, it did not take national dissolution lightly.

A memorial to General Robert E. Lee at Gettysburg National Military Park.

Pennsylvanians reacted angrily to the United States Supreme Court's infamous Dred Scott decision of 1856, invalidating an act of Congress—the Missouri Compromise—and permitting the spread of slavery into the American territories. In 1860, Pennsylvania's vote was pivotal to Abraham Lincoln's election as president. Powerful Southern leaders had declared their region would secede from the Union if Lincoln were elected, and when he was, Southern states began to carry out that threat.

When Lincoln called for troops to support the Union in 1861, no other state was as ready as Pennsylvania to go to arms. The president requested 14 regiments; volunteers filled 25 regiments almost immediately.

Pennsylvania also became the site of the war's most devastating battle when Confederates led by Gen. Robert E. Lee crossed the narrow sliver of Maryland that separates Virginia from Pennsylvania and brought the war to the sleepy farming community of Gettysburg. The ferocious Battle of Gettysburg, which lasted from July 1 through 3, 1863, caused more than 51,000 Confederate and Union casualties, almost all under the age of 21.

■ CAPITALISTS AND UNION MEN

The Civil War had stimulated Pennsylvania's industrial might. With the end of the war came an era of industrial expansion led by entrepreneurs who built the mills, mines, and factories of the late 19th century. Businessmen like Andrew Carnegie, Henry Clay Frick, Robert Hunt, Joseph Wharton, and William Scranton saw fortunes to be made in steel production and coal mining, and they set about building enormous empires. Along with them came some of the country's most innovative financiers—the Mellons of Pittsburgh and the Cookes of Philadelphia.

Factories need laborers, and they came to Pennsylvania by the thousands: blacks from the South, Irish Catholics, the Welsh and the Scots-Irish, Russian Jews and Eastern Europeans. Pennsylvania owes much of its cultural wealth and economic success to these people, who did all the heavy lifting—mining coal and laying track, stoking the coke furnaces and pouring the molten iron ore into ingots.

In these "beehive ovens," coal was baked into coke, which burns at the high heat necessary to produce steel. (Library of Congress)

Ironworkers at a factory in Sharon. (Carnegie Library of Pittsburgh)

As the titans of industry exercised largely unfettered control over their workers, Pennsylvania became the testing ground for the American trade union movement. Several important labor struggles took place among the burgeoning semiskilled labor forces of railroad, mining, and steel manufacture, most notably the Homestead Steel Strike of 1892.

■ THE MODERN ERA

Pennsylvania followed an almost predictable course for an industrial state in the first half of the 20th century. Economic slumps were devastating, and wars were financially invigorating. The Great Depression brought unemployment as high as 80 percent in the steel and railroad industries. World War II eliminated unemployment with a vengeance: factories ran around the clock and women were recruited into the work force.

So much is said about the "Rust Belt" in the post-industrial age that it is surprising to learn there are still steel mills and coal mines in Pennsylvania. But steelmaking and other heavy manufacturing have declined steeply in the past three or four decades, and services now play a much larger role in a diversified economy. Government initiatives encourage growth in such high-technology industries as electronics and biotechnology.

The decline of heavy industry made it possible to undo some of the environmental damage wrought by mining and manufacturing. As a result, agriculture and tourism, now two of the state's major industries, have benefited from improvements in air and water quality.

Pennsylvania grapples with problems that vex every state—public safety, race relations, and educational opportunities. An additional problem for Pennsylvania has been the "brain drain" of talented people who have moved away from its urban areas or out of the state altogether. The steady trickle leaving Philadelphia and Pittsburgh is, some sociologists hypothesize, a by-product of the cities'— especially Pittsburgh's—transformation from manufacturing-based economies to more multifaceted ones.

The diversification may take several decades to fully unfold, but both cities show evidence that the most difficult parts of the process are behind them. Revitalized downtowns and new sports stadiums and arts centers have attracted new business, which in turn has brought hotels, restaurants, and housing to previously blighted areas. And both cities, capitalizing on their proximity to top-notch universities and research institutes, have emerged as

A promotional piece for the Pennsylvania Railroad.

key players in the new economy. Pittsburgh is among the largest software employers in the nation, has a budding robotics industry, and in 2000 was selected by Rand, the renowned research and development "think tank," as the site for a satellite office. Furthermore, both Pittsburgh and Philadelphia have become hotbeds of activity in the budding biotechnology industry, in part because of the high concentration of PhDs in both of them and their proximity to universities, businesses, and media. Reflecting Philadelphia's new prominence in the field, the Biotechnology Industry Organization chose it as the site of its 2005 convention.

Philadelphia and Pittsburgh's ability to adapt to industrial and demographic changes is indicative of the resilience and creativity of Pennsylvanians as a whole. That's an assertion with some basis in historical truth. The citizenry of this state did, after all, play a key role in creating the United States and an equally pivotal one later in the development of the nation's industrial might. At the start of the 21st century, new challenges loom, but if the past is the road map to the future, there can be little doubt that Pennsylvanians have what it takes to meet them.

A dramatic sunset over Lake Erie, as viewed from Presque Isle.

HISTORICAL AND CULTURAL TIME LINE

1643 Governor Johan Printz of New Sweden establishes his capital at Tinicum Island within the present limits of Pennsylvania.

1654 British seize control of New Sweden.

1681 Charles II of England grants land to William Penn.

1682 William Penn and Friends aboard the *Welcome* land at Newcastle, Delaware.

1683 Penn purchases land from Indians in the Delaware Valley.

1701 Penn grants charter to the city of Philadelphia.

1774 The first Continental Congress convenes at Carpenter's Hall in Philadelphia in response to new taxes imposed on colonists by the Crown.

1776 Commonwealth of Pennsylvania is established in June during conference at Carpenter's Hall.

1776 On July 4, Declaration of Independence is signed at Independence Hall in Philadelphia.

1777 The British occupy Philadelphia. News of the French alliance with the colonies, negotiated by Benjamin Franklin, leads to withdrawal of British forces from the city in the spring of 1778.

1784 Treaty of peace with England ratified by Congress in Philadelphia.

1787 The Constitution of the United States is adopted at Independence Hall in Philadelphia.

1793 Yellow fever kills 4,000 in Philadelphia. The health crisis results in improved sanitation and the opening of a hospital, in 1810, devoted to the study of infectious disease.

1814 Domestic use of anthracite coal begins, resulting in the organization of important mining companies throughout the state.

1848 Andrew Carnegie and family arrive in Pittsburgh from Scotland.

1850 Women's Medical College is founded in 1850, opening the medical profession to women.

1856 Pennsylvania organizes new Republican Party, with former Democratic leader Simon Cameron throwing his support to the new party.

1860 Republicans dominate in the state and nation with the elections of Gov. Andrew Gregg Curtin and President Abraham Lincoln.

1863 Battle of Gettysburg marks a change in fortune for the Union.

1868 Women in Philadelphia organize the Pennsylvania Women's Suffrage Association.

1876 In Philadelphia, on July 4, Susan B. Anthony reads her "Declaration of Rights for Women" at Independence Hall.

Centennial Exhibition, with at least 30,000 displays of science, art, industry, and agriculture representing all the U.S. and many nations, opens in Philadelphia.

1877 Strikes and bloody flare-ups lead to the creation of the United Mine Workers union in 1890.

1892 Carnegie Steel Company chairman Henry Clay Frick orders 300 armed Pinkerton guards to repel strikers at the Homestead Steel Works. Sixteen workers are killed.

1940 The Commonwealth is the second-most populous state in the nation, after New York.

1948 In Donora, 20 people are asphyxiated and 7,000 are hospitalized because of severe pollution from zinc factories. Public outcry results in federal and state laws to control air pollution.

1952 Jonas Salk develops a vaccine against polio in the Virus Research Lab at the University of Pittsburgh.

1954 WQED in Pittsburgh pioneers community-sponsored educational television.

1959 Steel strike puts many Pennsylvanians out of work; President Eisenhower invokes Taft-Hartley Act to end 116-day walkout.

Twelve workers die in the Knox Mine flood disaster, marking the end of deep mining in the anthracite region.

1962 Pennsylvania-born Rachel Carson publishes *Silent Spring*, which challenges the widespread use of pesticides in agriculture and calls for increased government action against pollution.

1967 Hurricane Agnes devastates Lebanon County.

1976 Members of the Pennsylvania American Legion contract a previously unknown form of pneumonia, at a convention at Philadelphia's Bellevue Stratford Hotel. Of the 221 stricken, 34 die.

1979 Reactor 2 at the Three Mile Island nuclear facility experiences a partial meltdown, beginning an ongoing debate about the safety of nuclear energy.

1985 A city block in West Philadelphia burns after city officials bomb a house in an attempt to dislodge the radical MOVE group.

A fence in Shanksville becomes a memorial to those who died aboard Flight 93 on September 11, 2001.

1990 Pittsburgher August Wilson wins Pulitzer Prize for Drama for *The Piano Lesson,* one year after winning the same prize for *Fences.*

1991 Philadelphia architect Robert Venturi wins the prestigious Pritzker Prize in recognition of his career accomplishments.

2000 Republican Convention meets in Philadelphia, the sixth time in a century and half that the party has met in the city.

2001 On September 11, United Airlines Flight 93 takes off from Newark, New Jersey, and is hijacked by terrorists en route to San Francisco. The plane crashes near Shanksville.

2002 Nine miners assumed dead after an accident at the Saxman Mine, in Somerset County, are saved after three days underground.

PHILADELPHIA
AMERICA'S FIRST CAPITAL

Philadelphia has appeared in many different guises over the past 300 years. Once as proper and upright as its English Quaker founders, the city has relaxed under the influence of immigrants from all over Europe as well as African-Americans who migrated from the South before and after the Civil War. A center of revolutionary fervor in the late 18th century, by the late 19th Philadelphia was basking in the prosperity of the Gilded Age. In the 1920s, the city was known in movies and novels for its "Main Line" upper-crust society, but by the 1980s Philadelphia was down at the heels. Today, the city is on the upswing, rebuilding its urban landscape and buffing up its many fine buildings, which constitute a nearly complete history of American architecture.

The mixed population of this casual yet energetic city has cultivated an eclectic blend of tastes. Residents can be found patronizing top-notch art museums or having art tattooed right onto their bodies; listening decorously to a world-class orchestra or screaming at the top of their lungs for (and sometimes against) the

Boathouse Row, at the southern end of Fairmount Park.

The printmakers Currier and Ives created this city map in 1875. (Library of Congress)

Phillies baseball team; dining in an excellent restaurant or tucking into that most Philadelphian of concoctions, the cheesesteak sandwich. Elegant and proletarian, haughty and earthy, Philadelphia is a city of complementary contradictions.

■ HISTORY

■ WILLIAM PENN'S VISION

When William Penn arrived aboard the *Welcome* at a quay along the Delaware River in 1682, he found 10 small houses along a wooded shore and a settlement that had foundered for 44 years, first as a Swedish trading post and later as the Dutch outpost of New Amsterdam. Penn, then 38, a devoutly religious and idealistic aristocrat, stepped ashore possessed of a powerful humanitarian vision: he wished to build a society based on trust in man's better instincts. He stated his goals in a letter written a year earlier:

> I purpose that which is extraordinary and leave to myself and successors no power of doing mischief, that the will of one man may not hinder the good of an whole country.

That he did not falter in this purpose was remarkable, given his aristocratic background and the potential for abuse inherent in authority. Penn held to a vision of mankind as essentially good and deserving of dignity, a vision that would sustain his spirits as he struggled to apply high principles to real life.

Penn laid out detailed plans for his town, one in which commerce would prosper, all religions would be tolerated, and order and Christian rectitude would prevail. Philadelphia (Greek for "brotherly love") was also to be, if not fireproof, fire resistant. Heeding the advice given by Sir Christopher Wren after the great London fire of 1666, Penn designed a city with straight streets intersecting at right angles— considered an improvement on the curving lanes of European cities. Houses were to be placed at the center of their lots, with open space between them, for it was to be "a greene Country Towne, which will never be burnt, and always be wholesome." To that end he also proposed public parks for the commercial center, something unknown in English cities at the time.

■ PROSPERITY AND IDEALISM

With its access to shipping routes through the Chesapeake Bay and its proximity to trappers, hunters, and wheat farmers in the surrounding countryside, Philadelphia began to flourish. The city exported lumber and furs from the western forests, wheat from what are now Lancaster and Bucks Counties, and cast iron and flour from city mills.

By 1700, Philadelphia's population had reached 6,000, and the pastor of Old Swedes' Church was writing proudly: "All the houses are built of brick, three or four hundred of them, and in every house a shop, so that whatever one wants at any time he can have, for money."

This high chest, made in Philadelphia around 1770, is a fine example of the sophistication of both craftsman and merchant in the city at that time. (Philadelphia Museum of Art)

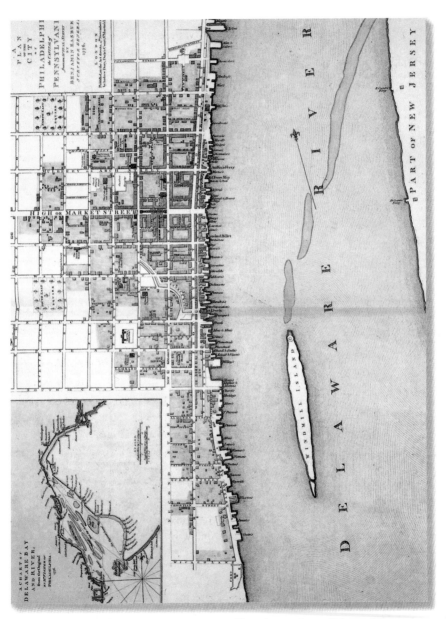

Penn's right-angled streets and green spaces remain visible in this 1776 map. (Library of Congress)

NOT SO PLAIN PEOPLE

English and French visitors were amazed by the luxury displayed in the city. President Washington's splendid coach and his liveried footmen; staid Quakers carrying gold canes and gold snuffboxes, and wearing great silver buttons and buckles; ladies with sky-high coiffures, in costumes of costly brocades and velvets, silks, and satins; the grand wigs and queues, new buckles and silk stockings, worn by the men. "Ladies paid their French maids no less than two hundred pounds a year; and there were statesmen like Gouverneur Morris who had his two French valets and a man to buckle his hair in paillots." So long as the capital was in Philadelphia and the Federalists were in power, social life was luxurious and stately.

—Clarence P. Hornung, *The Way It Was*, 1978

If Quakers were the backbone of the early city, their tolerance brought in their wake Anglicans, Catholics, Jews, and "Plain People"—including Mennonites and Pennsylvania Germans, or "Deutsch." Newly prosperous merchants patronized equally prospering craftsmen: silversmiths, cabinetmakers, and coach makers. (If the Quakers' philosophy of simplicity led them to avoid ostentation, the Anglicans had no such scruples.)

Philadelphians were well abreast of the egalitarian and democratic ideas circulating during the mid-18th century. By the time of the Revolutionary War, theirs was the wealthiest city in the colonies and, with 24,000 residents, the most populous. These residents were by some accounts the most outspoken and opinionated on the continent. The Rev. Jacob Duche wrote in 1772:

> The poorest labourer upon the shore of the Delaware thinks himself
> entitled to deliver his sentiments in matters of religion and politics
> with as much freedom as the gentleman or the scholar. Indeed there is
> less distinction among the citizens of Philadelphia than among those
> of any civilized city in the world. . . . For every man expects one day
> or another to be upon a footing with his wealthiest neighbor.

(preceding pages) The city skyline, reflected in the Schuylkill River. On the left are a house in Fairmount Park (outlined in lights), the Philadelphia Museum of Art, the PSFS Building (with its letters in neon), and, to its right, City Hall.

The first federal bank in the United States opened in Philadelphia in 1791, though the need for such an institution was a matter of great debate. (New York Public Library)

These self-confident people established libraries and discussion clubs; patronized societies studying science, painting, and music; undertook reform and civic improvement; and, as they drank ale in pubs, talked politics. Why shouldn't they govern themselves, and establish a democracy?

So the character of the city, and not just its location, helped to make it the birthplace of the American republic, beginning with the First Continental Congress in 1774. During the hot, sticky July of 1776, Benjamin Franklin, Thomas Jefferson, George Washington, John Adams, John Hancock, and other representatives from 12 of the 13 colonies composed and signed the document we know as the Declaration of Independence.

On July 8, their declaration was read to an enthusiastic group of citizens. A year later, when General Howe led the British Army into Philadelphia, the active patriots fled, and the city's thousands of loyalists welcomed the British with open arms. Yet the occupation of Philadelphia served no strategic purpose for Britain, and when Howe was dismissed from his command in May 1778 for "inactivity," it was widely said that Philadelphia had captured him rather than the reverse.

■ EPIDEMICS AND GAMESMANSHIP

Centrally located among the 13 colonies, Philadelphia became the new nation's capital in 1779. The city's reputation was so positive that immigrants sailed in by the shipload, disembarking at Water and Market Streets. Many of the new arrivals were willing to indenture themselves for years in order to live here.

As businesses mushroomed and skilled workers were enticed to make their fortunes, the city struggled to keep pace. Housing was scarce, and crowding favored the spread of disease and fire. Outbreaks of yellow fever occurred frequently, with each epidemic killing thousands. Still, the city managed to move ahead.

After the U.S. Constitution was ratified in 1789, New York briefly became the country's capital, but by 1790 Philadelphia had regained the title. The city's return to political prominence, though, was fleeting. The new U.S. government decided to move the nation's capital 144 miles south, to a marshy site where the Potomac and Anacostia Rivers converged. By 1800, Philadelphia was no longer the capital, and by 1823 it was no longer the country's most populous city, either. New York had edged out Philadelphia in population.

But though it had lost these distinctions, William Penn's town retained its reputation for innovation and was known as the City of Firsts—in public safety, education, the arts, and business. The Pennsylvania Academy of Fine Arts, the country's first art school, opened here in 1805, and during the 19th century, Philadelphia became a leading center for the manufacture of textiles, apparel, shoes, machinery, tools, iron, steel locomotives, and ships. Philadelphians formed the Anti-Slavery Society in 1833, and Philadelphia regiments answered the Union call to arms.

Pennsylvania Academy of Fine Arts.

After the Civil War the city continued to thrive. The telephone and the auto-mated building elevator accelerated the pace of commerce, and the first medical college for women in the United States was founded.

■ THE MODERN ERA

As a major manufacturing area, Philadelphia drew thousands of immigrants, each group settling into its own neighborhood: Italians in South Philly, Chinese in part of Center City, African-Americans in North Philly, Irish in Olney, Jews in the Northeast, and, much later, the Vietnamese in West Philly. Old-time Philadelphians—those who traced their lineage directly to the city's founders and prominent early leaders—were already well established in Chestnut Hill.

Mayors Richardson Dilworth and Joseph Clark presided over something of a golden age between 1951 and 1962, when the city was flush and civic pride ran high. The 1970s and 1980s proved a depressing contrast, as the politics of race and the reality of crime and poverty divided the city, especially during the tenure of Frank Rizzo, a combative mayor whose admirers cheered his tough-guy approach to politics and crime.

Replacing Rizzo in the 1980s was Wilson Goode, an African-American former city manager who enjoyed the support of the city's black community. That support survived the bombing by the police department of the headquarters of the radical black MOVE organization in 1985. The explosion accidentally destroyed an entire city block of 60 houses, earning Philadelphia the sobriquet "The City That Bombed Itself."

By the end of the century the city had rebounded once more. Much of the credit is given to the administration of Ed Rendell, a Democrat known for an aggressive style and a knack for getting things done. Under Rendell, Philadelphia, which has been steadily losing population—according to the 2000 census, about 1.5 million people live within the city limits, down from nearly 1.95 million in 1970—began encouraging economic growth in fields such as warehousing and dis-tribution, education, health care, and tourism. The Rendell administration breathed new life into Center City, creating the Avenue of the Arts along South Broad Street to support an emerging arts district of theaters and performance cen-ters. Hundreds of millions of dollars, both private and public funds, are being invested in sports stadiums and other building projects.

(following pages) The Kimmel Center and the Avenue of the Arts.

■ INDEPENDENCE NATIONAL HISTORICAL PARK
map page 55, E/F-3

Philadelphia may be evolving into a future that measures up to its heritage, but for many visitors the city's past is the real draw. Perhaps no place in the country has more of an emotional grip on America's historical psyche than Independence National Historical Park in Center City. The place where some of the greatest events in American history occurred, it is where any tour of Philadelphia should begin. This is where Americans initiated their war for independence from England and where the foundations were laid for a democratic form of government admired around the world.

Half a century ago, the area around Independence Park was a dank industrial zone, cluttered with factories and abandoned warehouses. The site has since been turned over to the federal government for maintenance as a national treasure. The friendly green-uniformed rangers who patrol, maintain, and conduct tours at the site refer to their workplace as "Independence Mall," but the national park actually spreads out over 42 acres and encompasses several city blocks of an area known as Old City.

DECLARATION OF INDEPENDENCE

When, in the course of human events, it becomes necessary for one people to dissolve the political bands which have connected them with another, and to assume, among the powers of the earth, the separate and equal station to which the laws of nature and of nature's God entitle them, a decent respect to the opinions of mankind requires that they should declare the causes which impel them to the separation.

We hold these truths to be self-evident, that all men are created equal, that they are endowed by their Creator with certain unalienable rights, that among these are life, liberty, and the pursuit of happiness. That, to secure these rights, governments are instituted among men, deriving their just powers from the consent of the governed. That, whenever any form of government becomes destructive of these ends, it is the right of the people to alter or to abolish it, and to institute new government, laying its foundation on such principles, and organizing its powers in such form, as to them shall seem most likely to effect their safety and happiness.

—Thomas Jefferson, 1776

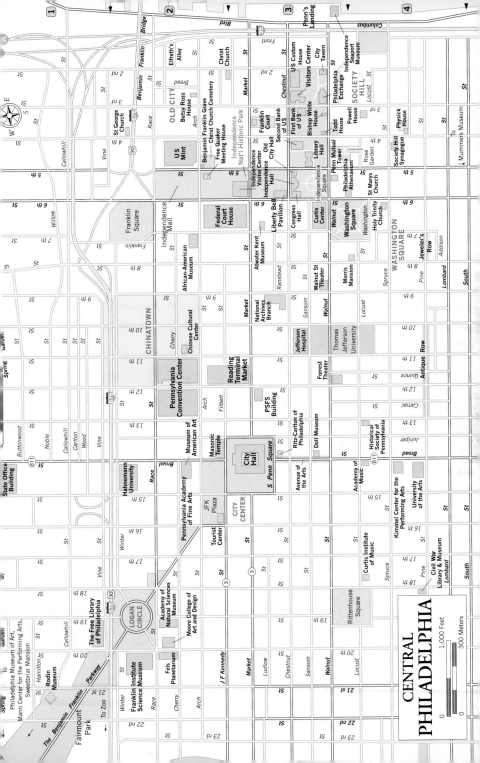

CENTRAL PHILADELPHIA

Most of Independence Mall is closed to traffic and protected by a combination of 8-foot-high brick walls and colonial-era buildings. Inside this area, the noise and bustle of modern life are left behind, and the ghosts of colonial Philadelphia seem to come to life.

■ TOURING THE PARK

Independence Visitor Center *map page 55, E-3*
The visitors center was the first building to open as part of the renaissance of Independence Mall. The 50,000-square-foot facility contains historical exhibits and provides information about tourist activities in the Philadelphia area. A short film that plays continuously throughout the day will orient you to Old City's sights and the history that played out here. Maps, available at the center, include historical tidbits and easy-to-follow directions. There are also rest rooms and a well-stocked bookstore. *Sixth and Market Streets; 215-597-8974.*

Independence Hall *map page 55, E-3*
In the center of the park is Independence Hall, a two-story red brick building with white wood trim and gable roof. Startling in its simplicity, the structure, built between 1732 and 1756, was originally called the State House of the Province of Pennsylvania. Planned and designed by Andrew Hamilton, it is considered a fine example of Georgian architecture. A square tower and octagonal steeple at one end were added in 1753 to hold the Liberty Bell.

It was in the assembly room of this building that the Declaration of Independence was adopted on July 4, 1776, stating that the colonies would no longer abide by the laws of England. George Washington received formal command of the Continental Army in the same assembly room, and the Articles of Confederation were ratified here in 1781.

The room is also where, between May and September of 1787, delegates from 12 states (Rhode Island did not send a representative) met to frame a thoroughly original instrument of government: the Constitution of the United States of America. In closed sessions, during long, hot days, delegates argued over and agreed upon the basic tenets of government, the balance of powers between branches of the government, and the civil protections accorded citizens.

The straightforward architecture of Independence Hall echoed the urgency and forthrightness with which the American Revolution was undertaken.

The 55 men who met here included Alexander Hamilton of New York, Bostonian John Adams, Virginians Thomas Jefferson and James Madison, and Pennsylvania delegates James Wilson, Robert Morris, and Benjamin Franklin, then 70 years old. They constituted an intellectual elite astonishing even at the time. Louis Otto, the French *chargé d'affaires,* commented to his superiors at home:

> If all the delegates named for this Convention at Philadelphia are present, we will never have seen, even in Europe, an assembly more respectable for the talents, knowledge, disinterestedness, and patriotism of those who compose it.

The nicks and warping in the floor of the assembly room will help you to visualize the likes of Thomas Jefferson and Benjamin Franklin pacing back and forth between their desks and conferring with supporters while James Madison, seated at the main table, tried to move delegates toward consensus. *Groups admitted every 15 minutes. Chestnut Street between Fifth and Sixth Streets; 215-597-8974.*

Independence Hall connects with **Congress Hall,** the meeting place of the country's fledgling legislative body between 1790 and 1800. Two presidents were inaugurated here: George Washington (for his second term) and his successor, John Adams.

Outside Independence Hall, close to the statue of George Washington, are two bronze plaques set in the brick sidewalk. One is where President Abraham Lincoln stood when he visited Independence Hall and raised a flag here in February 1861. The other is where John F. Kennedy, then still a senator from Massachusetts, delivered an address on July 4, 1956.

Liberty Bell *map page 55, E-3*

One block north of Independence Hall is one of our nation's most significant icons, the Liberty Bell. Since the terrorist attacks against the United States in 2001, the Liberty Bell has become even more of a touchstone for patriotic expression than it already was.

The bell's history is a nearly impenetrable blend of fact and fiction. Originally called the State House Bell, it was cast in England in 1752 to commemorate the 50th anniversary of the Charter of Privileges, the democratic constitution that William Penn granted his colony in 1701. It cracked, however, soon after it arrived in Philadelphia. Local craftsmen John Pass and John Stow recast the bell and engraved its famous inscription: "Proclaim liberty throughout all the land, unto all the inhabitants thereof" (Leviticus 25:10).

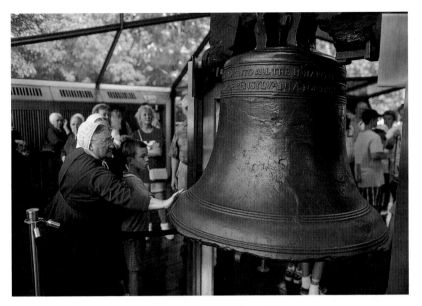

Throughout its history the Liberty Bell has been a touchstone for patriotic expression.

The recast bell was hung in the tower of the State House and rang on July 8, 1776, to call the citizens of Philadelphia. Shortly after noon, a crowd having gathered, Col. John Nixon climbed up onto a wooden platform and read "The unanimous declaration of the 13 United States of America." Later that afternoon, at the green-covered tables in the Assembly Room, the parchment copy of the Declaration of Independence was signed by delegates.

During the Revolutionary War, the bell was moved to Allentown and hidden in a cellar until the British evacuated Philadelphia. By the 1830s, when abolitionists who were inspired by its inscription began calling it the Liberty Bell, it had begun to crack again. It is long believed the crack occurred while the bell tolled during the funeral of Chief Justice John Marshall in 1835, but this is considered historically questionable. It rang for the last time in 1846, in celebration of George Washington's birthday. In 1852, the bell was placed in the "Declaration Chamber" of Independence Hall, where it remained until 1976, when it was moved to the glass Liberty Bell Pavilion for the U.S. Bicentennial.

The Liberty Bell Pavilion is scheduled to move and reopen at the site of the Independence Visitor Center, at Sixth and Markets Streets, by the end of 2003. The bell will be placed so that when visitors view it close up, Independence Hall and other centuries-old structures will form the backdrop. The site of the new pavilion is near the house, owned by businessman Robert Morris, where President George Washington lived from 1790 to 1797. The proximity of the Liberty Bell to a house in which the country's first president was known to have kept slaves underscores for many a paradox at the heart of the American independence movement. Many African-Americans and others in Philadelphia have called for acknowledgment of this historical fact at the pavilion. *Market Street between Fifth and Sixth Streets.*

Franklin Court *map page 55, F-3*

East of Liberty Bell Pavilion on Market Street is Franklin Court, the site of the three-story, 10-room house that Benjamin Franklin shared with his wife, Deborah, and their two children. The original home was torn down in 1812, but for the U.S. Bicentennial architect Robert Venturi re-created in white steel the outline of the house and two nearby structures from Franklin's era. Carved on slate tiles

placed where the house's wood flooring would have been are quotations by and about Franklin and selections from his correspondence with Deborah about the furnishings and maintenance of the house. (Franklin spent a good deal of time in London as a representative of Pennsylvania and several other colonies, but wrote frequently to Deborah about the house.)

Glass sections interspersed among the rectangles of slate provide views into Franklin's privy pits and wells. Venturi's "ghost" structure, as it is called, stands in the middle of a garden. Through the courtyard to the north, on Market Street, are row houses whose ground floors contain a post office, a postal museum, and a printing office and bindery with period equipment.

"Ghost" structure in Franklin Court.

Inside the printing office at Franklin Court.

Below the courtyard in the **Underground Museum** are paintings, objects, and various Franklin inventions, including what he said was the invention that gave him his "greatest personal satisfaction," the armonica, a musical instrument composed of glass bowls. An 18-minute film sketches Franklin's life, and on a bank of telephones the testimonials of famous historical figures, read by actors, can be heard. *314–322 Market Street, between Third and Fourth Streets (additional entrance on Chestnut Street); 215-597-8974.*

■ Old City and Other Historic Neighborhoods

Philadelphia extended only as far as Old City and Society Hill in the 18th century. The natural relationship of these neighborhoods to the city's port on the Delaware River was evident until the 20th century, when they were cut off from the river by I-95.

In addition to Independence National Historic Park, **Old City,** which extends from Market Street to Spring Garden Street, and from the Delaware River to Seventh Street, includes other historic sites and neighborhoods. North of Chestnut between Front and Fifth Streets, two- and three-story brick houses,

CHARMING BEN FRANKLIN

Benjamin Franklin (1706–1790) arrived in Philadelphia from Boston in 1723, stopped at a baker's shop, and bought "three great Puffy Rolls." With a roll under each arm and munching on the third, he made his way up Market Street, where he passed his future wife, Deborah Read, at the door of her family's home. She watched him "& thought I made as I certainly did a most awkward ridiculous Appearance."

Franklin moved into Deborah's father's house and courted the young woman, but when he left for London, she married John Rogers, who, as it turned out, already had a wife. Eventually Rogers deserted Deborah and Franklin took her as his common-law wife. Their marriage lasted until her death in 1774, although they were frequently apart.

Franklin's versatility and long life defy summary. He did everything it is possible to do on the printed page, as writer, editor, publisher, and printer. He served his city, colony, and new nation as postmaster, assembly delegate, and foreign envoy. He founded a library and a fire insurance company. He was as versatile and accomplished as a scientist as he was as a writer and statesman. He was also the life of the party, to judge from all accounts, as well as from this lyric he wrote:

> There's but one Reason I can Think
> Why People ever cease to Drink
> Sobriety the Cause is not
> Nor Fear of being deam'd a Sot,
> But if Liquor can't be got.

> If on my Theme I rightly think
> There are Five Reasons why Men drink:
> Good Wine, a Friend, because I'm dry,
> Or least I should be by and by
> Or any other Reason why.

The list of Franklin's innovations includes not just bifocals and the Franklin stove, but also shuttle diplomacy and international superstardom. He commuted between England and the colonies during the decade before the American Revolution. Once that conflict was under way he spent his time in France, seeking aid for the war effort. That the French gave generously testifies both to their animosity toward the British and their infatuation with the American envoy. As the historian Page Smith writes in his history of the American Revolution, *A New Age Now Begins:*

Franklin, a man as subtle and devious as a French diplomat, as sophisticated in his tastes as the most decadent aristocrat, was nonetheless cast by the French in the role of a simple American agriculturalist. And Franklin—editor, author, courtier, scientist, inventor, sensualist, and roué—played the role with zest. He even wore a beaver cap, which was more enchanting to his admirers than the most bejeweled crown could have been. Everywhere in Paris he was honored, admired, and acclaimed. His picture was reproduced on snuffboxes, plates, vases, and commodes and sold by the thousands. Enterprising businessmen sold seats at places where the people of Paris could watch him ride by in his coach. Elegant ladies vied for his favors.

At Franklin's death in 1790, the French National Assembly took time out from its own tumultuous affairs to observe three days of mourning for a man they praised for "the simplicity and sweetness of his manners . . . the purity of his principles, the extent of his knowledge, and the charms of his mind."

—Jessica Fisher

Benjamin Franklin, whose accomplishments included being named the first Postmaster General of the United States, was honored by having his portrait adorn the nation's first official postage stamp, in 1847. Less official likenesses of Franklin appeared on more pedestrian objects abroad.

many of them two centuries old, are typical of the area. Factories and warehouses also line Old City streets, and many of these old commercial structures have been converted into attractive loft spaces by artists, architects, and young professionals. On weekends, people from all over Philadelphia and its suburbs flock here to go museum- and gallery-hopping and sample Old City's restaurants and bars.

■ OLD CITY SIGHTS

Betsy Ross House   *map page 55, F-2*

Historians can neither confirm nor deny that Betsy Ross sewed America's first flag, and they are equally unsure whether George Washington came secretly to her house just before he went to war and gave her his roughly sketched design. Whatever the truth about Ross's flag-making, she was well known to 18th-century Philadelphians as a tough-minded draper's widow who appeared regularly at patriot rallies.

Betsy Ross liked to tell friends and family of the day in 1776 when three members of a secret committee from the Continental Congress—George Washington, Robert Morris, and George Ross—came to her home and asked her to sew a flag for the colonies.

On June 14, 1777, members of the Continental Congress, in Philadelphia, officially recognized the flag design that is said to be Ross's. Thus: "the flag of the thirteen United States be thirteen stripes, alternate red and white; that the union be thirteen stars, white, in a blue field representing a new constellation."

The Ross house, built in the Georgian style around 1740, has few furnishings and does not suggest comfort. The contrast between these spartan digs and the fine homes of the local gentry is startling. The house has a Flag Room, which holds many of Ross's personal belongings, and an Upholstery Shop, where Ross and her husband, John, managed the family business. There is also a Musket Ball Room, where Ross sewed soldiers' uniforms and other clothing. *239 Arch Street, between Third and Broad Streets; 215-686-1252.*

Elfreth's Alley   *map page 55, F-2*

Cobblestone-paved Elfreth's Alley is one of the oldest residential streets in America. At least one home here dates back to 1720. In the 1930s and 1940s, a preservation group, the Elfreth's Alley Association, saved six homes along the historic street. Two can be toured year-round, but if you're visiting on the second weekend in

Elfreth's Alley is the oldest continuously occupied residential street in the United States.

June, during Fête Days, when locals dress up in period costumes and demonstrate crafts, you can tour 32 of these architectural gems. *Front and Second Streets between Arch and Race Streets; 215-574-0560.*

Christ Church *map page 55, F-2*
Christ Church was built between 1724 and 1744 to replace a rickety wooden structure modeled after the post-Baroque style of English architect Sir Christopher Wren.

Look for the brass plaques that mark the pews of George and Martha, Benjamin and Deborah, and Betsy Ross. Benjamin Franklin was an active member of the church, and a series of lotteries he ran helped pay for the 196-foot steeple and its bells. *Second Street one-half block north of Market Street.*

You cannot walk through **Christ Church Cemetery,** but you can peer through the wrought-iron fencing at the grave markers of seven signers of the Declaration of Independence. The Franklins are buried near the fence on Arch Street, a few steps east of Fifth Street, next to a son who died at age four. Visitors toss pennies on Franklin's marker in remembrance of his famous adage, "A penny saved is a penny earned." *Fifth and Arch Streets.*

BLACK PHILADELPHIANS

In 1780, Philadelphia's African American population of about 3,000 was concentrated in the area between Fifth and Ninth Streets, from Pine to Lombard. . . . The population doubled in the next ten years, spreading west across Broad Street to form a center of African American business activity at Sixteenth and Seventeenth Streets and a residential district in the southwestern section of the city. By 1793, the spread took a northward trend, when one-quarter of the African American population was living between Market and Vine Streets.

The growing African American community, though degraded and subjugated, became more valuable to whites during this time, and they proudly served their adopted country. The part African Americans played in defense of the United States goes back to the American Revolution. Over 5,000 African Americans throughout the colonies fought in the Revolution. They were fighting side by side with their white comrades in most units of the Continental Army. By the summer of 1778, hardly a ship sailed in the Continental Navy without an African American gunner, officer's helper, or seaman. Among the brave was James Forten. Forten served as a powder boy under Stephen Decatur, commander of the *Pennsylvania Royal Louis*. As an adult, Forten became Philadelphia's most influential African American citizen.

—Charles L. Blockson, *Philadelphia 1639–2000*, 2000

African-American Museum in Philadelphia   *map page 55, E-2*
Inside a modern four-story structure a few blocks north of the Liberty Bell, the African-American Museum celebrates the contributions of blacks to the city since colonial times. The museum's collection includes more than a half-million items; exhibits might cover anything from the role religion has played in the lives of the city's African-Americans to the Civil Rights movement, the Negro baseball league, and the fabled Philly sound of the 1970s. *701 Arch Street; 215-574-0380, ext. 224.*

Bishop White House   *map page 55, F-3*
Pennsylvania's first Episcopal bishop, William White, lived in this Georgian-style abode for half a century, beginning in 1786. The three-story house, with dormered attic and fine carvings around the windows, is typical of Philadelphia's upper-class residences in the late 1700s. The bishop hosted many famous statesmen here, holding forth in a beautifully appointed parlor that has been restored by the

National Park Service. White was known for keeping a tight rein on his priests—it was not unusual to see several of them fidgeting in hardback chairs in the second-floor hallway outside his library, waiting to face him.

Tickets to tour the house, which is generally considered the most historically accurate re-creation of all the historic residences in Old City, may be purchased at the visitors center. The ticket also includes a tour of the Todd house (343 Walnut Street), a more modest home once occupied by Dolley Madison, whose second husband, James, was the nation's fourth president. *309 Walnut Street, between Third and Fourth Streets; 215-597-8974.*

Pennsylvania's first Episcopal bishop lived in this house for half a century.

City Tavern *map page 55, F-3*

Built in 1773 by the "principal gentlemen" of Philadelphia, City Tavern was for three decades a social, political, and economic center with several large meeting rooms, lodgings, two kitchens, and a bar. John Adams called it "The most genteel tavern in America." At a famous meeting here in May 1774, radicals pushed the heretofore moderate colony of Pennsylvania into the forefront of the dispute with England. In 1775, George Washington had dinner here before leaving as the newly elected commander of the Continental Army.

The tavern was a gathering place for members of the Continental Congresses, the Constitutional Convention, and officials of the federal government from 1790 to 1800. In 1834, it was partially destroyed by fire, and in 1854 the original structure was demolished.

A replica of the original tavern was completed in 1976. Furnished with period reproductions, the tavern once again serves lunch and dinner. The menu successfully re-creates the cuisine of 18th-century America, though many locals find the attempts to mimic the ambiance of the period a bit forced. *Second and Walnut Streets; 215-413-1443.*

The father of American surgery lived and worked in the Physick House.

■ SOCIETY HILL *map page 55, F-3/4*

If there is one neighborhood that has endured in station and purpose, it is Society Hill, the wealthy enclave of early-19th-century Philadelphians and an exclusive, meticulously preserved district today. Society Hill extends from Walnut Street to Lombard Street, between Front and Eighth Streets. More a rise in the road than a hill, within its streets are several historic churches, many Federal-style brick row houses, and the **Society Hill Synagogue** (418 Spruce Street; 215-922-6590). The society the neighborhood is named after is the Free Society of Traders, a consortium of business investors who moved here on William Penn's advice.

The **Physick House** is the only freestanding Federal-style mansion left in Society Hill. The square three-story house, built in 1786 by wine merchant Henry Hill, reflects London architecture at the time. Philip Syng Physick, the father of American surgery—the stomach pump and catgut sutures are among his innovations still in use today—lived here from 1815 to 1837 and saw patients that included Dolley Madison and the future president Andrew Jackson. Restored in the 1960s, the Physick House contains some of the finest period antiques in historic Philadelphia. *321 South Fourth Street; 215-925-7866.*

Stroll along **Delancey Street,** a side lane, to view its colonial and contemporary structures. Other streets worth investigating are **American, Cypress,** and **Philip.** Subtle architectural details to notice include chimney pots and roofs with copper of a nice patina. Many of the courtyards on these streets have breathtaking gardens.

■ PENN'S LANDING *map page 55, F-3*
Society Hill's waterfront along the Delaware River is known as Penn's Landing, a 37-acre river park east of Christopher Columbus Boulevard between Spring Garden and Lombard Streets. This is where William Penn stepped ashore from the *Welcome* in 1682 and took possession of Pennsylvania.

Penn's Landing has been sliced out of the working waterfront. If you look north toward the magnificent Ben Franklin Bridge, you'll see cargo ships and tankers loading and unloading. Looking across the granite-blue Delaware River, you can see New Jersey's waterfront about a half-mile away.

Back on the Pennsylvania side of the river, you'll see the masts of fine old sailing vessels, some of which can be toured. Among these is the 394-foot-long *Moshulu* (Columbus Boulevard, Pier 34). Built in 1904, the vessel is among the world's

Exhibits at the Independence Seaport Museum tell the story of Philadelphia's waterfront.

biggest and oldest four-masted ships. Other boats you can board include the *Spirit of Philadelphia* (Pier 3) and, when in port, the 177-foot-long *Gazela,* built in 1883.

Exhibits at the **Independence Seaport Museum** illuminate the Philadelphia waterfront's place in American history. Admiral George Dewey's 1892 cruiser *Olympia* is berthed directly behind the museum in the Delaware River. One of the first ships to be made of steel, the *Olympia* served as an escort ship in the Atlantic Ocean during World War I. The vessel's last assignment, in 1921, was to carry home from Europe the body of the Unknown Soldier, which rests now in Arlington National Cemetery.

Alongside the *Olympia* floats the *Becuna,* a 308-foot-long submarine that was part of the Pacific fleet during World War II. The sub destroyed many Japanese naval ships during the war, after which it was redesigned to carry nuclear warheads. The sub was decommissioned in 1969. On the tour you'll get a feel for the cramped conditions sailors endured. *211 South Columbus Boulevard, at the foot of Walnut Street; 215-925-5439.*

The **Great Plaza** amphitheater hosts events from May through September, including multicultural festivals, children's theater, concerts, and Philadelphia's Fourth of July celebration. In good weather, it's a popular spot for strolling or picnicking.

Columbus Boulevard itself is in a state of transition. The first stage was the completion of the Hyatt Regency Philadelphia at Penn's Landing. A luxury apartment building, the Dockside, went up in 2002, and plans are under way for a family entertainment center. Nightclubs and more than a dozen restaurants—some good, many less so—can be found along this 3-mile stretch.

■ WASHINGTON SQUARE DISTRICT   *map page 55, D/E-3/4*

Washington Square, one of Philadelphia's original five squares, is a large park at Walnut and Sixth Streets. Though not far from the hubbub of Independence Hall, the park is often quite serene. The Tomb of the Unknown Soldier, the only such monument to Revolutionary War soldiers, is here.

The Washington Square District, bounded by Market, Sixth, Lombard, and Broad Streets, connects the historic and commercial sections of Center City. Curtis Publishing, responsible for the *Saturday Evening Post, Ladies Home Journal,* and other popular magazines of the 19th and 20th centuries, had its headquarters in what is now the **Curtis Center** (Sixth and Walnut Streets) office building. In the

Gems for sale on Jeweler's Row.

center's Sixth Street lobby is *The Dream Garden,* a 15- by 49-foot glass mosaic by Louis Comfort Tiffany based on a Maxfield Parrish painting. The lobby is accessible during business hours and on Saturday until mid-afternoon.

West of Seventh Street on Sansom Street is **Jeweler's Row,** where jewelers and importers have been doing business since 1852. **Antique Row** is between Ninth and 12th Streets along Pine Street.

A short detour north nearly to Market Street brings you to the quirky **Atwater Kent Museum,** in an 1826 Greek Revival–style building designed by John Haviland. The museum's namesake, who made his fortune manufacturing radios, collected all sorts of Philadelphia-related items, from Stetson hats to souvenirs from Philadelphia's Centennial Celebration in 1876. The museum's entire second floor is given over to a gallery of Norman Rockwell images that graced *Saturday Evening Post* covers. *15 South Seventh Street; 215-685-4830.*

Two cultural venues in the Washington Square area are the **Walnut Street Theatre** (825 Walnut Street; 215-574-3550) and the **Forrest Theater** (1114 Walnut Street; 215-923-1515), which present touring Broadway shows, light comedies, and dramas.

■ SOUTH STREET *map page 55, A/F-4*

The shift in tone can be downright jarring when you pass from Old City's sedate colonial-era enclaves into the antic South Street area, the closest thing Philadelphia has to New York's Greenwich Village or San Francisco's Haight-Ashbury. Tattoo parlors and record shops abound along and just off the stretch of South Street between Front Street and Seventh Street, and there are fringe-art galleries, scores of ethnic restaurants, bookshops devoted to New Age philosophies, and even a supply store for witches. In the early 1980s, property here was going at fire-sale prices after city officials let it be known they planned to raze the neighborhood to make room for an expressway overpass. The flyover never happened, but the low prices remained, and the funky financially challenged moved in. Since the Gap and other chains began appearing on South Street it has lost some of its low-rent cachet, but parallel Lombard and Bainbridge Streets have taken up the slack. The area gets successively rowdier as weekend evenings wear on.

(above) The Mummers Parade, held in Philadelphia every New Year's Day, might best be described as the city's version of Mardi Gras. (opposite) A colorful emporium on South Street.

■ CENTER CITY

Stand between Broad and 15th Streets along Market Street to take full measure of the fanciful office towers of Liberty Place. The steel tower of One Liberty Place (1650 Market Street) was constructed in the 1980s. At 945 feet, it is the tallest building in Philadelphia and the first to violate the long-standing gentleman's agreement among architects and engineers not to exceed the height of the William Penn statue atop City Hall. Two Liberty Place (1601 Chestnut Street) is slightly shorter (848 feet) than One Liberty Place.

■ CITY HALL AREA

City Hall *map page 55, C-3*
Until 1987, City Hall was the most prominent feature of the Philadelphia skyline, the bronze statue of William Penn rising above all else from the 548-foot-tall clock tower. Designed by sculptor Alexander Milne Calder, the grandfather of the modernist sculptor Alexander Calder, this 37-foot-tall statue is one of the largest single pieces of sculpture on any building in the world (Penn's nose alone is 18 inches long). The impressive granite and white marble City Hall edifice, adorned with a not entirely coherent mix of columns, pilasters, pediments, dormers, and sculptures, was built between 1871 and 1901. Despite wear and tear and more recent architectural competition, it remains the visual centerpiece of downtown Philadelphia. Free tours are conducted every 15 minutes on weekdays. *Broad and Market Streets; 215-686-2840.*

Masonic Temple *map page 55, C-2*
Membership in the Philadelphia Free and Accepted Masons, a fraternal society founded in the Middle Ages, was coveted in colonial times. Many statesmen of the Revolution, including George Washington, belonged to the Philadelphia Guild and supported building the temple as a statewide meeting place. The temple is divided into seven lodge halls, all ornately decorated in the styles of various cultures, including Egyptian, Asian, and Gothic. On display in the building's museum is a Masonic apron embroidered for George Washington by the wife of the Marquis de Lafayette. *One North Broad Street; 215-988-1917.*

Bright lights, big City Hall tower.

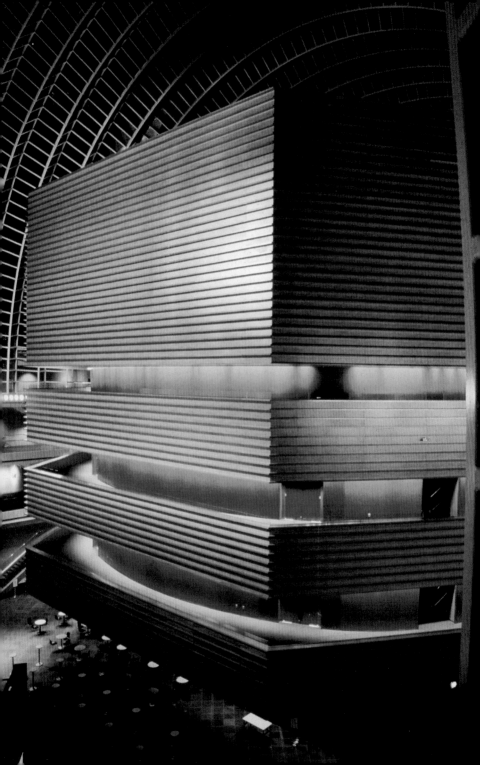

Pennsylvania Academy of Fine Arts *map page 55, C-2*
America's first art museum and art school was founded in 1805 by a group of artists and entrepreneurs that included the painter Charles Willson Peale and the sculptor William Rush. The academy had several addresses during the 19th century, but in 1876 architects George Hewitt and Frank Furness designed the school's current home, a stunning example of Victorian Gothic, complete with a mahogany and bronze staircase, Gothic arches trimmed in gold, and a blue vaulted ceiling with painted stars. So taken with the academy was the modernist architect Louis I. Kahn that he called the building "life-giving and life-inspired."

The academy's collection looks at American art from the 1760s to the present and includes work by, among others, William Merritt Chase, Cecilia Beaux, Thomas Eakins, Winslow Homer, Andrew Wyeth, Georgia O'Keeffe, John Singer Sargent, and James Whistler. Contemporary American artists represented include Richard Diebenkorn, Alex Katz, Raymond Saunders, and Frank Stella. *118 North Broad Street; 215-972-7600.*

Kimmel Center for the Performing Arts *map page 55, C-4*
In 2001, Philadelphia realized one of its long-cherished goals—an arts complex that lives up to the city's cultural aspirations. The New York–based architect Rafael Viñoly designed this $250 million structure, named after local philanthropist Sidney Kimmel. The center has two concert halls: 2,500-seat Verizon Hall, where the Philadelphia Orchestra and Philly Pops perform; and 650-seat Perelman Theater, which hosts performances by smaller ensembles, among them the Chamber Orchestra of Philadelphia and the Philadelphia Chamber Music Society. The Kimmel's atrium, whose most dynamic feature is a vaulted glass roof reminiscent of European train depots, instantly became one of the city's great public spaces. *260 South Broad Street; 215-790-5800.*

Academy of Music *map page 55, C-4*
The former home of the Philadelphia Orchestra is a block from the Kimmel Center. The 2,900-seat hall, built in 1857 and the oldest opera house in America, takes its architectural cues from Milan's La Scala opera house. Richly detailed murals by Karl Heinrich Schmolze and an impressive chandelier are among the hall's noteworthy features, but equally impressive is the list of American premieres

The Kimmel Center's glass-enclosed atrium is one of Philadelphia's great public spaces.

Verizon Hall.

that have taken place here, among them Verdi's opera *Il Trovatore,* Gounod's *Faust,* Strauss's *Ariadne auf Naxos,* and Wagner's *The Flying Dutchman.* Many of the world's greatest musicians and singers have graced this stage, including Maria Callas, Enrico Caruso, Vladimir Horowitz, Gustav Mahler, Leontyne Price, Artur Rubinstein, Richard Strauss, Igor Stravinsky, and Pyotr Ilich Tchaikovsky. The Academy of Music presents performances by the Opera Company of Philadelphia and the Pennsylvania Ballet, along with touring Broadway shows and other productions. *Broad and Locust Streets; 215-893-1955.*

Two History Museums *map page 55, B/C-4*
In operation since 1824, the **Historical Society of Pennsylvania** (1300 Locust Street; 215-732-6200) has original manuscripts and other artifacts related to the founding of the United States, the evolution of its cities and industries, and the wars and other conflicts that have defined the country. Founded in 1888, the **Civil War Library and Museum** (1805 Pine Street; 215-735-8196) houses more than 12,000 volumes pertaining to the War between the States, along with 5,000 photographs documenting the war, its battlefields, generals, and soldiers. Weapons, flags, and uniforms are among the many items displayed, and an entire room is devoted to Abraham Lincoln.

Reading Terminal Market *map page 55, D-2*
Many Philadelphians say the best cure for the blues is a visit to this enormous indoor market, whose nearly 100 vendors have been serving up fresh meats, poultry, fruit, seafood, baked goods, and crafts since 1892. Amish families sell produce from Wednesday through Saturday, and restaurants serve everything from Pennsylvania Dutch to Middle Eastern cuisine. The market is closed on Sundays.

Reading Terminal Market, another magical downtown space, attracts food lovers from all over Philadelphia and beyond.

Built as a train shed for the Reading Railroad in 1889, the red brick terminal has a fanciful Italian Renaissance–style facade that livens up its stretch of Market Street. *Reading Terminal Market entrance, 12th and Arch Streets; 215-922-2317.*

PSFS Building *map page 55, C-3*

Architectural styles range freely in Philadelphia, from Georgian and Federal to Romanesque, Beaux Arts, and modernist. Diagonally across from the Reading Terminal and in nearly every way its antithesis, the PSFS Building, completed in 1932, was designed by the firm of Howe & Lescaze. With its spare vocabulary of glass and glazed brick, the structure, one of the country's earliest examples of the International style, made perhaps too stark a statement. A critic in 1985 described Howe & Lescaze's creation as being "too coolly self-possessed to start a trend," and indeed there is nothing quite like it in Philadelphia. Originally the headquarters of the Philadelphia Savings Fund Society, it was restored in 2000 and converted into a hotel. Still coolly self-possessed, with crisp art deco interior detailing and austere lines, the building is well worth investigating. *1200 Market Street, at 12th Street.*

A lion dance during the Chinese New Year's parade.

■ CHINATOWN *map page 55, D-2*
People have been coming to Chinatown to eat since the first Chinese restaurant, Mei-Hsian Lou (913 Race Street), opened in 1870. A plaque on the building pays homage to the eatery and to the first Chinese immigrants to America. Chinatown is loaded with small shops and restaurants, and in recent years a few bars here have been taken up by college students, lending the neighborhood a zippier feel than it has had in the past. The dining scene here is also more eclectic these days, including inexpensive Vietnamese, Thai, and Chinese restaurants. *From Ninth Street to 12th Street, between Vine and Arch Streets.*

■ FAIRMOUNT PARK *map page 85, A-2/4*
On land purchased by the city in the mid-1800s, Fairmount Park provides Philadelphians with 14 square miles of space to run, stroll, bicycle, or picnic. The **Philadelphia Zoo** (3400 West Girard Avenue) is here, as is the **Philadelphia Museum of Art.** Open-air concerts take place in summer at the **Mann Center for the Performing Arts** (52nd Street and Parkside Avenue), and 10 Victorian structures, known as **Boathouse Row,** front Kelly Drive. These are the headquarters of

the city's popular rowing clubs, whose members can be seen slicing through the glasslike river water on many early mornings. You can rent bicycles along Kelly Drive. Ask for directions to the Forbidden Trail—it's so undeveloped you'll swear you're in central Pennsylvania rather than a major metropolis. Along Kelly and West River Drives are more 18th- and early-19th-century houses, "rural" retreats for well-to-do families. Most of these 90 historic homes are open for tours. **Lemon Hill, Cedar Grove, Mount Pleasant,** and the fanciful **Strawberry Mansion** are among the most famous. *For park information, call 215-685-0000.*

Typical of the upper-class homes is **Sweetbriar,** now a popular house museum. It was built on the Schuylkill River's west bank by Samuel Breck, a wealthy merchant who served in the state legislature, where he wrote the bill calling for the emancipation of the state's slaves. Many of Sweetbriar's rooms were decorated in 18th-century French style, probably due to Breck's friendship with Lafayette, Talleyrand, and other French notables. The house's south parlor is supremely elegant, with floor-to-ceiling windows framing views of the exterior gardens. *Sweetbriar Hill, off Lansdowne Drive; 215-222-1333.*

A solitary sculler toils on the Schuylkill River below the Philadelphia Museum of Art.

A Calder mobile graces the airy interior of the Philadelphia Museum of Art—appropriate, because Alexander Calder was a Philadelphia native.

Philadelphia Museum of Art *map page 85, A/B-4*
The vast holdings of this outstanding museum include more than 300,000 works, encompassing 300 years of European decorative arts, Renaissance drawings and sculpture, art from East Asia, and European painting from the 15th to the 20th centuries. The painting collection alone could swallow up several days of concentrated viewing. Highlights include works by Fra Angelico, Botticelli, Bronzino, Chardin, Poussin, Renoir, Monet, Cézanne, and van Gogh. The museum's modern, Pop, and postmodern holdings include pivotal works by Brancusi, Duchamp, Matisse, Léger, Rauschenberg, Pollock, Twombly, Warhol, and many more. Traveling exhibitions are top-notch. *26th Street and Benjamin Franklin Parkway; 215-763-8100.*

Rodin Museum *map page 85, B-4*
The Rodin Museum, four blocks east of the Philadelphia Museum of Art on Benjamin Franklin Parkway, houses 124 Rodin sculptures, the largest collection of the sculptor's oeuvre outside Paris. Among the works displayed are *The Kiss, The*

Burghers of Calais, and *The Gates of Hell,* on which Rodin labored from 1880 until his death in 1917. A part of the Philadelphia Museum of Art, the Rodin Museum was created in the mid-1920s by the movie-theater entrepreneur and philanthropist Jules Mastbaum. In 1926, Mastbaum hired the French architects Paul Philippe Cret and Jacques Greber to design the building, an austere temple surrounded by a garden, but Cret died before its completion. *22nd Street and Benjamin Franklin Parkway; 215-763-8100.*

■ SOUTH PHILADELPHIA *map page 85, A-5*

The oldest district in Philadelphia County was settled by Swedish immigrants in the mid-17th century. Today, South Philadelphia—or South Philly as it is more often called—consists of small city blocks lined with row houses. Often called "old school" by locals, this area is best known for the Italian Market, Italian restaurants, and genuine Philly cheesesteaks. What's in a cheesesteak, you ask? Here's the high-calorie recipe: take a thinly sliced steak, top it with grilled onions and smother it with Cheez-Whiz (the authentic choice) or provolone; and add lettuce, tomato, mayonnaise, and pizza sauce and place the mixture inside a bun.

Italian Market *map page 85, B-5*
Still in business after 100 years, this market along Ninth Street offers the best of many cultures and cuisines to locals and tourists. High-quality produce, seafood, pastries, coffees, cheeses, pastas, kitchenwares, herbal remedies, sporting goods, and antiques make for a great shopping expedition. *Ninth Street between Washington Avenue and Christian Street.*

Mummers Museum *map page 85, B-5*
This museum celebrates Philadelphia's Mummers and the unique parade they put on each year as they strut along Center City's usually freezing streets on New Year's Day. First in the line of march are the comics, followed by the fancies and the string bands, all in humorous or lavishly beautiful costumes composed of sequins, spangles, and seemingly billions of multi-colored feathers. (So elaborate are some, in fact, that winds high enough to render them airborne are cause to postpone the parade.) Larger groups and the string bands are not only costumed, but also choreographed and equipped with props and backdrops, which they set up and knock down at intervals along the way and in front of the judges stand—instant stage sets. Mummery is a way of life for participants, who begin work on next year's

South Philadelphia is famous for its sports stadiums, Italian restaurants, and the engaging Italian Market, pictured above.

event the day after. If you can't make the parade—which so far is televised only locally—this diverting museum is worth a visit. The city officially began sponsoring the parade in 1901, but the Mummers' history goes back well into the 19th century. The museum is a fairly long way from the Old City, but if you do walk, it is safer to use Second, Third, or Fourth Street instead of the streets farther west. *1100 South Second Street, at Washington Street; 215-336-3050.*

Sports Stadiums

South Philly is also where professional sports are played. Until 2004, when they move into a 43,000-seat stadium at 11th and Darien Streets, major-league baseball's Philadelphia Phillies make their home at **Veterans Stadium** (3501 South Broad Street). The 76ers basketball team and Flyers hockey team play at **First Union Center** (3601 South Broad Street). The Philadelphia Eagles take on the rest of the National Football League at the recently built 55,000-seat **Lincoln Financial Field** (11th Street at Pattison Avenue).

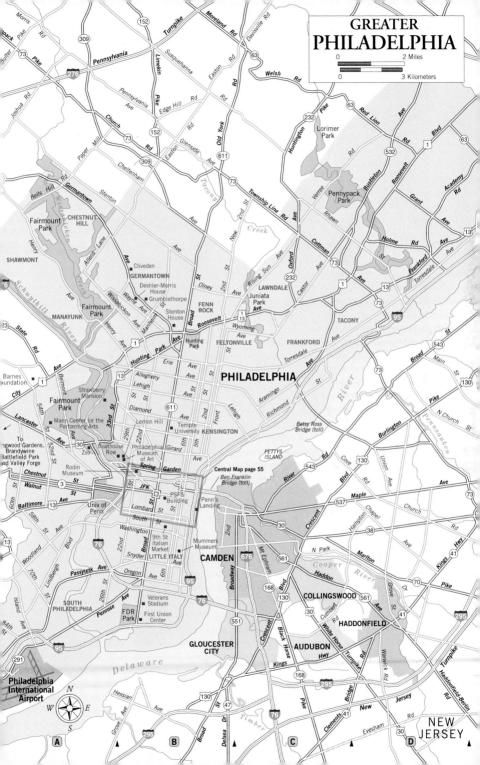

South Philadelphia row houses.

■ CHESTNUT HILL *map page 85, A-2*

This serene neighborhood, northwest of Center City, has homes that date back to the 18th century, when the quarter was a small colonial settlement of farmhouses and taverns. Many houses in the area are architectural gems and can be viewed on pleasurable bus tours offered by the **Chestnut Hill Historical Society** (215-247-0417) or the **Chestnut Hill Visitors Center** (215-247-6696).

■ MANAYUNK *map page 85, A-3*

Taken from a phrase of the Lenni Lenape Indians for "where we go to drink," Manayunk, on the Schuylkill River, was once connected to the Pennsylvania canal system built in 1819. Manayunk's factories have all closed, but the town has become a hip neighborhood, with boutiques, contemporary restaurants, and snazzy nightclubs and bars in and around the remains of mills and other structures from the 19th century. The community hosts a well-attended arts festival on the last weekend in June each year. Area restaurants supply the edibles and local artists and craftspeople display their works.

■ GERMANTOWN *map page 85, B-3*

When it was settled in 1683, Germantown was a separate village from Philadelphia, its citizens a mix of German Quakers and Mennonite farmers who proved to be even more progressive and welcoming than many mainstream Philadelphians. European immigrants with differing religious beliefs and cultural mores settled here and prospered. Residents of Germantown were quietly supportive of the Revolution, although as Quakers they were pacifists.

Because of the village's industrial facilities, the British army made a beeline for Germantown after routing George Washington's army and occupying Philadelphia in 1777. The Battle of Germantown, actually a series of attacks on the British troops by Washington, was a bitter early defeat for the revolutionaries.

Many fine house museums in Germantown reflect the influence of German architecture on American residential design before and after the Revolutionary War. **Cliveden** (6401 Germantown Avenue; 215-848-1777), at the north end of Germantown, is a 1763 country house occupied by the British during the Revolutionary War. The amusingly named **Grumblethorpe** (5267 Germantown Avenue; 215-843-4820) has a fairy tale–like quality amplified by its stone exterior and dark-red trim. George Washington lived in the **Deshler-Morris House** (5442 Germantown Avenue; 215-596-1748) for a spell, supposedly to avoid the dampness of sea-level Philadelphia.

Stenton (4601 North 18th Street; 215-329-7312), an early Georgian-style brick house, was built by James Logan in 1727 when he found himself "no longer in love with life." Sparsely ornamented, with light-filled parlors and a capacious library, the house makes a convincing case for the healing powers of solitude. For more information about house museums, contact the **Germantown Historical Society** (215-844-0514).

■ BARNES FOUNDATION *map page 85, A-4*

Dr. Albert C. Barnes developed Argyrol, an antiseptic widely used prior to the introduction of antibiotics, and he used the fortune it made him to finance his passions: collecting art and educating people about art. He bought well, acquiring works by van Gogh, Matisse, Monet, Cézanne, Seurat, Renoir, Picasso, and others. A populist, Barnes scorned art historians and refused them access to his collection. The critic Clement Greenberg reputedly disguised himself as a worker to gain

The Barnes Foundation's collection includes paintings by Degas, Monet, Picasso, and Cézanne.

entrance, but was discovered and ejected. He and other critics were desperate to see the collection because so many of its works reflect crucial moments in the development of artists and modernism. Henri Matisse's *The Joy of Life* (1905), for instance, marks the painter's transition from talented young painter to mature artist.

Barnes's antipathy toward art historians and critics resulted in part from an exhibition he curated in 1923 for his alma mater, the University of Pennsylvania. The exhibition was panned, and the University later added insult to injury by rejecting his offer to bequeath it his collection, a gift easily worth a billion dollars today.

Also on the Barnes grounds is the 12-acre Joseph Lapsley Wilson Arboretum, the passion of Mrs. Barnes. Highlights include a teahouse, a spring-set pond, and more than 200 varieties of lilacs. To visit the Barnes Foundation, which is 10 miles west of Center City in the town of Merion, requires planning. The museum's days and hours of operation are restricted (the neighbors aren't crazy about the traffic), and reservations must be made a month or more in advance. The foundation has announced plans to move to downtown Philadelphia by mid-decade. Because this would require breaking Dr. Barnes's will, litigation will likely delay the move, which may never even happen. *300 North Latch's Lane, Merion; 610-667-0290.*

■ **BRANDYWINE VALLEY** *map page 97, D-4*

Twenty-five miles southwest of Center City, the urban landscape gives way to the verdant farm and horse country of the Brandywine Valley. In the spring, when the ponies are taking the first measure of their privileged lives and the air is thick with the fragrance of honeysuckle and mowed grass, it is difficult to imagine that this landscape once witnessed the deaths of thousands of young soldiers participating in the American War of Independence.

Country roads stretch into rolling honey-colored hills, past heavy green spruce trees and, in springtime, pastel wildflowers. To find rural beauty, turn north off U.S. 1 on Route 100 at Chadds Ford and drive along Creek Road toward West Chester. This is also the exit for the Brandywine Battlefield State Park, the site of the largest engagement of the Revolutionary War.

Just about any turn off U.S. 1 west of I-476 will put you on a rural road. Take the exit at Route 82, for example, 6 miles from the Brandywine River Museum, and you will be in the heart of a mushroom-growing region.

Mill on the Brandywine *(ca. 1830), by John Rubens Smith. (Library of Congress)*

■ CHADDS FORD *map page 97, D-4*

In 1967, a group of residents, many of whom could trace their family histories in the area back to colonial times, succeeded in putting a cap on development in this region. To defray costs of their efforts, they enlisted the talents of valley artists and opened the Brandywine River Museum in a converted 1880s gristmill. The glass-wall lobby frames views of the river and surrounding woods. On exhibit are paintings by Andrew Wyeth, his son Jamie, and others of the Wyeth clan, in addition to landscapes and portraits by other noted American artists. *U.S. 1 and Route 100; 610-388-2700.*

On September 11, 1777, on the site that is now the **Brandywine Battlefield Park,** George Washington, with half his army off defending Manhattan, faced a well-equipped British force and lost, forcing his retreat to Lancaster and then to Valley Forge. Without Washington's army to protect the city, the British captured Philadelphia, dealing the revolutionary cause an enormous blow. At the 50-acre park are reproductions of the farmhouses that Washington and Lafayette used as headquarters. *U.S. 1; 610-459-3342.*

Operating out of a renovated 17th-century barn, **Chaddsford Winery** produces about 30,000 cases of wine each year. Known for its cabernets and chardonnays, the winery, established in 1982, presents outdoor concerts during the summer. *U.S. 1, about 1.5 miles south of Route 202; 610-388-6221.*

■ LONGWOOD GARDENS *map page 97, D-4*

The 1,050-acre country estate of industrialist Pierre S. du Pont encompasses 20 outdoor gardens, 20 indoor gardens, 11,000 different types of plants, elaborate fountains, two lakes, and several large heated conservatories of exotic tropical vegetation. Although cultivation of this property had begun in the 1700s, du Pont began creating Longwood Gardens as it is today around 1907, with shrubs, rose-laden trellises, and garden flowers. After 1914, du Pont expanded his vision to include fanciful fountains. The Main Garden Fountain is epic, to say the least, spurting 10,000 gallons of water per minute as high as 130 feet.

In spring, the azaleas and rhododendrons are especially beautiful; in fall the blooms of chrysanthemums and the changing foliage steal the show. Water lilies with huge upturned leaves and large flowers flourish in the lakes. In the formal gardens are topiaries, and as you wander the paths you'll come upon sculptures that blend perfectly with the plantings. *U.S. 1, Kennett Square; 610-388-1000.*

The interior of the tropical plants conservatory at Longwood Gardens.

■ **WINTERTHUR** *map page 97, D-4*

A few miles from U.S. 1 across the Pennsylvania border in Delaware is the Brandywine Valley's most famous attraction: Winterthur Garden and Museum, the country estate of Henry Francis du Pont. H.F. du Pont, whose interests included antiques and horticulture, and his father, Henry Algernon du Pont, based the design of the nearly 1,000-acre Winterthur estate on English country manors of the 18th and 19th centuries. A man of exceedingly particular tastes, H.F. Du Pont owned hundreds of sets of china. He expected fresh flowers from his gardens to bedeck his dinner tables and dictated that the china match the flowers and that the food complement the plates.

Winterthur contains the world's finest collection of early American decorative arts, beautiful Wedgwood originals, paintings by John Singleton Copley, Rembrandt Peale, and Gilbert Stuart, and no end of glittering antiques from France, Germany, England, and elsewhere. As at Longwood Gardens, something is always in bloom—many people time their visits for May, when the dogwoods and azaleas are in full flower. *Route 52; 800-448-3883.*

George Washington's headquarters at Valley Forge.

■ **VALLEY FORGE** *map page 97, D-3*

After his defeat by the British at Brandywine, George Washington regrouped his forces briefly at Lancaster and then set up headquarters with 16 brigades across the Schuylkill River from Philadelphia at Valley Forge. A sculpture at one end of **Valley Forge National Historic Park,** the National Memorial Arch, honors the soldiers who endured the terrible winter encampment of 1777–78. Conditions were so debilitating that many soldiers deserted camp, and more than 2,000 soldiers died from malnutrition and disease. One officer, who spent the winter with them and trained in the cold, helped many find the will to survive. He was not an American, but a Prussian drillmaster, Friedrich von Steuben, and much of the tour material in the park is devoted to the role that foreign officers and soldiers played at this crucial point in the War of Independence.

Among the park's sites open for touring are several simple homes Washington and his officers used during that winter. The park also has picnic areas and a 6-mile hiking and biking trail. You can pick up audio driving tours at the visitors center. *Off I-76, Exit 26B; take Route 422 west 1 mile to Route 23 west; 610-783-1077.*

■ TRAVEL BASICS

Getting Around: Major highways in and near Philadelphia include I-95, I-676, I-76 (also known as the Schuylkill Expressway), and the Pennsylvania Turnpike. Laid out in a grid pattern by its founder William Penn, Center City is relatively easy to navigate. However, finding metered on-street parking can be challenging, so if you're arriving by car, and money is no object, you may want to park at one of the many garages available to the public, or use buses, taxis, subways, or your feet to get around. The streets are often one-way, and congested with traffic. There are many squares and circles, such as Rittenhouse Square and Logan Circle, that can confuse you by interrupting the grid pattern.

Arriving by train at the beautiful **30th Street Station,** the main train terminal, puts you right downtown—an easy cab, bus, or subway ride to most hotels, restaurants, and tourist attractions.

Philadelphia International Airport lies 6.5 miles south of City Hall. The SEPTA (Southeastern Pennsylvania Transportation Authority) airport rail line runs every half hour from 6 A.M. until midnight to three destinations, including 30th Street Station.

Philadelphia has excellent mass transit. Purple PLASH vans follow a Center City route to all the main downtown sights; you can buy an all-day pass. Buses, subways, and commuter trains travel the entire city and to nearby counties.

Climate: Summers can be hot and humid, with temperatures hitting between 80 and 90 degrees Fahrenheit (sometimes warmer). Spring and fall are the nicest times to visit. Winter rarely brings heavy snows but weather is unpredictable and can run from 25 to 40 degrees Fahrenheit in the daytime.

S O U T H E A S T

In Pennsylvania Dutch Country, about an hour's drive from Philadelphia, a modern couple in a convertible BMW, fleeing the city for a posh country inn, breezes by an Amish family in horse and buggy as it clings to the berm. In the more rural sections of Bucks County, also about an hour's drive from the city, stone farmhouses older than the Declaration of Independence stand near pricey new gated housing developments. Near Reading, a town founded by William Penn's sons, the old iron furnace that produced cannons and shot for the Continental Army sits peacefully just a mile away from one of the most monstrous and bustling outlet malls in the country.

Throughout this bucolic region of rolling hills, farmland, and quaint little towns that work hard to stay that way, rich pockets of early American history coexist with the trappings of modern life. In some places, the pairings seem oddly contradictory, but in others the conjoining of the American past and present provides the traveler with a harmonious blend of creature comforts and fascinating historical sites.

The understated beauty of southeastern Pennsylvania's landscape—the earthy browns and dark greens of the hills interrupted by huge swaths of neatly tilled farmland—has a mesmerizing effect on those who pass through. So mesmerizing, in fact, that some of these travelers put down anchor; the placid country towns of the southeast are seeing more and more urbanites from Philadelphia, New York, and New Jersey snatching up homes and property.

■ LAND AND PEOPLE

Southeastern Pennsylvania lies within the fertile Piedmont Plateau, between the Delaware River in the east and the Susquehanna River in the west. The immigrants who first settled here bought their land from William Penn's sons, whose advertisements promised rich harvests on tracts of land that extended as far as the eye could see. The settlers did find plenty of forests, but once the land was cleared these rolling hills—a nutrient-rich limestone substrata watered by abundant streams—proved exceptionally fertile. Before the Midwest opened to settlement, this region was known as the breadbasket of the United States.

Today, several thousand small farms cover the area and only patches of the once thick woodland remain. Much of the land is worked by descendants of the

Mennonite girls pose for a picture along the Appalachian Trail at the Blue Rocks overlook, in Berks County.

German Protestant settlers who began moving into southeastern Pennsylvania in the late 1600s and spread out over Berks, Bucks, Lancaster, Lebanon, Lehigh, and York Counties—people who have come to be known as Pennsylvania "Dutch," derived from *Deutsch*, the German word for Germans. In Lancaster County, the epicenter of Pennsylvania Dutch Country, many of the farmers are Amish and Old Order Mennonites, the plainest of the Plain People who came to Penn's woods seeking refuge from religious persecution. Their agricultural methods to this day are not far removed from those they employed in colonial times.

Southeastern Pennsylvania communities remain favored places of refuge and rejuvenation. The crisp country air and deep snows attract visitors in winter, and the river-cooled breezes and tree-shaded streets of quaint towns do so in summer. Bucks County has been especially attractive to the artistic set since the 1930s. The Pulitzer Prize–winning authors Pearl S. Buck and James A. Michener had homes here, as did the composer Oscar Hammerstein. Many artists have been drawn here by the quality of the light, the magical way it dances upon the Delaware River and weaves through the branches of the bankside trees.

sts who took advantage of the Penn family's land offering were
_enni Lenape Indians they displaced, "neither having much nor
expecting much," as William Penn described the Indians. In treaties negotiated in
William Penn's time, the Lenni Lenapes owned the land and leased it to settlers,
usually trading it for goods. But by the time of Penn's death in 1718, a steady
stream of settlers was moving in, picking the forests clean of wildlife and chopping
down huge areas for farming. It wasn't long at all before the treaties were ignored
and the Lenni Lenapes were pushed off their land and forced to move beyond the
fertile valleys.

Among the settlers who poured into the region in the decade after Penn's death
were Quakers, Mennonites, Amish, and members of other religious sects, attracted
by a spirit of tolerance that allowed them to practice their beliefs in the open.
During the French and Indian War and, later, the Revolutionary War, some of the
Quakers and others with pacifist beliefs refused to join the war effort, although
they did supply food and clothing to the Continental Army. Other religious communities openly supported the British.

The southeast figured prominently in several of the Revolution's key military
encounters, supplying fresh frontiersmen-soldiers and supplies to counteract
British gains in New York and New England. The only significant inroad the
British made into Pennsylvania territory during the war occurred two months after
the signing of the Declaration of Independence, when British forces landed on the
upper Chesapeake Bay and marched 57 miles north to capture Philadelphia.
George Washington's attempt to stave off the invasion failed; after hours of fighting at Brandywine Creek, he withdrew to Valley Forge and the Continental
Congress fled to York.

The regrouping and retraining of troops at Valley Forge and France's decision to
side with the Americans led to several key American victories and forced the
British to negotiate peace. After the war ended, southeastern Pennsylvania's farmers
and craftsmen returned to their homes to enjoy relative prosperity. In the 1820s, a
wave of immigration pushed the Pennsylvania frontier farther west, and a new railroad system spurred economic growth.

(following pages) Many have been drawn to southeastern Pennsylvania by the quality of light.

SOUTHEAST PENNSYLVANIA

Edward Hicks's depiction of David Twining's farm in 1787 (painted circa 1845–47) idealized the farmers of Bucks County, where Hicks grew up. (Abby Aldrich Rockefeller Folk Art Center)

In the years leading up to the Civil War, the region's economy grew steadily, and so, too, did the political and religious movements that aimed to set a moral compass for the country. The Quakers and other local pacifist sects were abolitionists, instrumental in keeping Pennsylvania an antislavery state. Many farm communities and small towns along the Delaware River became part of the Underground Railroad, establishing networks of safe houses to help slaves from the Southern states make their way to freedom in New England and Canada.

After the Civil War, during which Quaker and Amish farmers once again supplied food for an army—the Union Army this time—southeastern Pennsylvania played a leading role in the industrialization of the nation. Although farming continued to dominate the economy, steel mills, iron works, and mining operations were set up here because of the area's proximity to coal fields and to the Delaware River (and later to railroads), which provided efficient means to transport goods. While residential and commercial areas have grown significantly along the "Main Line," the collective name for a series of communities that sprouted up along Route 30, the country's first toll road, the rural-agrarian nature of the southeast remains. Two-thirds of the land is still farmed—and although that's much less than even a decade ago, you can still drive for miles across wide open spaces and take in the sights, sounds, and smells of rural life.

■ **BUCKS COUNTY** *map pages 97, E/F-1/3, and page 102*

Bucks County is perhaps best known for idyllic scenes of farm life and quaint little towns that fill up on weekends with urbanites escaping city life. The stretch of Route 32 (often signposted as River Road) that follows the Delaware River from Washington Crossing Historic Park north to Erwinna winds through one of the most history-laden sections of the state.

The two-lane road hugs the towpath of the old Delaware Canal, and a few hundred yards beyond that, often hidden in spring and summer by leafy birch, oak, and hickory trees, the shallow Delaware River rolls leisurely toward its outlet into Delaware Bay.

In the early morning and at dusk, deer gather along the towpath to graze or sneak into the organic gardens of the local inns. In summer, hummingbirds flit through wildflower patches near the riverbank and geese overtake the towpath.

In late fall and winter, the river views are unobstructed. The soft afternoon light reflecting off the river is so unusual that painters have flocked to these Delaware banks hoping to capture it on canvas, and many have ended up settling here. Amid the views of the trees, water, and light are glimpses of riverfront homes, some dating back to the early 1700s. Some have been restored to perfection; others have been long abandoned.

During the hour-long drive from Washington Crossing Historic Park to Easton, you can stop along the way at roadside produce stands, antique stores, and several wineries open for tastings and tours. Many of these attractions are located in tiny, picturesque villages—most of them former mill towns that have aged gracefully.

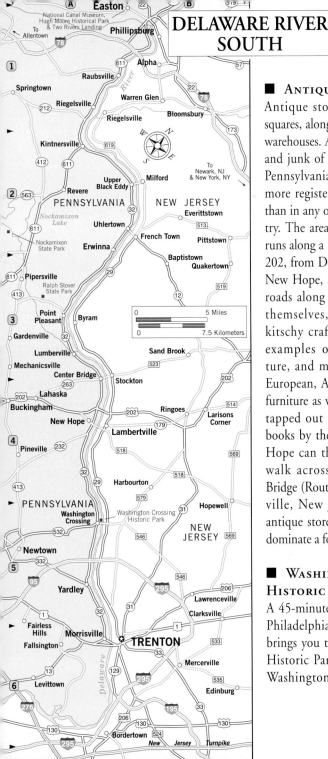

DELAWARE RIVER SOUTH

■ ANTIQUES ROW

Antique stores abound in village squares, along highways, and in giant warehouses. All are stuffed with gems and junk of Revolutionary War–era Pennsylvania. There are said to be more registered dealers in this area than in any other region of the country. The area's premier antiques row runs along a 15-mile stretch of Route 202, from Doylestown to Lahaska to New Hope, spilling onto a few side roads along the way. The antiques themselves, run the gamut from kitschy crafts to museum-quality examples of colonial-era furniture, and many dealers here offer European, Asian, and Scandinavian furniture as well. Buyers who haven't tapped out their energy or checkbooks by the time they get to New Hope can then take a five-minute walk across the Delaware River Bridge (Route 202 East) to Lambertville, New Jersey, where upscale antique stores and furniture studios dominate a four-block area.

■ WASHINGTON CROSSING

HISTORIC PARK *map page, 97, F-2*
A 45-minute drive northeast out of Philadelphia's Center City on I-95 brings you to Washington Crossing Historic Park, where Gen. George Washington and his demoralized,

haggard troops rallied on the freezing Christmas night of 1776 to fight one of the decisive battles of the Revolutionary War. Climbing into cargo boats, 2,400 soldiers set out across the Delaware in a snowstorm, using poles to bash their way through a river choked with chunks of ice. After landing at Johnson's Ferry on the other side, the ragtag forces marched to Trenton, surprised the garrison of Hessian soldiers celebrating the holiday there, and captured the base in less than an hour.

The battle was Washington's first clear-cut victory, and it was a crucial one, giving the Revolutionary cause much-needed momentum—both physically and emotionally. Because of it, the colonial forces were bolstered by an influx of new recruits, and the French government was eventually influenced to back the American army in its fight against the British.

The park is split between an upper and a lower section, which are about 5 miles apart. Heading north on Route 32 you'll come first to the lower park, the McConkey's Ferry section, which is the best place to start a tour. The rangers are informative, and a 30-minute film recounts the surprise attack. From the visitors center, walk to the Memorial Building to see a reproduction of the famous painting by Emanuel Leutze of Washington's crossing, then proceed down to the Durham Boat House to view reproductions of the cargo boats that carried the troops to battle.

Five miles farther north on Route 32 is the upper part of the park, the Thompson's Mill section, which includes an 80-acre wildflower preserve and the 18th-century Thompson-Neely House, which looks much as it did the night that Washington and his officers sat in the kitchen hashing out the details of their attack plan. *Lower Park: 7 miles south of New Hope on Route 32, near junction of Route 532; Upper Park: 2 miles south of New Hope on Route 32; 215-493-4076.*

■ **NEW HOPE** *map page 97, F-2*
Seven miles north of Washington Crossing (and roughly 45 minutes north of Center City), on Route 32, you'll enter the town of New Hope, often referred to as the "jewel of Bucks County," where white clapboard and brick houses spread out along the banks of the slow-rolling Delaware River and its canal. Once known for its mills, which processed goods ranging from grain to metals, New Hope is now part artist colony, part historic site, and part shopping mall. Art galleries and boutiques line Main Street, interspersed with tacky T-shirt shops and hamburger joints. In summer, art lovers, souvenir hunters, history buffs, and city-weary wanderers clog town streets, and on weekends hordes of motorcyclists roar into town.

One of the great pleasures of visiting Bucks County is boarding a mule-drawn barge and riding down the Delaware Canal.

The village has been attracting offbeat characters for decades, and locals like to think of themselves as a people tolerant of unconventional lifestyles. Townspeople also figured prominently in several controversial events of the nation's past. In the summer of 1804, the town's most prominent citizens hid Aaron Burr from pursuing authorities after the fateful duel in which Burr mortally wounded Alexander Hamilton. In the Civil War years, many of the town's homes were used as safe houses along the Underground Railroad.

In the early 1900s, New Hope became a favored destination for artists and actors fleeing New York for the summer, lending the village a bohemian air. The area has more recently become a popular destination for gay and lesbian tourists.

Touring New Hope

You can tour the New Hope area by rail, foot, and even barge. At one time New Hope was an important transportation center along the Delaware Canal—handling between 2,500 and 3,000 barges a month at its peak in 1862. The **New Hope Canal Boat Company** (215-862-0758) brings this aspect of the town's past to life; old mule-drawn coal barges now ply the Delaware Canal to offer day rides, complete with tour guides singing folk songs.

The canal system met its demise with the advent of rail transport, but the town continued to prosper with the arrival of the **New Hope and Ivyland Railroad** (215-862-2332). Today you can take a 9-mile ride along the river in restored 1920s passenger cars pulled by a steam locomotive.

Perhaps the best way to see New Hope is to stroll down any side road off Main Street: you'll encounter 18th-century stone houses with intriguing courtyards, alleys lined with cozy row houses, and cobblestone walkways that lead to the wooded trails that workers once followed out of town to various mills.

The entire town is listed on the National Register of Historic Places, and at the **New Hope Visitors Center** you can pick up a free guide or buy a "Walking Tour of Historic New Hope" map with the important sights highlighted. *1 West Mechanic Street, at Main Street; 215-862-5030.*

The stone **Parry Mansion** was built in 1784 for a wealthy lumber mill owner whose descendants occupied it until the New Hope Historical Society bought it in the 1960s. On weekends from late April to early December, you can tour eight rooms that reflect several generations of its occupants' decorating styles. *45 Main Street, at Ferry Street; 215-862-5652.*

In the 1920s, an old grist mill was converted into the nationally recognized **Bucks County Playhouse,** which presents Broadway-caliber musicals and dramas to packed houses year-round. *70 South Main Street; 215-862-2046.*

Exotic is indeed the word at **Gerenser's Exotic Ice Cream,** a family-owned and -operated ice cream shop that has been selling out-of-the-ordinary flavors since the 1940s. Among the selections: Polish plum brandy, African violet, and Indian loganberry. *22 South Main Street; 215-862-2050.*

■ **LUMBERVILLE** *map page 97, F-2*
About a 10-minute drive north from the bustle of New Hope is quiet, tidy Lumberville, where you can leave the car and view the old homes crowded together on the main street. Lumberville has been a one-industry town since it was known as Wall's Saw Mills in the late 18th century, and its old buildings are on the National Register of Historic Places.

Buy a picnic lunch at the **Lumberville Store** (3741 River Road; 215-297-5388), in operation since 1770, and enjoy it on the New Jersey side at Bull's Island, accessible by way of a sturdy footbridge over the river. Older even than the store, and just across the street (at the footbridge), is the atmospheric **Black Bass Hotel** (3774 River Road; 215-297-5770), which has been hosting travelers since 1741. A B&B these days, the hotel is a splendid place to stop for lunch, Sunday brunch, or dinner.

■ **POINT PLEASANT** *map page 97, F-2*
Should you grow tired of driving along the river and want to get into it, the mellow reach of water near Point Pleasant, just north of Lumberville, is perfect for the decidedly nonadventurous sport of "tubing." The folks at Bucks County River Country will get you outfitted with a truck inner tube—or a canoe or kayak—and they also conduct guided raft trips. It's wise to call the company ahead of your visit. *Byram Road off River Road; Point Pleasant; 215-297-8181.*

■ **ERWINNA** *map page 97, E-1*
A quaint town situated along the twists of River Road as it follows the river's sharp curves, Erwinna has several inns that serve lunch and dinner. There are also antique stores, the renowned **Tinicum Park** (River Road; 215-757-0571), which has well-marked hiking trails, and the **Sand Castle Winery** (755 River Road; 610-294-9181), which has a tasting room and offers tours.

■ **EASTON** *map pages 97, E-1, and page 102, A/B-1*

Just over the Bucks County line in Northampton County, Easton was, on July 8, 1776, the site of the second public reading of the Declaration of Independence. Those fateful words, "We hold these truths to be self-evident," were shouted from the steps of the Northampton County Courthouse on Centre Square.

The land for the square had been presented to city founders in 1765 by William Penn's sons under a bill of sale that required the city to pay the Penn family an annual fee of one red rose. By the early 1800s, in large part because of its prime location at the confluence of the Lehigh and Delaware Rivers, Easton had become an important link in the Pennsylvania canal system—Lehigh Navigation, known as the Lehigh Canal, and the Delaware Canal connected here. In the 1830s, railroad companies began constructing lines here, and by the mid-1860s, when the iron horse superseded canals as the favored mode of shipping transport, Easton was already securely established as an interchange point for five separate railroads.

Red crayon liquid is poured on a belt at the Crayola factory in Easton.

Today, after a solid century of industrialism, the town is in the early stages of an economic and cultural renaissance. New high-tech industries are setting up shop in old factory sites; tourism is on the rise, and city-funded renovations are slated for many of the town's historic buildings.

■ **TWO RIVERS LANDING** *map pages 97, E-1, and page 102, A-1*
An abandoned department store in downtown Easton has been reclaimed and put to new use as the Two Rivers Landing complex, whose three tenants are the Delaware and Lehigh National Heritage Corridor Visitor Center; the Crayola Crayon Factory; and the National Canal Museum. *30 Centre Square; 610-515-8000.*

The **Delaware and Lehigh National Heritage Corridor Visitor Center,** on the first floor, has exhibits and a short film about the history of Easton and the Lehigh Valley, including displays on the area's ethnic groups, historic canals, and main industries.

On the second floor at the **Crayola Factory** you'll learn everything you want to know and then some about crayons and Crayola, including that the product's name derives from *craie,* the French word for chalk, and "ola," from the English word "oleaginous." The first box of Crayola crayons, containing eight colors—red,

CANALS

Pennsylvania's canal system was actively used between 1826 and 1900, and in its heyday had 900 miles of state-owned and 300 miles of privately owned canals. Charles Dickens was 30 years old when he traveled on the canal in 1842.

There was much in this mode of traveling which I heartily enjoyed at the time, and look back upon with great pleasure. Even the running up, bare-necked, at 5 o'clock in the morning from the tainted cabin to the dirty deck; scooping up the icy water, plunging one's head into it, and drawing it out, all fresh and glowing with the cold; was a good thing. The fast, brisk walk upon the towing-path, between that time and breakfast, when every vein and artery seemed to tingle with health; the exquisite beauty of the opening day, when light came gleaming off from everything; the lazy motion of the boat, when one lay idly on the deck, looking through, rather than at, the deep blue sky; the gliding on, at night, so noiselessly, past frowning hills, sullen with dark trees, and sometimes angry in one red burning spot high up, where unseen men lay crouching round a fire; the shining out of the bright stars, undisturbed by noise of wheels or steam, or any other sound than the liquid rippling of the water as the boat went on: all these were pure delights.

Canal Scene on the Juniata, *by George Storm. (State Museum of Pennsylvania)*

orange, yellow, green, blue, violet, brown, and black—was produced in 1903 and sold for a nickel. The **National Canal Museum,** on the third and fourth floors, charts the history of the country's extensive waterways transport system in the 19th century. The inland canal network is detailed in wall-size panels and in displays of equipment used to build the canals. Hands-on exhibits allow you to operate a model lock and pilot a scaled-down canal boat.

■ HUGH MOORE HISTORICAL PARK *map page 97, E-1*
Named after the Easton businessman who made his fortune selling Dixie cups, and who also happened to have a fondness for canal history, this historic park runs along the banks of the Lehigh River for 6 miles on land bought by the city from the Lehigh Coal and Navigation Company. It includes a restored portion of the Lehigh Canal—on which you can take a ride aboard a mule-drawn canal boat, the *Josiah White II*—as well as the 1890s lock-tender's house, now a museum. Outside the house, canal boats enter Lock 47 and rise 8 feet in about five minutes as a hydrostatic valve is opened. Company founders Josiah White and Erskine Hazard invented the valve, which helped give the Lehigh Canal the largest carrying capacity of any canal in the country. *2.5 miles north of I-78; 610-515-8000.*

■ DELAWARE LOOP DRIVE *map page 102*

A popular day trip with New Yorkers, Philadelphians, and other travelers is the drive up the Pennsylvania side of the Delaware River through Bucks County, following Routes 32 and 611 to Easton, then crossing into New Jersey on I-78 and lazily following Route 29 back down the other side, stopping to scout antique stores and crafts shops en route. Before you get as far south as Trenton, New Jersey, you'll come to a bridge that will take you back over the Delaware to Washington Crossing. From there you can venture inland and absorb the rest that Bucks County has to offer.

■ BUCKS COUNTY WEST *map page 97, E-2*

Many people argue that the most bucolic region in Bucks County is along the Delaware, but some of the region's best sights and museums—among them the Moravian Pottery and Tile Works, the James A. Michener Art Museum, and the Pearl S. Buck House—lie well west of the river in Doylestown.

■ **DOYLESTOWN AREA** *map page 97, E-2*

Even though it's less than an hour's drive from Center City Philadelphia, the first thing you realize when you reach Doylestown's central business district is that the foot traffic on the tree-canopied streets eases along at a languid pace. First settled in the 1730s, and once a stop on the stagecoach line between Philadelphia and Easton, Doylestown is steeped in early American history, and much of the town is on the National Register of Historic Places. Take a stroll through downtown to see the hundreds of preserved and carefully restored buildings, many of which now house boutiques, cozy cafes, and restaurants.

Mercer Mile

Doylestown native Henry Chapman Mercer (1856–1930), a Harvard-educated millionaire, was a historian, archaeologist, and ceramist—"Renaissance man" is the term usually used to describe him—as well as a dedicated collector. Fascinated by the objects used in everyday life in pre-industrial America, he began to collect them in 1897, visiting junk dealers and selecting pieces that would tell the story of work and leisure in the American experience.

Today more than 50,000 objects reflecting Mercer's objective—the tools of more than 60 Early American trades and crafts—are in the collection of the **Mercer Museum,** a large reinforced-concrete "castle," begun in 1913, completed in 1916, and constructed without the assistance of architects or blueprints. Some people find it bizarre, others unique. It is one of three buildings by Mercer, all now National Historic Landmarks and known collectively as the Mercer Mile. *84 South Pine Street; 215-345-0210.*

Artisanal crafts were Mercer's first love, and in 1898 he established the **Moravian Pottery and Tile Works**—named for his collection of Moravian stove plates—to produce ceramic tiles. In 1903, commissioned with creating tiles for the floor of the new state capitol building in Harrisburg, he turned out 377 tiles depicting Pennsylvania flora, fauna, and history. The reinforced-concrete building housing the factory, built in the style of a U-shaped California mission church, was completed in 1912. Today it is a combined museum and manufacturing plant specializing in the production of distinctive decorative tiles using traditional crafting and firing methods. A slide show and lecture introduces Mercer's world. Tours include a walk through the factory. *130 Swamp Road; 215-345-6722.*

Henry Chapman Mercer's Fonthill castle is an exuberant mix of sand, concrete, wood, and thousands upon thousands of decorative tiles.

The third concrete "castle," **Fonthill,** was Mercer's residence, built between 1908 and 1910 and inspired by whimsy rather than by any architect's plans. Mercer sketched it from the inside out and hired local laborers, none of whom had ever built a house before, to build it. The overall effect is of a haphazard, multitextured extravaganza. The basic structure is concrete, but other building materials include sand, grass, Mercer's precious tiles, and wooden posts. With 44 rooms, 18 fireplaces, 200 windows, and 32 stairwells, Fonthill is impressive in an odd sort of way, but exhausting to visit, and most people breathe a sigh of relief when they leave. The museum here includes Mercer's vast collection of decorative tiles, pottery, lighting devices, and prints. *East Court Street at Swamp Road; 215-348-9461. Guided tours only, reservations required.*

The late James Michener, the author of mammoth novels like *Hawaii, The Source, Centennial,* and *Chesapeake,* was raised in Doylestown, and the town's regional art museum is named after its famous native. The **James A. Michener Art Museum,** inside the former Bucks County Jail, built in 1884, contains seven galleries of 19th- and 20th-century American art. The museum, which has an outdoor sculpture garden, often exhibits the works of Bucks County artists. *138 South Pine Street; 215-340-9800.*

Pearl S. Buck House   *map page 97, E-2*

Six miles north of Doylestown (take Route 313 to Dublin and turn left onto Dublin Road) is Green Hills Farm, former residence of the Nobel laureate and Pulitzer Prize–winning author of *The Good Earth* and *My Several Worlds.* Born in 1892 to parents who were missionaries, and raised in China from the age of four, Buck made her experiences with China and Chinese life the focus of much of her writing.

Buck and her second husband, Richard Walsh, purchased this 48-acre farm (dating from 1835) in 1934, as a home for themselves and their family, which included seven adopted children. The house, fancifully filled with American and Asian antiques, remains much the same as when Buck lived and wrote here.

In 1949, Buck founded Welcome House, to find homes for "unadoptable" mixed-race children, and in 1964, she formed the Pearl S. Buck Foundation to assist primarily Asian children not eligible for adoption. She died here in 1973 and is buried on the property, which is now the headquarters of Pearl S. Buck International, a humanitarian assistance organization that carries on her charity work. *520 Dublin Road, Hilltop Township (Perkasie); 215-249-0100.*

■ BERKS COUNTY DUTCH HEX SIGNS

The Pennsylvania Germans who began settling in southeastern Pennsylvania in the late 1600s and early 1700s brought with them their language, their old-world customs, and their decorative arts—unique painted furniture, quilts, and other household articles with distinctive, geometric designs. In the mid-19th century (paint was too costly before then), these colorful designs began to appear on barns. For the Plain People of Lancaster County, such decoration would have signified vanity, so you will see more of this folk art in areas inhabited by the "fancy" Dutch, their less conservatively religious cousins. Berks and Lehigh Counties have a lot of barn art.

Use of the term "hex" to describe these designs has been traced to a guidebook of the 1920s. Presumably, they were meant to ward off the influence of the devil. The symbolic meanings attached to them—stars for good fortune, hearts for love, tulips for faith, the stylized bird known as the *distelfink* for happiness—may well have roots in superstition. But it's more likely that when a Pennsylvania Dutch farmer sets out to touch up his barn stars today, he's doing it "chust for nice."

A farmer and his chickens in front of a barn in Berks County.

BERKS COUNTY HEX BARN TOUR *map page 97, C-1/2*

The following tour will take you through a wonderful region of the state, an area with more than a few memorable examples of Berks County hex signs. Maps for this drive are available from the **Reading and Berks County Visitors Bureau** (352 Penn Street, Reading; 610-375-4085 or 800-443-6610; www.readingberkspa.com— click on "Getaway Ideas").

Continuing north from the western Bucks County area, take the Kutztown Road exit off U.S. 222, take a right, and drive through town, cutting through the leafy campus of Kutztown State University, then continuing to the junction of Kutztown Road and Crystal Cave Road. Set your odometer to zero and take a right toward Crystal Cave park. You'll roll through wooded countryside interspersed with open farms and fields, and at 5.0 miles **Barn One,** on the Stutzman farm, will be tucked behind a clump of trees on the right. The winding road crests out on a open hilltop, offering views to all sides, then descends rather steeply, and at 5.5 miles you'll see **Barn Two,** the monstrous, weathered white barn of the Dreibelbis farm, with its fading but intricate hexes, sitting quaintly in the middle of a luxuriantly green pasture.

After 6 miles, take a left onto Route 143 south, and after another half-mile, **Barn Three** will be on the left; **Barn Four** is perched on a rise to the right at the 6.9-mile point. At 8.1 miles, keep your eyes peeled for easy-to-miss Route 662, and after turning right onto it proceed 0.3 miles, where just off the road on the right you'll find **Barn Five,** a beautiful red barn with four hexes painted on its broad side. There's a place to pull the car over and see it relatively close up, without being overly invasive.

The next 3.5 miles are barn-free, so take in the quiet, hilly countryside, stealing glances skyward for hawks riding on thermals, or looking into roadside thickets to spy whitetail deer snacking on vegetation. At the 12-mile mark you'll pass **Barn Six** on the right; then swing immediately right onto Windsor Castle Road and you'll pass **Barn Seven,** which is on the Christman farm, at the 12.2-mark on the right. When you hit the 13.7-mile marker, turn right onto Virginville Road. On the left side of the road, between here and mile 14.0, are **Barns Eight, Nine,** and **Ten.** They're all huge dairy barns painted with hexes of horse heads (the Amish Carriage Horse hex protects horses and livestock) and rows of hexes with birds (the Double Distlefink hex, for double good luck), as well as the more standard star patterns. At the 14.9- and 15.0-mile points, **Barns Eleven** and **Twelve,** both on the Miller farm, will be on your left.

At 16.4 miles turn left onto Route 143 North. The Sunday farm barn is on the left at 16.7 miles and the Leiby farm is on the left at 17.2 miles. Off to the right at 18.4 miles is the **Dreibelbis Covered Bridge,** which bears a colorful, star-shaped hex over the entrance. At mile 20 you'll come to Old Route 22, also known as the Hex Highway, where you'll go left, continue one block to Deitsch Eck Restaurant, and turn right onto Route 143 North, which will take you to **Barn Fifteen. Barn Sixteen**, at 20.3 miles, is just ahead on the left, and, after passing under I-78, **Barn Seventeen** is also on the left, at 22.9 miles.

You'll wind past farms and scattered woods, then, after taking a left at mile 24.2 onto Hawk Mountain Road (just past Raberts Garage on the right), **Barn Eighteen** will be on the right at 24.5 miles. The land starts to be a bit more steep and wooded now as you follow along Kittatinny Ridge to your left. Coming through here in the late evening, the fading sunlight covers the countryside with subtle bursts of color, and in the distance the spire of a church and a small, rounded hill studded with tombstones are illuminated in the glow.

Climbing slowly up the ridge, you'll come to mile 28.1 and **Barn Nineteen**, the shop of Robertsons Restoration, which is on the right and covered with a variety of hex designs. The final barn of the tour, **Barn Twenty,** sits 0.3 miles farther along on the right side of the road and is adorned with two freshly painted starburst-design hexes.

Birders on the North Overlook at Hawk Mountain Sanctuary.

■ **HAWK MOUNTAIN SANCTUARY** *map page 97, C-1*

The drive on Route 895 along Kittatinny Ridge passes through open farm country until you reach the 2,400-acre Hawk Mountain Sanctuary. Each year between mid-August and mid-December, more than 18,000 birds, including 16 species of raptors, pass by here on their annual migration to Central and South America. The preserve was founded by local conservationist Rosalie Edge in 1934 to save these magnificent creatures from hunters who slaughtered them wholesale for "sport" and under the guise of protecting their livestock. It was the first refuge for birds of prey in the world.

The best time to spot ospreys, American kestrels, and broad-winged hawks is in late August and September; peregrine falcons and merlins visit in October; and red-winged hawks and golden eagles in November and early December. The best viewing points are from the South and North Lookouts. From the visitors center, it's an easy five-minute stroll along a well-groomed path to the South Overlook, where a panoramic vista reveals the rolling farm country below. The trail to the North Overlook is rockier and a more strenuous 45-minute climb, but worth every

Double your pleasure at the Kutztown German Festival.

step when you arrive at the top and gaze out over the sheer cliffs, rocky outcroppings, and dense forest in the valley below. *1700 Hawk Mountain Road, off Route 895, Kempton; 610-756-6000.*

■ **READING AREA** *map page 97, C-2*

Reading is a struggling post-industrial city reinventing itself to fit into a new economic niche—outlet shopping. Ten million consumption-crazed visitors flock here every year to grab bargains at the 300 outlet stores around the town. Reading was once a center for the manufacture of textiles, and its new incarnation is a fairly natural outgrowth of the sale of mill overruns and irregulars to employees. Just west of Reading in nearby Wyomissing, the VF Outlet Village, which has about 90 stores and offers some of the best selections and prices, occupies the old Berkshire Knitting Mill, once the largest hosiery mill in the world. The smaller Reading Outlet Center is also housed, in part, in an old factory that once produced silk stockings. The Reading Station Outlet Center, on the other hand, was the headquarters of the Reading Railroad.

■ THE PAGODA *map page 97, C-2*

The Pagoda is a seven-story Japanese castle perched on top of Mount Penn, just south of Reading. It was built in 1908 by Reading businessman William A. Witman, who made his fortune as the owner of a rock quarry on the mountain. Concerns that the operation was turning the area's highest point into an eyesore prompted Witman to close the quarry, after which he built a resort modeled after a castle of the Shogun dynasty.

The resort failed, and the castle was neglected and abandoned by a series of owners until it was renovated by a local preservation group in 1969. It is now home to the Berks Arts Council. The second-floor gallery presents fine exhibits, but the real treats here are the peaceful Oriental garden and panoramic views of the Reading area. *98 Duryea Drive; 610-655-6374.*

■ DANIEL BOONE HOMESTEAD *map page 97, C-2*

About 8 miles east of Reading, the Daniel Boone Homestead provides a unique view of what rural life was like for Pennsylvania families in the mid-1700s. Dense woodlands make up most of the 579-acre park, and you can see the foundation of the cabin where Boone lived until the age of 16. The remote feel of the area—it's a 3-mile drive from the entrance to the visitors center—makes it easier for the visitor to imagine how early settlers had to fend for themselves in remote sections of southeast Pennsylvania.

Boone gained the foundation of his legendary frontiersman skills while growing up here. Writes John Mack Faragher in his 1992 book, *Daniel Boone,* the young Daniel "found his forest teachers" among "backwoods hunters descended from European colonists, many of them of Scandinavian background, whom the Delawares called *nittappi,* or friends. There were Indians of many ethnic varieties who also called friend this young hunter....These men of the forest frontier instructed Daniel in a way of life that combined elements of both cultures and bridged many of the differences between Indian and European."

In 1750, Boone's parents had a falling out with the Quaker church, which disapproved when first one of their daughters and then a son married "worldlings." The family headed for North Carolina. The remains of the homestead they left behind include 14 miles of wooded trails, the ruins of the original cabin, and a two-story stone house built in the late 1700s after the Boones had moved on. *Daniel Boone Road off Route 422; 610-582-4900.*

■ HOPEWELL FURNACE NATIONAL HISTORIC SITE *map page 97, D-2/3*

One of the earliest and now best-preserved iron manufacturing furnaces in the United States, the Hopewell Furnace, 17 miles southeast of Reading, churned out cannons and shot during the Revolutionary War and cooking stoves and farm tools during peaceful colonial times.

The furnace was built in 1771 by Mark Bird and operated until 1883, though its peak years were between 1820 and 1840. It is considered a fine example of a 19th-century iron "plantation," an entire community devoted to iron making. Such communities had to be built near good sources of iron ore (there were three mines nearby); wood, which was used to make the charcoal that fueled the furnace; and water. A waterwheel powered the bellows that blew air into the furnace, keeping it at nearly 3,000 degrees. The cast house, the big white building with the steeple containing the 32-foot stone furnace, is the centerpiece of Hopewell, but you can also visit the remaining three of 14 workers' houses, the ironmaster's mansion, the wheelhouse, and other buildings. The surrounding French Creek State Park was the source of Hopewell's raw materials; a century ago it was virtually denuded, but the forest has returned. *2 Mark Bird Lane, Elverson; 610-582-8773.*

■ PENNSYLVANIA DUTCH COUNTRY *map page 97, B/C-3/4*

Travelers from around the world flock to this region of southeast Pennsylvania to catch a glimpse of the quaint and simple life led by the Plain People, the members of several religious groups that have been quietly going about their business in this countryside for close to 300 years. Their plain dress, which makes them the most distinctive of the Pennsylvania Dutch, is the outward sign of their austere lifestyle, marked by separation from society and solidarity with their own community. They include the Old Order Amish (the large majority of the Amish), Old Order Mennonites (about a third of the Mennonites), and a few Old Order Brethren.

The Mennonites trace their origins to the Swiss Anabaptist movement of early 16th-century Europe. Their belief in adult baptism set them off from the mainstream Protestantism that emerged from the Reformation, and in 1693, the more rigorous Amish split off from the Mennonites. Fleeing religious persecution in the Rhineland-Palatinate and Alsace areas of present-day Germany and France, the first sizable groups of Amish and Mennonite settlers arrived in Lancaster County in the early 1700s. They were attracted by the promise of William Penn's "Holy Experiment" in religious tolerance and by the region's fertile soil.

About 22,000 Old Order Amish live in Lancaster County. They constitute 90 percent of Lancaster's Amish—more progressive groups make up the remainder. (About half the Amish in Pennsylvania live in Lancaster County.) They live in the countryside, especially southeast of Lancaster, around the towns of Ephrata, Bird-in-Hand, Intercourse, Paradise, and Strasburg, making this the second-largest Old Order community in the country, next to Holmes County, Ohio.

It's easy to spot the Amish: men and boys wear dark suits topped with broad-brimmed hats of straw or black felt; women and girls wear modest, solid-color, mid-calf-length dresses covered with an apron and a cape whose apex is fastened at the waistline in back and whose two sides are brought up over the shoulders, crisscrossed, and fastened. Black is the predominant clothing color; gray, green, blue, wine, and purple are also typical. No zippers hold things together, just safety and straight pins, buttons, snaps, and hooks and eyes. Men have untrimmed beards, but no mustaches, which these pacifists deem militaristic. Women never cut their hair, and wear it in a bun on the back of the head. If married, they wear a

(above) A team of horses pulls a plow for this Amish farmer. (opposite) An Amish family out for a spin in Lancaster County, home to an estimated 22,000 Old Order Amish.

An Amish driver takes his buggy over the Jackson Mill covered bridge in Bart Township.

white prayer covering; if single, a black one. Over all goes a shawl, and a bonnet is worn. They do not wear jewelry, even wedding rings. The Amish feel their simple clothes encourage humility and signal their separation from worldly society.

Old Order groups drive horses and buggies and do not have electricity in their homes, although they may use electricity in their businesses, provided they generate it themselves and are not connected to the public utility lines. Their children attend school only through the eighth grade, in private, one-room schoolhouses—their fight for exemption from compulsory public school attendance resulted in jail time for many Amish people until the Supreme Court ruled in their favor in 1972. One of the subjects they study in school is English, because until they go to school, the Amish speak only Pennsylvania Dutch, the old dialect of German they use in everyday life—another sign of separation from the larger society. After school they work on the family farm or in the family business until they marry.

Traveling in this region, you'll notice a host of seeming contradictions: families in horse-drawn buggies clopping past the monstrous Wal-Mart store on Main Street in Ephrata; a young girl in a homemade dress, pigtails streaming behind her,

Amish children attend school only through the eighth grade, in schoolhouses like the one above.

schussing down a side road on a pair of Rollerblades. You'll witness the incongruity of a religious people seeking to distance themselves from the modern world, while the inhabitants of that very same world clamber for a closer look. There's a further paradox: As the Amish population grows, the four million tourists who head this way each year are helping more and more of them make a living.

The Amish are anything but a dying community. Families with from five to seven children are common. At the same time, Lancaster County is one of the fastest-growing areas in the state, leading to a serious loss of farmland and raising land prices to unaffordable levels. The World Monuments Fund has placed Lancaster County on its list of endangered sites, and the National Trust for Historic Preservation has put the county on a similar list. During the 1990s the county developed a master plan to channel growth and safeguard its unique heritage. Preserving farmland by buying up development rights is part of the effort. Nevertheless, more and more Old Order groups are turning to nonfarm work. Fortunately, the crafts and baked goods that the tourists lap up are products suitable to their way of life.

■ **LANCASTER** *map page 97, B-3*

Lancaster, pronounced LANK-uh-stir, was founded in 1710 by lieutenants of William Penn and named by the town's chief magistrate, John Wright, for his home shire of Lancaster, England. Lancaster is known as the Red Rose City because the symbol of the English House of Lancaster was the red rose. By 1760 Lancaster had become the largest inland city in the colonies, with 4,200 people and 600 houses. With an abundance of craftsmen and nearby iron ore furnaces, it had become a gun-producing center: Swiss and German weapons makers developed the highly accurate Pennsylvania long rifle here.

During the Revolution, Lancaster supplied the Continental Army with high-quality arms and ammunition. The city was, for one day only—September 27, 1777—the capital of the colonies, after George Washington failed to stop the British advance at the Battle of Brandywine, which forced the members of the Continental Congress to flee Philadelphia. They paused to hold a session in the courthouse on Lancaster's Penn Square, thus making the city the temporary capital, and then went on to York, where they convened for nine months before heading back to Philadelphia. From 1799 to 1812, though, Lancaster served as the capital of Pennsylvania.

Lancaster's economy is based on agriculture, light manufacturing, retail trade, and tourism. The city of 56,000 people has a pleasant center with tree-shaded streets and rows of majestic colonial- and Victorian-era homes and historic churches. There is plenty to see, which makes Lancaster a good place to kick off a visit to Pennsylvania Dutch country.

Smack in the center of town is **Penn Square,** and two blocks south, in the old red brick and gabled Southern Market building, is the **Lancaster Visitors Center,** run by the Lancaster Chamber of Commerce and Industry and bursting with information on what to see and do. Here you can sign up for the **Historic Lancaster Walking Tour** (717-392-1776; daily from April through October and by reservation the rest of the year). You can also pick up maps and brochures for the **Victorian West Chestnut Street Walking Tour** and the **Freedom of Religion Walking Tour,** which will take you past some of the city's very fine 18th- and 19th-century churches. *South Queen and East Vine Streets; 717-397-3531.*

Martin's Pretzel Factory in Akron, outside Lancaster, is owned and run by Mennonites.

After walking your feet off, you might want to join the life-size bronze statue of a newspaper reader sitting on the park bench at the entrance to **Steinman Park** (22 West King Street). The brick-paved and tree-shaded vest-pocket park is next door to the building occupied by Steinman Hardware from 1886 to 1965. The company is said to have been founded in 1744. Look above the door, and you'll see a Conestoga wagon in stained glass. The red wheels, white cover, and Prussian blue body were the standard colors of this early American freight hauler, which was invented in the nearby Conestoga Valley and for which Steinman Hardware used to supply parts.

The cavernous building is now occupied by the **Pressroom** (26–28 West King Street; 717-399-5400) restaurant, whose decor has a newspaper theme. It's fitting, because Lancaster has three newspapers, and they're all published by the Steinman family. The oldest, the *Intelligencer Journal,* established in 1794 and bought by the Steinmans in 1866, is the morning paper, with a Democratic/liberal bent, while the *Lancaster New Era,* the afternoon paper, has a Republican/conservative bent. The *Sunday News* is nonpartisan.

■ LANCASTER AREA SIGHTS

At the heart of downtown, in two old buildings dating from the 1790s—the old City Hall and Masonic Lodge Hall (where both the Marquis de Lafayette and President James Buchanan attended ceremonies)—the **Heritage Center Museum** brings Pennsylvania Dutch history to life with fine examples of regional furniture, tall-case clocks, redware pottery, *Scherenschnitte* (scissor art), metalwork, needle-work, and birth and baptismal certificates and other documents in the decorative *Fraktur* style. The museum shop sells the works of local artisans, including Ned Foltz, a well-known creator of Pennsylvania redware pottery. The museum is closed during the winter. *13 West King Street, at Penn Square; 717-299-6440.*

Central Market, behind the museum in a redbrick Romanesque Revival building erected in 1889, is the country's oldest publicly owned farmers market. Open on Tuesdays, Fridays, and Saturdays, the market is a worthy attraction for tourists, though it is much more than that, as the procession of locals entering it with shopping baskets tucked under their arms will tell you. Inside is booth after booth of locally produced meats, sausages, and cheeses, fresh fruits and vegetables, prepared foods, baked goods, flowers, and craft items. Many of the vendors are Amish or Mennonite, and although you can buy a bagel, a southern sweet-potato pie, or gourmet coffee, this is really the place to stock up on local items like scrapple, corn

Amish and Mennonite bakers sell their edibles at the Romanesque Revival Central Market.

on the cob "pulled this morning," and shoo-fly pie. Scrapple, consisting of slices of pork mush (made of the leftovers of the pig after butchering) that are usually fried, is a breakfast staple for many in these parts. Shoo-fly pie is a gooey concoction, heavy on the molasses. *Penn Square; 717-291-4723.*

The history of the **Fulton Opera House** is the history of the American theater, they'll tell you, and as you read the names of those who have appeared here, you realize that's no idle claim: Tom Thumb, Mark Twain, Buffalo Bill and Wild Bill Hickok, John Phillip Sousa and the U.S. Marine Band, the Barrymores, W.C. Fields, Sarah Bernhardt, and Al Jolson. The theater was built in 1852, and early audiences had to put up with smoke and gunpowder drifting down from a shooting gallery on the top floor and the smell of fertilizer and tobacco stored in the basement. A drastic remodeling in 1873 transformed the structure into a European-style "opera house," although operas were not performed here immediately. Another renovation in 1904 added a second balcony with pew seating to accommodate the growing audiences attracted by vaudeville and, later, "talkies."

By the 1960s the theater was slated for the wrecking ball. Saved by community spirit and designation as a National Historic Landmark, the building is now fresh

museu 1 - 4 Sunday.

from a multimillion-dollar restoration, once again a gem of plaster rosettes, scrolls, and cherubs decked out in gilt and Victorian-correct colors, with red velvet seating and chandeliers imitating the original gaslight. You can tour the building daily year-round or see it during one of the shows put on by the Actors Company of Pennsylvania, which performs from September through May, or during the brief fall and spring seasons of the Lancaster Opera Company. *12 North Prince Street; 717-397-7425.*

The paintings of Lancaster native Charles Demuth, a pioneer of modernism, are in museums all over the world. Most of them were created in his studio on the second floor of the 18th-century **Demuth House.** Demuth gained early recognition for his watercolors of flowers, fruits, and vegetables—subjects he could see in the flower garden his mother, Augusta, tended in the courtyard beneath his window and in the farmers markets not far away. Later, influenced by exposure to cubism during travels to Europe, he turned to architectural themes and became known for his precisionist style. His famous *My Egypt,* in New York City's Whitney Museum of American Art, depicts the Eshelman grain elevators that once stood nearby; *Chimney and Water Tower* depicts the Armstrong plant; and *Welcome to Our City* the Lancaster Courthouse. Once a year, for two months around June, about 30 Demuth works owned by the Demuth Foundation are brought out of storage and put on display here.

Next door is the **Demuth Tobacco Shop,** opened in 1770 by Christopher Demuth and now the oldest continuously operated tobacco shop in the country. It was the prosperity of this enterprise that spared Charles Demuth, who was sickly and suffered from diabetes, the worries of earning a living, allowing him to paint. The shop displays some ancient smoking bric-a-brac (plus some antique firemen's hats) and sells mainly pipe tobacco and cigars, including the locally made Amish Fancy Tails and Amish Palmas. The shop keeps regular business hours; the house is closed in January. *114–120 East King Street; 717-299-9940.*

James Buchanan, the only president from Pennsylvania (1857–1861) and the only bachelor president—he often said

This late-19th-century weathervane reveals the craftsmanship of Pennsylvania Dutch metalworkers. (Heritage Center Museum)

This Lancaster County birth record is an example of the Pennsylvania Dutch art of decorative illumination known as Fraktur. *(Heritage Center Museum)*

John Bachman A son of Jacob Bachman and wife Barbara A Daughter of Christian Kindig was born on the 10th Day of June In the year of our Lord 1832 In the Township of Lampeter in the County of Lancaster in the State of Pennsylvania in North AMERICA

Thou with thy counsel while I live wilt me conduct and guide And to thy Glory afterward receive me to abide

Whom have I in the heaven high but thee O Lord alone And in the earth whom Ideʃire beʃide thee there is none

publicly that he entered politics in his 30s as a diversion from grief after the death of his fiancée, a Lancaster woman—bought **Wheatland,** a Federal mansion, in 1848. He lived in it, except for his term as the 15th president, until his death. Buchanan's presidency was marred by dissension over states' rights and slavery issues, and many historians rank him among the worst of presidents. Others judge him a victim of circumstances. A scholar of constitutional law, he felt that slavery was morally wrong but protected by the Constitution where it already existed. He also felt that it was up to new territories to choose to be free or slave states. His attempts to strike a "sacred balance" between pro-slavery and anti-slavery factions succeeded only in angering both sides, and by the time he left office, his efforts to preserve the union through compromise had failed to prevent the secession of six states. The Civil War broke out shortly thereafter.

Yet he was one of the best prepared of presidents, having been a representative, senator, minister to Russia and Great Britain, and secretary of state. On his diplomatic missions he was accompanied by his orphan niece, Harriet Lane, who also served as his First Lady in the White House. She lived at Wheatland until her

inherited it, and used it as a summer house until she sold it in
⟩ry house, built in 1828, reflects her sophisticated style—it was
⟩ho bought her uncle the desk at which he wrote his memoirs,
ministration on the Eve of the Rebellion. Everything but the floor
coverings and draperies is of the period, and many of the larger pieces of furniture
are original to the house. The Wilsons, who occupied it from 1884 to 1934,
upgraded the bathroom: note the wood-encased tin tub and the bidet. Then go
out back to the original privy, with three adult seats on one side—for servants, perhaps?—and two adult and three smaller seats of graduated heights on the other.
Well-marked herb and flower gardens are behind the estate. The house is closed in
winter. *1120 Marietta Avenue; 717-392-8721.*

The outdoor **Landis Valley Museum,** 2.5 miles north of Lancaster, depicts the
rural life of the Pennsylvania Dutch from the 1740s through 1940. It consists of
about two dozen buildings, some original to the area and some relocated, laid out
to form a crossroads village and its adjoining farms. You can wander from barn to
blacksmith shop, from tavern to tin shop to print shop, and listen to costumed
docents explaining the work of artisans and farmers. The museum also has several
Conestoga wagons; these massive covered vehicles, developed in Lancaster County
in the mid-18th century, were the tractor-trailers of their day, hauling freight
between Lancaster and Philadelphia and points west. The museum is home to the
Heirloom Seed Project, which seeks to preserve vegetables, herbs, and flowers lost
to the effects of hybridization and mechanized agriculture.

Save time to browse through the museum's shop, whose inventory includes
handmade dolls, beeswax candles, shirts and bonnets, handwoven linens, paintings, and some of the crafts—wood carvings, paper cuttings, paintings on tin, and
others—demonstrated by artisans at the museum. *2451 Kissel Hill Road (Route
272/Oregon Pike); 717-569-0401.*

■ INTO THE COUNTRYSIDE

Anyone interested in getting a taste of the authentic Amish experience must venture
out to the smaller towns and gently rolling farm country where the Amish live and
work. There's really no "best way" to tour the region, but the relative proximity of
the towns, and the small area that contains them, tends to encourage you to follow
your own impulses. Good places to start are the corridors heading east out from

Lancaster: toward Bird-in-Hand and Intercourse along Route 340; toward Paradise along Route 30; and toward Strasburg, at the junction of Routes 896 and 741.

In Lancaster County, handmade Amish quilts and Mennonite furniture—more like works of art than household goods—are sold from the makers' own homes and at retail outlets that come recommended by visitors bureaus. Other valued Pennsylvania Dutch crafts include needlework, such as tablecloths and napkins; gardening tools; leather goods; pottery; and toys. Primary locations include Lancaster, Intercourse—where the Amish conduct much of their regular business—and Bird-in-Hand.

Visitors centers throughout the region carry standard warnings that while there are reputable dealers who offer the best Pennsylvania Dutch craftwork, imitations are common, so the buyer must beware. Another reality check: much of the best work here passes by the local market and is handled through galleries in large cities such as Philadelphia and New York.

The sights below are organized roughly in a counterclockwise spiral that begins southeast of Lancaster.

Five miles south of Lancaster, the stone **Hans Herr House** was completed in 1719. The oldest building in Lancaster County, it is one of the best examples of medieval German architecture in North America. Hans Herr was the patriarch of a group of Swiss Mennonites who arrived in the area in 1711, and the house, built by his son, Christian, was probably lived in by both men and their families. Because they were both Mennonite bishops, the house was used for services, making it the oldest Mennonite meeting house in

This hope chest, crafted about 1792 in Lehigh or Berks County, exemplifies the furniture built by German craftsmen from the late 18th to the early 19th century. (Philadelphia Museum of Art)

the Western Hemisphere. Artist Andrew Wyeth, a descendent of Herr, included the house, which is open from April through November and by appointment the rest of the year, in several of his paintings. *1849 Hans Herr Drive, in the town of Willow Street; 717-464-4438.*

About 3 miles east of Lancaster via Route 462, the **Mennonite Information Center** is a good place to get background information on the lives and history of the Mennonites. There are audiovisual displays and a 20-minute film plays regularly. Contact the center if you wish to stay in a Mennonite guest home or find a Mennonite tour guide. *2209 Millstream Road, Lancaster; 717-299-0954.*

■ STRASBURG AND INTERCOURSE   *map page 97, B/C-3*

At the **Amish Village** you can take guided tours through a farmhouse from the 1840s that has been authentically furnished as an Old Order Amish home. A barn with animals, a blacksmith shop, a one-room schoolhouse, and a smokehouse are also on the site. To get to the village, head east from Lancaster along U.S. 30. *Route 896, about 2 miles north of Strasburg.*

The state-maintained **Railroad Museum of Pennsylvania** charts railroad history from its beginnings in the early 1800s to the present and does a great job of showing how the railroads transformed the state's economy and the face of the nation. You can climb into a caboose at the museum, or walk beneath a 62-ton steam locomotive. About 60 meticulously preserved locomotives and rail cars are on display in the cavernous original Rolling Stock Hall and the newly built New Railroaders Hall. Another 40 or so are outside in the Restoration Yard, where there's a working Reading Railroad turntable from 1928. *Route 741, Strasburg; 717-687-8628.*

Just down the road from the museum is the antique **Strasburg Rail Road,** whose trains wind for 9 miles round trip between Strasburg and Paradise, passing through beautiful farm country. On view through the windows are horse-drawn buggies paying no mind to cars swooshing by on backcountry roads and Amish men in their wide-brimmed straw hats directing horse-drawn plows along ever-so-neat rows. Before or after you board the train, inspect the opulent private coach that catered to the president of the Reading Railroad. The car, which is on static display, cost more than $100,000 to build back in 1913 and contains separate sleeping, dining, and meeting compartments. The lavish decor includes cut-glass chandeliers and floor-to-ceiling mahogany paneling. *Route 741, Strasburg; 717-687-7522.*

A Strasburg Rail Road train passes a corn maze near Paradise.

You can dine while you ride on the Strasburg Rail Road in the **Lee E. Brenner dining car** (717-687-6486 for reservations) or pack a lunch: the train stops at a picnic area just before Paradise. Or you can stick to the railroading theme and eat on the outskirts of Strasburg in the Victorian dining car that serves as the restaurant of the **Red Caboose Motel** (316 Paradise Lane; 717-687-5000), so-called because its rooms are in recycled cabooses, mail cars, and baggage cars.

The **People's Place** heritage center and bookshop, in Intercourse, is one of the better places to get a good understanding of the Amish and other Plain People sects. The 30-minute documentary *Who are the Amish?* plays continuously, and there is an interactive museum that answers the 20 most frequently asked questions about the Plain People. Next door is the **People's Place Quilt Museum,** plus the **Old Country Store,** an outlet for locally made crafts, including quilts of exceptional value. You can also purchase quilts in the museum shop, although these tend to be art pieces, not in traditional style and not necessarily locally made. The adjacent **Village Pottery** sells the works of various American potters. *3510 Old Philadelphia Pike (Route 340), Intercourse; 717-768-7171.*

THE AMISH AND THEIR QUILTS

The story begins in Switzerland, where in 1525 a group called the Brethren separated from the state church. They eventually became known as Mennonites, after Menno Simons, one of their early leaders. The Mennonites believed in separation of church and state, saying that man couldn't swear an oath of allegiance to anyone but God. They also espoused adult rather than infant baptism, since a child didn't know enough about true faith to make a commitment. The state church banned the new religion and a long, bloody history commenced. . . .

In 1693, Jacob Ammann, a Mennonite elder, formed his own splinter group. He felt that the Mennonites were too worldly. He also wanted to instigate the practice of shunning, whereby transgressors were ostracized. The Amish, as they became known . . . eventually migrated to America, seeking religious freedom. . . .

The Amish goal is to be self-sufficient from the outside world. They don't want to be part of the government structure. They pay taxes, but build and maintain their own schools. They don't collect welfare, pensions, or social security. They won't hold public office, although some of them vote. The Amish are conscientious objectors, serving in hospitals if drafted. They won't go to court if sued, and won't file suit themselves if wronged.

Amish women often love to embroider and to quilt. As always, since there must be a utilitarian function, the embroidery is done on tea towels and bed linens. Quilts are used for warmth, and are made at times of birth or marriage, and when old ones wear out. . . . The Diamond and Bars quilts are as unique as the Amish themselves. They are simple and unlike any other quilts in the mainstream of American quilting. Even

when the Amish work with familiar patterns, their version will be unusual because of their use of only solid colors. Prints are considered too worldly. No one knows for sure why the Amish have chosen to use color as they do. The end result is very strong and powerful. Perhaps that is reason enough.

—Roberta Horton, *An Amish Adventure*, second edition, 1996

A center diamond pattern quilt, ca. 1930. (Heritage Center Museum)

The Ephrata Cloister is now open to the public.

■ **BACK ROADS TO EPHRATA** *map page 97, C-3*

Some of the most appealing, authentically Amish farm country lies between Intercourse and the town of Ephrata to the north. There are endless combinations of back-road routes that wind lazily through the heart of this bucolic countryside dotted with white farmhouses. Arm yourself with a good map and follow whatever route strikes your fancy.

The **Ephrata Cloister,** a community of religious celibates, was founded in 1732 and practiced a no-frills existence with an emphasis on self-denial. Unlike other strict religious societies of the times, however, the group believed they honored God and themselves best when they were singing or engaging in artistic pursuits. The members, who numbered about 300 at the community's peak, held to rigid dietary restrictions in the belief that singing through the discomfort of a near-empty stomach made voices purer. Ephratans were admired for their skill in a form of calligraphy known as *Frakturschriften*—broken lettering. The cloister has a library filled with hand-lettered books, and many others that were produced here are held in rare book collections and research libraries.

me to tour the cloister is on a cold, gray winter's day, when you'll get
sense of how drafty and austere the medieval-style buildings can be.
walk the entire length of the narrow corridors and imagine being reminded day
after day that the path of virtue and humility is also straight and narrow—this
according to the preaching of founder Conrad Beissel, who wrote much of the
music sung by members. Also be sure to walk the grounds around the complex—
still set off from modern society by a wooded park—and visualize how much more
remote the community was more than 250 years ago. The last celibate member
died in 1813, but the cloister continued to be occupied until 1934 by married
members of the German Seventh-Day Baptist Church. *At Routes 322 and 272,
Ephrata; 717-733-6600.*

■ **LITITZ** *map page 97, B-3*
Just a few miles west of Ephrata along quiet Route 772, at the intersection with
Route 501, is peaceful Lititz, founded by a religious group, the Moravians, that
originated in Moravia and Bohemia in what is the present-day Czech Republic.
The Moravians may be the oldest of the Protestant denominations. Followers of
John Hus, a Protestant reformer who predated Martin Luther and was burned at
the stake for heresy in 1415, the Moravians came to America by way of Germany,
where they had sought refuge from persecution in the early 18th century.
Moravian missionaries arrived in the Lititz area in 1746 and, among others, converted a local farmer who deeded his property to the congregation 10 years later. A
church was built and a town laid out, and until 1856 only church members were
permitted to own land and live in Lititz.

The town really deserves to be described as "charming." The clean, tree-shaded
streets are lined with beautiful 18th-century buildings of fieldstone and aged red
brick, many housing antique stores and craft shops.

You can pick up a walking-tour map of the Main Street at the Lititz **Welcome
Center** (Lititz Springs Park), housed in a replica of the 1884 Lititz train station.
Before you even start your stroll, however, you may find yourself following the
sweet smell of chocolate that wafts from the Wilbur Chocolate Company's **Candy
Americana Museum & Factory Candy Store.** Here, next door to the train station, you can see the confections being made, sample some Wilbur Buds—which
the company has been making since 1894—and stock up on enough chocolate to
last you until you get to Hershey. *48 North Broad Street; 717-626-1131.*

The Wilbur Chocolate Company has been a Lititz institution for nearly a century.

The first site on the walking tour map is the **General Sutter Inn** (14 East Main Street; 717-626-2115), at the intersection of Broad and Main Streets. Established in 1764 as the Zum Anker Inn, it was renamed in the 1930s to call attention to the fact that the man who set off the California Gold Rush spent the last several years of his life in Lititz.

The walking tour wraps up at the spiritual heart of town, the wonderfully preserved **Moravian Church Square.** Bordering the square are the Moravian Church, built in 1787 but not the first on the spot, and Linden Hall, which was founded by the church in 1746 and is the oldest girls' boarding school in the United States.

Across the street are two old gray stone buildings owned by the Lititz Historical Foundation. One, built in 1793, houses the **Lititz Museum** (145 East Main Street; 717-627-4636), with historical artifacts. The other building, the **Johannes Mueller House** (137–139 East Main Street), was built in 1792 and is furnished as it would have been when its original occupant, a Moravian cloth dyer, lived there. The house was inhabited until 1962, and so little had been done to it over the years that it hardly needed restoration. The museum and house are both open from Memorial Day through October; the museum stays open on weekends to mid-December.

The **Sturgis Pretzel House** is the first commercial pretzel bakery in the country. The nominal tour fee gets you not only a pretzel as a ticket but also the chance to make your own pretzel. As the story goes, Julius Sturgis was baking bread in this 18th-century stone house in 1850 when, in thanks for a kindness, a stranger gave him the recipe for pretzels. They proved so popular that by 1861 the bakery was twisting pretzels full time. Nowadays the hard pretzels are made by machine, but the soft pretzels are still done by hand and baked in the old brick oven. *219 East Main Street; 717-626-4354.*

■ **MOUNT JOY** *map page 97, B-3*

Leaving Lititz on Route 772 and heading west toward the Susquehanna River, you enter the town of Mount Joy, where you can sample pleasantly unpretentious Mennonite cuisine—though "cuisine" really is too chichi a word for the down-home meal served at **Groff's Farm Restaurant** (650 Pinkerton Road; 717-653-2048), where the specialty is Betty Groff's creamed chicken.

For a pint and a tour, stop in at **Bube's Brewery.** German immigrant Alois Bube brewed lager here from 1876 until he was forced to close down in 1917 because of Prohibition. The 19th-century brewery survives in nearly intact condition, and in 2001 beer-making resumed in its ice house. The tour leads down narrow, winding passages to vaults 40 feet below street level that held the original brewery's fermentation tanks and may once have sheltered slaves moving along the Underground Railroad. Now the tanks sit alongside the tables of the complex's Catacombs restaurant. Bube's Brewery also holds the Bottling Works bar and restaurant, in the old bottling plant (with an adjacent Biergarten in good weather), plus the Alois restaurant, formerly the dining room of a Victorian-era hotel that Alois Bube opened to round out his business. *102 North Market Street; 717-653-2056.*

■ **MARIETTA** *map page 97, B-3*

After a 10-minute drive southwest of Mount Joy, at the junction of Route 772 and Route 441, you'll find the sleepy riverfront town of Marietta, where at least half of the buildings have earned designation on the National Registry of Historic Places. Stroll along Norman Rockwell-esque streets lined with elegant colonial, Federal-style, and Victorian homes, complete with manicured lawns, towering shade trees, and huge American flags flying from front porches. That this newly polished former mill town is nurturing a growing artist's community is evident in many galleries, studios, and antique shops in the village center.

If you have time on your hands, visit the National Watch and Clock Museum in Columbia.

■ CHICKIES ROCK COUNTY PARK *map page 97, B-3*
Give the Amish a break and pull off at this riverfront park to gawk at the swans
and green herons gracefully plying the slow-rolling waters of the Susquehanna and
at the ospreys and bald eagles skimming the surface to snatch fish in their talons.
You may see rock climbers (humans, not birds) scaling the walls at Chickies Rock
itself, because this is considered the best place for the sport in the area. The 444-
mile-long Susquehanna River is shallow and rocky here, its flow contained by
hydroelectric dams. The park has two spectacular overlooks from which you can
observe the wildlife along the steep banks of the river. *Route 441 between Marietta
and Columbia; 717-295-2055 or 717-299-8215.*

■ COLUMBIA *map page 97, B-3*
Two easy miles south of Marietta on Route 441 is the placid town of Columbia,
stretching languidly along the riverfront and peppered with B&Bs, good restaurants,
and antique shops. The town is best known for the more-interesting-than-it-sounds
National Watch and Clock Museum, with 8,000 items in the collection. Hanging
over the reception desk is the Latin motto *Tempus vitam regit*—"Time rules life."

But time gets lost here amid the various timepieces, which include an Egyptian pot that measures time with dripping water, American railroad watches, an entire room of cuckooing cuckoo clocks, and, perhaps the museum's greatest treasure, the Engle Clock, the first American-made monumental clock, an 11- by 8- by 3-foot timepiece in an exquisitely carved case. Made by Stephen Engle, a clock-maker from Hazleton, it has 48 moving figures, including Jesus, the 12 Apostles, and Engle himself as one of the three Ages of Man. Engle worked on the clock for 20 years before completing it in 1877; he then turned it over to a pair of Philadelphia entrepreneurs, who took it on tour around the eastern United States, advertising it as the Eighth Wonder of the World. *514 Poplar Street, Columbia; 717-684-8261.*

■ **HERSHEY** *map page 97, A-2*

The smell of chocolate permeates part of Lititz, but here's a town where, no matter the direction of the wind or time of day, the aroma of chocolate wafts through the air. It has a main street named Chocolate Avenue, and street lights in the shape of foil-wrapped Hershey's Kisses. Chocolate addicts following their noses directly to Hershey's Chocolate World may not fully appreciate the significance of the place, but the man who built the world's largest chocolate factory produced a lot more than just chocolate. Hershey is basically a factory town, sweetened with a tourist destination that draws 1.5 million visitors a year.

After failed attempts to manufacture and sell candy in Philadelphia and New York City, native son Milton Snavely Hershey returned to Lancaster County, where his innovative use of fresh milk in making caramels proved highly successful. In 1900 he sold his Lancaster Caramel Company for $1 million, and in 1903 he bought a cornfield in his Derry Township birthplace, constructed a manufacturing plant, and set out to perfect the chocolate bar. The rest is history, but only part of the story.

A Pennsylvania Dutchman of Mennonite stock, Milton was not only hard working but also endowed with a strong sense of moral responsibility. For his employees, he built a model company town, full of comfortable, worker-owned one- and two-family homes, tree-lined streets, and landscaped grounds. He built a bank, an inn, churches, schools, a trolley system, and a community center. He opened a park with a swimming pool, a ballroom, and a zoo. He kept on building

At Hersheypark, Reese's Peanut Butter Cups dance, chocolate bars hop, and Hershey's Kisses dispense hugs.

through the Depression, to keep everyone working. He and his wife, Catherine, were childless, but he founded a vocational school for orphaned boys in 1909 and endowed it, nine years later, with all of his Hershey Chocolate Company stock. Today, the Milton Hershey School serves 1,100 disadvantaged boys and girls from kindergarten through grade 12.

■ THE HERSHEY COMPLEX

To get to the Hershey attractions, take Hersheypark Drive exit off Route 322. *Call 800-HERSHEY for more information, directions, and lodging reservations.*

Chocolate World

The official visitors center of the Hershey Foods Corporation serves as an introduction to the chocolate-making process. You board a car that takes you along a conveyor belt on a free tour—not of the company's actual factory but of a simulation. At the end you get a little reward. There's also a shop in which to buy chocolate souvenirs. *800 Park Boulevard; 717-534-4900.*

Hersheypark

Candy man Milton S. Hershey opened the park in 1907 as a recreational area for his workers. Dancing Reese's Peanut Butter Cups and Hershey Bars bop around this 110-acre amusement park, which has more than 60 rides and attractions—including nine roller coasters, from vintage through state-of-the-art, seven water rides, and a carousel from 1919 decked out with 66 hand-carved wooden horses. *100 West Hersheypark Drive.*

Hershey Gardens

Purge the aroma of chocolate from your nose with a stroll through these 23 acres of stunning and fragrant botanical gardens. They've come a long way since the site's establishment as a rose garden in 1936. *170 Hotel Road; 717-534-3492.*

Hershey Museum

A memorial to Milton Hershey's life, the museum exhibits wonderful black-and-white photographs of the town's progression from a one-horse way station to a world-famous city. The collection of folk art, furniture, and other artifacts of early Pennsylvania Dutch life is another highlight, and there are exhibits of 19th-century firefighting equipment and Native American objects. *170 West Hersheypark Drive; 717-534-3439.*

■ **TRAVEL BASICS**

Getting Around: Since the real allure of the region lies on the back roads, and since Pennsylvania Dutch Country and Bucks County are hardly touched by mass transit, a car is a necessity. A good, detailed map will help you navigate the well-marked back roads that snake throughout the countryside. The Pennsylvania Turnpike (I-76) travels east-west across the northern part of Lancaster County, with Exit 20 (Route 72, Lancaster-Lebanon), Exit 21 (U.S. 222, Lancaster-Reading), and Exit 22 (Route 23, Morgantown) the most convenient to the area.

Amtrak serves Philadelphia from New York City and Washington, D.C.; Amtrak's *Keystone* train service, from New York through Philadelphia, stops in Lancaster, Mount Joy, and Harrisburg. The *Pennsylvanian,* coming to Philadelphia from Chicago and Pittsburgh, also stops in Harrisburg and Lancaster, as does the *Three Rivers,* also from Chicago and Pittsburgh. Capitol Trailways buses connect New York and Philadelphia with Lancaster, Reading, Hershey, and Harrisburg. Bieber Tourways buses connect New York and Philadelphia with Kutztown and Reading. Doylestown is reachable via SEPTA trains from Philadelphia.

Climate: Summer is T-shirt and shorts weather, with temperatures averaging in the 80s Fahrenheit. Humidity is unpredictable, but in general July and August are the most oppressively hot. Spring and fall are the most comfortable for traveling and hiking, with temperatures ranging from nighttime lows in the 50s to daytime highs in the upper 60s to low 70s. Winters are milder here than in any other part of Pennsylvania, with temperatures in the upper 30s to below freezing for most of December and January. Snowfall is not particularly heavy, averaging about 25 inches per season. Pack an umbrella, as rainy days are common year round.

NORTHEAST
& THE POCONOS

In northeastern Pennsylvania, forested mountains with spectacular views rise up from all directions. In the eastern section are the steep ridges of the Poconos; in the west, the hills of the Appalachian Plateau. Exit the interstate anywhere in the Poconos and you'll be rewarded with a back-road drive through mountain forests.

The Delaware Water Gap is where the Delaware River slices through a ridge a thousand feet high that runs across the borders of Pennsylvania and New Jersey. Views of the mountains and river are spectacular.

Roads west of the Delaware River will take you past former coal towns, such as Scranton and Jim Thorpe, and the heavily forested nature areas of Lehigh Gorge State Park and the "Endless Mountains" of the western Appalachian Plateau.

■ LANDSCAPE

The dominant landform in northeastern Pennsylvania is the heavily forested Appalachian Plateau. A narrow section of the Allegheny Mountains reaches in from the southwest to touch the region around Scranton. The Poconos stretch from the Allegheny Mountains in the south to the Moosic Mountains in the west, near Lehigh Gorge State Park, gradually subsiding into lower Wayne County in the north. They are bounded by the Susquehanna River to the west and the Delaware River to the east. The Pocono Escarpment plunges from 2,300 feet above sea level down to the Delaware River, creating dramatic vistas along the way.

In the north, the Poconos are covered by second-growth forests of pine, beech, birch, oak, and maple; in the south and east with hickory-mixed oak; in Monroe and Pike Counties with hemlock and white pine. These are still young woodlands, as the virgin forests were cut down during the 19th and early 20th centuries.

The Delaware River forms the border between Pennsylvania and New Jersey, cutting through the mountains at a spot known today as the Delaware Water Gap, but originally called "Pohoqualine," or "river passing between two mountains," by the indigenous Lenni Lenape Indians. English trappers and settlers shortened the name to the Poconos, a term that later came to refer to the entire area.

The northeast's forested Poconos and the shores of the Delaware and Susquehanna Rivers have remained beautiful and, for that reason, a place of

A bucolic scene along the Susquehanna in Bradford County.

retreat. In spring, creeks and streams swell from melting snow and carry icy water on a sharp, winding descent to the rivers. Marking the steeper drops along that journey are 30 waterfalls, nearly half of all the significant falls in Pennsylvania. Mountain meadows and fields here are dominated by the pinkish white mountain laurel, Pennsylvania's state flower, which blooms from May through July.

■ HISTORY

Before the first European settlers arrived, hunting trails used by the Lenni Lenapes crisscrossed northeastern Pennsylvania. Indigenous tribes must have heard rumors of the growing European presence in North America, but it was not until 1725 that a French Huguenot fleeing religious persecution became the first settler in the northeast. He was Nicholas DePui, who purchased 3,000 acres at the southern end of the Delaware Water Gap from the Wolf Clan of the Lenni Lenapes and established good relations with the native tribes. DePui and his wife raised nine children here and supported their family by hunting, farming, and growing apples.

If the settlers who followed had been as honorable and peaceful as DePui, Pennsylvania might have been a very different place. Instead, the English settlers who followed him drove out the region's Indians in order to claim the homesteads they had been promised by the Penn family and its agents in London. Angered, the Lenni Lenapes, Shawnees, and Nanticokes joined the French in fighting the English during the French and Indian War. Raiding parties descended upon small farms, terrorizing settlers. Entire families were butchered, farms burned, and children kidnapped.

■ CONNECTICUT VERSUS PENNSYLVANIA

In the mid-1700s, Connecticut challenged Pennsylvania for control of the Wyoming Valley. To establish his state's claim, Connecticut's governor sent hundreds of families to settle in the region that would later be called Wilkes-Barre. The arrival of these Connecticut settlers in the middle of the Wyoming Valley infuriated the Lenni Lenapes, who were already dispossessed of their original territory. In 1763, a Lenni Lenape war party went on the rampage, destroying hundreds of settlements.

Pennsylvania's new colonial governor, John Penn, grandson of William, exhorted settlers streaming into the region to respect American-Indian treaties, but to no avail. The Indian raids continued, and Penn descended to offering bounties for the scalps of Indian warriors. The conflict escalated into the Yankee-Pennamite Wars. The fighting was interrupted by the Revolutionary War, but it began again after the British surrendered. The dispute was ultimately resolved by the Decree of Trenton in 1782, ceding the valley to Pennsylvania.

■ REVOLUTIONARY WAR

In 1778, in the midst of the Revolutionary War, Native American tribes from the Northeast joined British loyalists in defending the area's grain stores from confiscation by the Continental Army.

On July 3, 1778, the British and their Indian allies attacked the colonists in the Wyoming Valley. Outnumbered three to one, the farmer-soldiers were overwhelmed and more than 220 of them were killed. The Indians proceeded to ravage the unprotected homesteads—events later referred to as the Wyoming Massacre.

After the Revolutionary War, the new American military forces retaliated by destroying scores of Indian villages. By 1795, Indian resistance had been overcome and peace finally came to the region. With borders secure and immigrants free to settle, farms prospered and towns expanded.

(following pages) This train belonged to the Jersey Central Lines, which were built in the 19th century to transport coal to and from cities throughout northeastern Pennsylvania.

NORTHEAST PENNSYLVANIA

Elevation
in feet
3,213
2,200
1,800
1,400
1,000
600
100

20 Miles
30 Kilometers
10 20
10 20
10

■ LOGGING, MINING, AND IRON

In the decade after the War of Independence, prospectors discovered huge anthracite coal deposits—"black diamonds" as this hot-burning and almost smokeless coal became known. In the decades before the Civil War, anthracite, along with timber, fueled Pennsylvania's economic expansion. Coal from Pennsylvania's new mines was hauled along makeshift roadways, and as access improved, logging operations flourished. Bark was stripped from oak trees to supply tannin for tanneries in Stroudsburg and Tannersville, and hardwood trees—lashed together as rafts and floated down the Delaware—were milled into lumber for homes in the rapidly developing western settlements. By the 1840s, virtually all usable timber had been logged from the Poconos.

As the demand for railroads expanded, so did the need for coal to fuel locomotives. The last barrier to widespread mining operations in the region—lack of a cost-effective transportation system—ended when railroad tracks were laid to the Pocono Plateau. With its plentiful coal, iron foundries, and rail system, Pennsylvania emerged from the Civil War with its economy roaring full steam ahead.

■ UNION MOVEMENT

The burgeoning mining industry was centered in Carbon County and in Jim Thorpe, known then as Mauch Chunk. Industrialists in this region amassed fortunes while miners toiled underground, going into debt buying their food in company stores. Many of the toughest mining jobs went to the Irish, who resented their treatment in the mines and saw it as a continuation of what they had endured under the British in Ireland. In the 1840s, laborers who dug coal were making 50 cents a day. There was no federal regulation of pay or working conditions, and the courts were vigorously anti-union.

A secret terrorist group, the Molly Maguires, formed in the coal-mining region, its roots in a similar violent gang that targeted land barons in Ireland for assassination. The name derived from a legendary Irish woman who brought murderous vengeance on those who had wronged her. Before long the Maguires had graduated from sending greedy mine owners to their graves to targeting people at all levels of mine management and community members seen as industry sympathizers. The gang's hold on the region was so strong that killings often took place in public, in front of dozens of witnesses, none of whom would cooperate with police.

Eventually, the public became fed up with the violence and began to testify at trials. Ironically, it was an Irish contingent of the Pinkerton Detective Agency—a private police force employed with bloody results decades later in Pittsburgh steelworker union strikes—that infiltrated the Maguires and brought them down.

In 1902, an emerging labor crusade against unsafe conditions in the coal mines and an increasing reliance on oil as an industrial fuel source brought coal production nearly to a halt. By the 1930s, underground coal mining had been followed by strip mining, which left large scars on the land. And by the 1970s, the iron foundries were idle and once-prosperous Scranton lay fallow in the heart of the "Rust Belt."

■ TODAY

The Lehigh and Wyoming Valleys and the forested Poconos bear little evidence today of the heavy industry of the past. In most valley communities, the rusty skeletons of old steel mills, iron foundries, and mining operations stand as depressing monuments to yesterday. But in Scranton and Jim Thorpe, those same facilities have been turned into museums. Other vacant industrial sites have been reborn as office parks for high-tech businesses.

In mountainous areas, forests cover most peaks and spectacular waterfalls drop precipitously through two major plateaus, wearing down their edges and adding to the drama of the landscape. Eight state parks preserve this natural beauty. Although development continues to encroach on animal habitats, this area of Pennsylvania is more protective of the environment than in the past. Community groups and state environmental workers have improved habitats for bald and golden eagles, ospreys, and white-tailed deer—the state animal, which was hunted almost to extinction in the 1800s.

In the former industrial centers of the northeast and in the most remote mountain communities, the cycle has come full circle, from exploitation and bloody confrontation to preservation and a willingness to share.

■ ABOUT THE POCONOS

Emerging from the Lehigh Tunnel on the northeastern extension of the Pennsylvania Turnpike (I-476), you will notice a dramatic change in the mountains. In this part of the Appalachian Plateau, the Poconos rise up steeply, in contrast to the long ridges of the Allegheny Plateau. These are hardly the Rockies,

PARALLEL RIDGES

What moved me most deeply about Pennsylvania as a boy, and still does today, is her ancient symbol of freedom, the mountains. The sight of their backs raised to the sky, sometimes humped or flared, green and lush in summer, brown and wild in winter, seldom failed to stir me. I liked to study them, learn how some ran parallel for twenty or even fifty miles and then turned or joined or threw out spurs to form coves and pinnacles or plateaus; how their aspect changed when seen from different angles; how the benches lay like smaller ridges, often with intervening forest swamps or wild hemlock hollows that the old mountain trails and early roads invariably followed; and how water from one mountain tasted sweeter and purer than that from another.

—Conrad Richter, *Pennsylvania*, 1947

however; the loftiest elevations are at best a few thousand feet. Drive through the back roads of these woodlands, and you'll come upon dairy farms, ski resorts, and, in the fall, a gorgeous display of foliage.

The reputation of the Poconos as a honeymoon destination began during World War II, when servicemen rushed here with their brides before leaving for war. In 1963, Morris Wilkins introduced the first heart-shaped bathtub at his Cove Haven Resort. A photo feature about the tub in *Life* magazine earned the area a reputation as the "Honeymoon Capital of the World." Today, more than 200,000 couples honeymoon in the Poconos ever year, many of them at various couples-only resorts. But the Poconos aren't just for lovebirds. The region is also popular with hikers, skiers, campers, and swimmers.

■ SKIING

Thanks to an average of 60 inches of snow per year, the Poconos have seven major winter recreation resorts, including Camelback Ski Area (800-233-8100) and Big Boulder Mountain (800-468-2442), two of the state's best places to ski. Whether your tastes lean toward fast downhill runs, groomed cross-country trails, or powdery snowshoe hikes, most resorts can accommodate you, whatever your skill level. *For skiing information, call 570-421-5565.*

A thrill ride at Knoebels Amusement Park in Elysburg. The Poconos have long been a family destination as well as a honeymoon retreat.

■ DELAWARE WATER GAP NATIONAL RECREATION AREA *map page 147, F-3, and page 154*

Unsuspecting travelers heading west on I-80 from New Jersey might not be prepared for the dramatic entry point into the state of Pennsylvania, a breach in the long ridge of Kittatinny Mountain made by the waters of the Delaware River and known as the Delaware Water Gap. How did the gap come to be? In a previous eon of geologic history, an uplift (a rise in the earth's surface in relation to adjacent areas) began beneath the river. The uplift was slow enough that the river's course eroded the rock underneath while the mountains rose on either side of it. As the mountains grew, so did the stone wall, creating a stunning cross-section. The twisted bands of metamorphic quartzite visible today cause geologists to pull off the highway for a closer look. Even those with little interest in geology stop to take in the views.

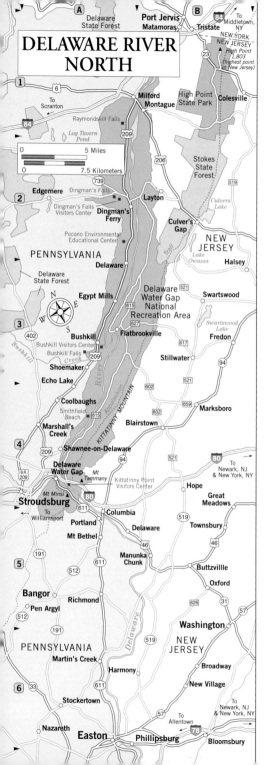

DELAWARE RIVER
NORTH

The 70,000-acre Delaware Water Gap National Recreation Area protects both sides of the Delaware River, which for 40 miles forms the border between Pennsylvania and New Jersey. The protected area is, at its widest point, about 6 miles across. You'll want to travel the back roads along the river, stopping at small villages, swimming beaches, or canoe launches. You can also hike in this area, starting at one of the many marked trail heads.

The upper Delaware River is slow-moving, shallow, and clear, lined with trees and filled with fishing birds, beaver, and, in season, Canada geese. Following a serpentine course, the river makes an S-curve on its mile-long journey through Kittatinny Ridge.

The Delaware is the only major waterway on the East Coast that has not been dammed. It narrowly escaped that fate 35 years ago when the federal government announced plans to flood the valley and create a giant reservoir. Opposition was fierce, and in the 1970s Congress added two sections of the Upper Delaware to the National Wild and Scenic River System, protecting 73.4 miles of natural resources along the New York–Pennsylvania border.

If you come west from New York City on I-80, or north from Philadelphia on Highway 33, you'll arrive at

A WALK NOT RECOMMENDED

The Appalachian Trail runs for 230 miles in a northeasterly arc across the state, like the broad end of a slice of pie. I never met a hiker with a good word to say about the trail in Pennsylvania. It is, as someone told a *National Geographic* reporter in 1987, the place "where boots go to die." During the last ice age it experienced what geologists call a periglacial climate—a zone at the edge of an ice sheet characterized by frequent freeze-thaw cycles that fractured the rock. The result is mile upon mile of jagged, oddly angled slabs of stone strewn about in wobbly piles known to science as *felsenmeer* (literally, "sea of rocks"). . . . Lots of people leave Pennsylvania limping and bruised. The state also has what are reputed to be the meanest rattlesnakes anywhere along the trail, and the most unreliable water sources, particularly in high summer. The really beautiful Appalachian ranges in Pennsylvania—Nitanny and Jacks and Tussey—stand to the north and west. For various practical and historical reasons, the AT goes nowhere near them. It traverses no notable eminences at all in Pennsylvania, offers no particularly memorable vistas, visits no national parks or forests, and overlooks the state's considerable history. In consequence, the AT is essentially just the central part of a very long, taxing haul connecting the South and New England. It is little wonder that most people dislike it.

—Bill Bryson, *A Walk in the Woods*, 1998

the southern end of the park, near Stroudsburg. To reach Kittatinny Point Visitors Center on the New Jersey side, take the last exit before you cross the river. U.S. 209 is the main Pennsylvania thoroughfare north through the park. Halfway along it, you'll find the Bushkill Visitors Center.

Swimming, Canoeing, and Tubing

In summer, you can swim, canoe, and ride inner tubes or rafts down the slow-moving Delaware. Access points to the river are located every 8 to 10 miles. Two beaches are recommended for swimming: Smithfield, at the south end of the park, near Shawnee-on-Delaware; and Milford, at the north end. These are family-friendly, with lifeguards, and get fairly crowded. Water temperatures rise from the mid-50s in late spring to the mid-70s in July.

(following pages) Interstate 80 follows the course of the river through the Delaware Water Gap near Stroudsburg.

It is easy to arrange one- to five-day canoe and raft trips. Look for Class I and Class II rapids. *For information on camping and canoe and raft trips, call 570-588-2451.*

Fishing

The Delaware River contains shad, trout, walleye, and bass. You can pick up the required license at tackle and hardware stores and even local Wal-Marts.

Trails

Sixty miles of hiking trails traverse the forest. Interesting day hikes include the trail up Mount Tammany (1,527 feet) and Mount Minsi (1,463 feet). A 42-mile segment of the Appalachian Trail, which in its entirety covers the East Coast from Maine to Georgia, winds through the park, most of it on the New Jersey side of the river. Bring a pack to hold food, a canteen, and a rugged pair of boots.

Visitors Centers

Bushkill Visitors Center. *On U.S. 209 along the Bushkill Creek; 570-588-7044.*
Kittatinny Point Visitors Center. *Off I-80 in New Jersey; open from spring through late October and on most weekends in winter; 908-496-4458.*
Park Headquarters. *On River Road, 1 mile off U.S. 209 in Bushkill; 570-588-2451.*

Camping and Lodging

Overnight accommodations here include cabins and campgrounds. In nearby towns, youth hostels and hotels abound.

■ BUSHKILL FALLS *map page 147, F-3*

Much of what is beautiful about northeastern Pennsylvania can be sampled at Bushkill Falls, a large park in the Poconos with eight roaring waterfalls. Known to many as the "Niagara of Pennsylvania," the waterfalls are easily reached by trails and bridges that take hikers through some of the state's most densely forested areas. It's an easy 20-minute walk to Main Falls, the highest of these cascades, where water plunges from a 100-foot-high cliff into a creek and then courses through a gorge strewn with gigantic boulders. Several trails (some challenging, some not) lead to the less vertigo-inducing Bridal Veil Falls and Bridesmaid's Falls. The most efficient way to get to Bushkill Falls is via I-80 to Stroudsburg, then heading north to U.S. 209. *Two miles northwest of U.S. 209; 888-628-7454.*

Bushkill Falls encompasses eight waterfalls; trails lead to them through densely wooded forests.

Deer abound in northeastern Pennsylvania.

■ **Pocono Environmental Education Center** *map page 154, A-2*
This 38-acre compound in the middle of the Delaware Water Gap National Recreation Area was once a well-known honeymoon getaway. In 1972 it was taken over by bird-watchers and environmentalists and is now the largest center for environmental education in the Western Hemisphere. More than 2,500 people come annually to study nature-related topics ranging from bird-watching to wildlife photography to the flora and fauna of the Poconos.

Trails within the complex cut across forests, open fields, and boggy wetlands. Otters, common in the Water Gap area, can be spotted here, as well as beavers, coyotes, foxes, porcupines, and snakes (timber rattlesnakes and copperheads). If lucky, you'll catch a glimpse of a bald eagle soaring in the late afternoon updrafts, searching for fish in the Delaware River.

A three-day, two-night stay at the center will cost a family of four about $700 for the seminar course (plus spartan bed and board, private bath, and daily meals). For those who don't fancy an overnight stay, day passes are available. *Off U.S. 209, north of Bushkill Falls; 570-828-2319.*

The golf course of the Shawnee Resort, one of the premier hotels along the Delaware River, can be seen on the island below.

■ **DINGMAN'S FALLS** *map page 154, A-2*

Close to the Delaware River and used as a canoe-launching site is the small town of Dingman's Ferry, where a privately owned toll bridge spans the river. Less than a mile west of U.S. 209 is Dingman's Falls, a tranquil place where a half-mile trail (keep the stream in sight) threads among rhododendrons and hemlocks to two waterfalls, the cascading Dingman's Falls and the more delicate Silver Thread Falls. There is a visitors center and a small picnic area.

■ **MILFORD** *map page 154, A/B-1*

Most first-time visitors to the Delaware Water Gap find Milford a convenient and congenial place. There are many motels, B&Bs, restaurants, and tree-shaded streets lined with handsome Victorians and antique shops. True to its name, Milford is also filled with mills. The first one was built in 1740, and by the 1800s, Milford had at least seven water-powered mills, in which flour and seeds were ground and wood was sawed and planed.

Autumn leaves form a carpet of gold, obscuring the green of a grassy meadow.

■ ALONG SCENIC U.S. 6 *map page 147, A/F-1/2*

U.S. 6 provides a scenic northern route across Pennsylvania. Its most beautiful stretch is from Milford west to the outskirts of Scranton. Don't be in a hurry if you take this route. The going may be slow but the views are splendid.

■ MILFORD TO WHITE MILLS *map page 147, E/F-2*

From Milford, U.S. 6 meanders west through forests of thick evergreens and hardwoods, country villages, and the occasional resort. Stop at the town of **Hawley** to visit antique shops and get a bite to eat. South of town is **Lake Wallenpaupack,** a 5,700-acre man-made lake formed by the Pennsylvania Power and Light Company in 1926. Fishing is a big pastime here, with typical catches yielding walleye, panfish, pickerel, largemouth bass, muskellunge, brown trout, and rainbow trout. The lake is surrounded by woodlands with walking trails and campsites.

Five miles north of Lake Wallenpaupack on U.S. 6 is White Mills, a homey burg with upscale antique stores and cozy restaurants. Getting here is a real treat because U.S. 6 travels though some of Pennsylvania's most drop-dead gorgeous countryside. It's a nice trip at any time of the year, but especially so in autumn, when leaves explode with color.

For information about fall foliage driving tours of the region, call the **Pocono Mountains Visitors Bureau** (570-421-5791).

In 1862, the world-celebrated glassmaker Christian Dorflinger bought 600 acres in White Mills to build a home and workshop for his glassmaking enterprise. When Dorothy Grant Suydam, the widow of Dorflinger's grandson, Frederick, died in 1979, she stipulated in her will that the property should become a wildlife sanctuary, and the land was donated to the community. Trails at the **Dorflinger-Suydam Wildlife Sanctuary** wind through generous forests and over fields bursting in spring and summer with flowers. There is a small lake, and deer, raccoons, foxes, and Canada geese live in peace. The grounds are open year-round, and in summer, music festivals and art shows take place.

The **Dorflinger Glass Museum,** near the entrance to the wildlife sanctuary, displays more than 700 pieces of cut glass and crystal, including etched vases, jewelry boxes, paperweights, and ornaments. The Dorflinger studio took commissions from U.S. presidents and other notables, and many of the pieces crafted for chiefs of state are exhibited here. The museum is open from mid-May through October. *Long Ridge Road and Elizabeth Street, White Mills; 570-253-1185.*

■ **ENDLESS MOUNTAINS** *map page 147*
The Endless Mountains region was named for its rolling forested hills, which appear to go on forever. A branch of the Allegheny Mountains, this 3,000-square-mile area cuts a wide swath through Bradford, Sullivan, Susquehanna, and Wyoming Counties.

Much of this territory was settled by Native Americans, but it later became the stomping ground of fur traders, French expatriates, European immigrants, farmers of all sorts, lumberjacks, industrialists, and coal miners. Sports enthusiasts and nature lovers are mostly what you will see today, as the mountains provide great opportunities for bird-watching, fishing, hiking, bicycling, and cross-country skiing. Game hunting is permitted on thousands of acres of state forest or game lands. *570-265-1528.*

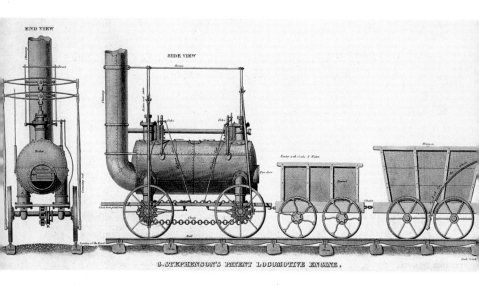

(above) Engineer and architect William Strickland's 1826 design for a locomotive steam engine. (Library of Congress) (below) Raymond Loewy, instrumental in defining the streamlined aesthetic of 20th-century industrial design, stands atop his prototype for the S-1 engine, created for the Pennsylvania Railroad. (Laurence Loewy)

■ COAL COUNTRY

West of the Poconos is the coal country of Lackawanna and Luzerne Counties. If you come from the Poconos, you'll pass low rolling hills and manicured farmland.

■ SCRANTON *map page 147, D-2*

Those interested in Pennsylvania's railway and mining heritage should visit Scranton, a city of 80,000 on the Lackawanna River. Scranton's history as an industrial town began in the 1840s, when it became a manufacturing center for iron rails. The success of the mills brought several railroads to Scranton. The city flourished in the 1850s when the town began mining and transporting anthracite coal.

Scranton also prospered during the late 19th and early 20th centuries. Vestiges of this gilded past can be seen in old neighborhoods like Greenridge and the Hills, where the mansions of onetime coal barons still stand. Most are private homes, but you can tour two fine ones, the **Tripp House** (1011 North Main Street; 570-961-3317) and the **Catlin House** (232 Monroe Avenue; 570-344-3841), a 16-room, English Tudor–style mansion.

The **Lackawanna Railroad Depot** is one of Scranton's architectural gems. The 1906 French Renaissance–style building was converted into a hotel in 1983, but most of the structure's original features remain intact, including the facade and the Grand Lobby, which has a mosaic-tile floor, marble walls, and a vaulted Tiffany stained-glass ceiling. *700 Lackawanna Avenue; 570-342-8300.*

A few blocks from the hotel is **Steamtown National Historic Site,** a steam-train museum operated by the National Park Service. The 52-acre yard has a fleet of vintage steam locomotives and passenger and freight cars, most of which can be boarded for close-up inspection. The history museum reveals railroad history with vivid displays of archival photographs, documents, and videos, and there's a 1930s-era roundhouse with locomotives. Sixty-minute steam train excursions to nearby Moscow are offered twice daily from July through October. *150 South Washington Avenue; 570-340-5200.*

The master magician Harry Houdini pulled off some of his most memorable contortionist tricks and speedy escapes in Scranton, which explains the presence of the **Houdini Museum** here. Created by adoring fans, the museum presents magazine articles, photographs, and film clips chronicling his exploits—which were often underwritten by Scranton businesses as a way to advertise their products. Workers at hardware manufacturer J.B. Woolsey & Co., for instance, shut him in a

FOREIGNERS

Theodore Dreiser was an Indiana native who often wrote about Pennsylvania. In 1915, he and a friend took a motor trip that covered most of the northeastern part of the state. Here are some of his reflections on the many foreigners he saw and met.

What becomes of all the Poles, Czechs, Croatians, Serbians, etc., who are going to destroy us? I'll tell you. They gather on the street corners when their parents will permit them, arrayed in yellow or red ties, yellow shoes, dinky fedoras or beribboned straw hats and 'style-plus' clothes, and talk about 'when I was out to Dreamland the other night,' or make some such observation as 'Say, you should have seen the beaut that cut across here just now. Oh, mamma, some baby!' That's all the menace there is to the foreign invasion. Whatever their original intention may be, they can't resist the American yellow shoes, the American moving picture... the popular song, the automobile, the jitney. They are completely undone by our perfections. Instead of throwing bombs or lowering our social level, all bogies of the sociologists, they would rather stand on our street corners, go to the nearest moving pictures, smoke cigarettes, wear high white collars and braided yellow vests and yearn over the girls who know exactly how to handle them, or work to someday own an automobile and break the speed laws. They are really not so bad as we seem to want them to be. They are simple, gauche, de jeune, 'the limit'. In other words, they are fast becoming Americans.

—Theodore Dreiser, *A Hoosier Holiday*, 1916

packing crate secured with seven pounds of nails. It took him six minutes to pop out. The museum is open on a regular basis during the summer and intermittently the rest of the year. *1433 North Main Avenue; 570-342-5555.*

McDade Park has 200 acres of beautiful woodlands and wetlands, picnic groves, an Olympic-size swimming pool, ball fields, and a fishing pond. Several nearby institutions relate the sometimes-harrowing story of coal mining in this region. *Off North Keyser Avenue; 570-963-6764.*

Photographs and archival documents at the **Anthracite Heritage Museum** reveal the difficult lives of the men and women who came to this region in the 19th and early 20th centuries to work in coal mines, mills, and factories. Particularly poignant are the stories museum guides tell about the hardships and

Eckley Miners' Village, a restoration of a 19th-century company town.

obstacles overcome by immigrants on the bottom rung of the employment ladder. *McDade Park, off North Keyser Avenue; 570-963-4804.*

At the **Lackawanna Coal Mine,** visitors descend 300 feet below ground in railcars to reach a former "working city" of underground stables, offices, storage rooms, and living quarters for hundreds of workers. Former miners lead the tour and give sobering lectures about the risks early miners faced, from poison gas eruptions to roof and wall cave-ins. *51 McDade Park, off North Keyser Avenue; 570-963-6463.*

■ **WILKES-BARRE** *map page 147, C-3*
Scranton and Wilkes–Barre are so close geographically it's easy to think of them as one city. The smaller of the two, Wilkes-Barre, was named in the late 18th century for John Wilkes and Isaac Barre, fellows of the British Parliament who lent sympathetic ears to the American colonies. A monument in the town square honors both men. Wilkes-Barre was considered tiny until thousands of immigrants came to the region in the early 1900s to work in the anthracite mines. By 1917, more than 100 million tons of coal had been mined in the Wilkes–Barre/Scranton area. Exhibits at the **Luzerne County Historical Society** (49 South Franklin Street; 570-823-6244) trace the history of the mining industry in Wilkes-Barre.

■ **ECKLEY MINERS' VILLAGE** *map page 147, D-4*

This 19th-century anthracite mining village, about 25 miles south of Wilkes-Barre in the little town of Eckley, is a fine example of the company towns of the industrial era, in which everything from the store to houses and schools was built and run by a single company. A walking tour of the town takes in about two dozen sites, including two churches, a miner's dwelling, and a general store. *Take 309 south from I-81, then Route 940 east; 570-636-2070.*

■ **LEHIGH GORGE** *map page 147, D-4*

Lehigh Gorge State Park follows the course of the Lehigh River for 26 miles, encompassing some of the most dramatic scenery in the Poconos. White-water rafting is popular here, and a typical raft trip organized by one of the companies operating in the park goes from White Haven to Jim Thorpe and takes 10 to 12 hours. (Inexperienced boaters should not attempt this trip without qualified guides. All boaters must enter and leave the Lehigh River at designated access areas.)

Abundant snowfall in the Poconos makes the region a prime destination for cross-country skiers.

The northern terminus of the **Lehigh Gorge Trail** is at White Haven. An abandoned railroad bed follows the river through the park, making it an ideal trail for hiking and mountain biking. Here, the landscape is a series of steep cliffs and jagged rocks. In the spring, rhododendrons bloom along parts of the trail. *Take I-80 to Exit 40, White Haven; 570-427-5000.*

■ **JIM THORPE** *map page 147, D-4*

The pioneers of this town on the Lehigh River named it Coalville, after the region's principal natural resource. By the time the first railroad arrived in the mid-19th century, the name was changed to Mauch Chunk, or "Bear Mountain" in the Lenni Lenape language. In 1954, three nearby towns merged into one self-governing district and named it after the country's most famous athlete, Jim Thorpe.

Born in Oklahoma of Fox and Sauk Indian lineage, Thorpe became one of the best all-around athletes in American history. He played football for coach Glenn Scobey "Pop" Warner at Pennsylvania's Carlisle Indian Industrial School, becoming an All-American in 1911 and 1912. Thorpe won the pentathlon and decathlon at the 1912 Olympic

Jim Thorpe was one of the best all-around athletes in American history. (Cumberland County Historical Society)

Games in Stockholm but was stripped of his two gold medals when Olympic Committee members discovered he had played a season of professional baseball. In 1982, nearly 30 years after his death, the Olympic Committee reinstated the medals. **Thorpe's mausoleum**—20 tons of granite—is in a park a half-mile from the town's east side.

The town of Jim Thorpe bills itself as "Little Switzerland," which is a bit of a stretch, but the setting is pretty and the town center is worth a walking tour.

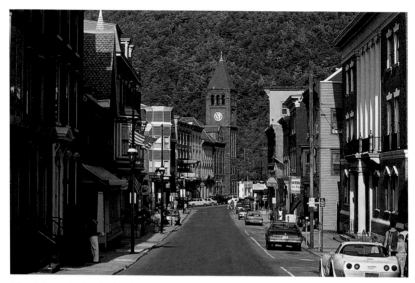

The citizens of Mauch Chunk, a gritty coal town, renamed their city after athlete Jim Thorpe.

From the 1888 Railroad Station you can take a leisurely 40-minute **train ride** over tracks that became part of the former Nesquehoning Valley Railroad in 1872. *Contact Rail Tours Inc.; 570-325-4606.*

St. Mark's Episcopal Church is a fine example of late Gothic Revival architecture, and one of the most intriguing structures in the area. The windows are Tiffany stained glass and the altar is white Italian marble. *21 Race Street; 570-325-2241.*

The **Asa Packer Mansion** is visible from just about anywhere in Jim Thorpe. Packer, an industrialist and philanthropist who founded the Lehigh Valley Railroad and Lehigh University, was worth $54 million in 1879. His mansion, built in 1850 and remodeled in 1877 for the then-staggering sum of $85,000, is worth a visit for its many beguiling and eccentric touches. The exterior is a playful cadenza of Gothic arches, gingerbread detailing, and embellishments like those seen on Italian villas. Inside, elegant wood carvings adorn the main hallway, and there are stained-glass windows in the dining room. One of the many chandeliers in the house served as a model for Tara's chandelier in the movie *Gone With the Wind*. The house can be toured from Memorial Day through October. *30 Elk Street; 570-325-3229.*

■ WEST AND SOUTH OF SCRANTON

Outside the metro area centered around Scranton and Wilkes-Barre, heading west on U.S. 11 toward Bloomsburg, urban sprawl gives way to rural hamlets, some with just one street or an abandoned house at the edge of town. Although picturesque, many of these towns have long since lost their economic anchors and exist by the grace of retirees' pension checks. Only a few have had success in reinventing themselves. These are working-class communities where laundry hangs from clotheslines and shopkeepers wander into one another's stores to chat when business is slow.

■ BLOOMSBURG AREA *map page 147, B-4*

The area where the Susquehanna River splits into its west and east branches developed largely because of lumber and agriculture, thus sparing it the disfigurement that coal mining brought to other sections of the state.

Bloomsburg, an attractive town of about 12,000, has a startling total of 650 buildings listed on the National Register of Historic Places. The town is known mostly for Bloomsburg University, founded in 1839 and now serving about 7,200 students.

Outside Bloomsburg, things get rural quickly. From late spring through early fall, most of the wonderfully aged covered bridges of the area are surrounded by green woodlands. For a pleasant drive, take Route 42 or Route 487 south from U.S. 11 and turn onto back roads like Shakespeare, Parr's Mill, Bethel, and Glory Lake.

■ LAKE CHILLISQUAQUE *map page 147, B-3*

In the broad Appalachian valley between Montour Ridge and Muncy Hills and about 10 miles northwest of Bloomsburg is a region of undulating hills that converge on Lake Chillisquaque.

The lake is an important stop for more than a dozen species of migrating waterfowl. Common birds include Canada geese and hooded gansers, and even brown pelicans from Florida have been spotted in recent years.

Hiking trails in the area vary in length from a quarter of a mile to 4.2 miles and pass through beds of thistle, daisy, and clover. From late spring to early fall, the preserve's wildflowers bloom in colors that range from deep violets and reds to light yellows and ivories.

Fields of Indian pipes and buttercups are bordered by hardwoods and conifers—red, silver, and sugar maples, groves of white oak, shag bark hickory, and birch. *From I-80 take Exit 54 north to the village of Washingtonville and follow signs.*

CENTRALIA

From the mid-1800s to mid-1900s, Centralia, about 15 miles south of Bloomsburg on Route 42, was a thriving town with a population of almost 2,000. Today that is all gone. What remains beneath the town are coal seams that have been burning since 1962.

The fire started when trash dumped at the edge of town caught fire and spread into the coal seams and abandoned mines. Over the next two decades, various plans were advanced to fight the fire. Huge volumes of water were poured onto the seams but simply evaporated due to the extreme underground temperatures. The only method proven effective against this sort of fire—digging out the blaze, extinguishing it, then refilling the dig area—proved the most expensive, and funding for Centralia ran out.

The area had become a frightening place to live, with ground temperatures recorded at close to 1,000 degrees Fahrenheit and glowing hot spots visible across the landscape at night. Sudden cave-ins claimed backyards and basements, and increasing levels of carbon monoxide seeping into homes made people sick.

In 1983, Congress allocated $42 million to purchase the town's homes, relocate its population, and bulldoze the buildings. The residents voted to accept the offer, and abandoned the town.

Today, all routes into Centralia are closed but remain passable. Its streets are deserted, driveways lead to empty lots, and only a few houses remain scattered around—some, amazingly, still occupied. An overall view of what's left of this once typical American town can be had from the mountain north of town. Some say the fire could burn another thousand years.

A subterranean fire has been burning in Centralia since 1962.

A sleigh rally in Forksville, Sullivan County.

■ TRAVEL BASICS

Getting Around: Many scenic routes wind through the region. Interstate 84 begins in Pennsylvania at Point Jervis and skirts the Poconos to I-380, which leads to Scranton. Scenic Route 6 (U.S. 6) begins in Milford and wends its way slowly across the northern half of the state, hitting some of the region's most wondrous natural settings, including the areas around White Mills, Carbondale, and Dixon. U.S. 6 also offers connections to the region's many lesser-traveled back roads, which lead through mile after mile of unspoiled wilderness and past small towns filled with friendly locals. Route 209, running the length of the New Jersey and Pennsylvania border, is the easiest route to the Delaware Water Gap, Dingman's Falls, Delaware State Forest, and Bushkill Falls. Martz Lines (800-233-8604) has regular bus service running through the Poconos from Stroudsburg to Wilkes-Barre and Scranton.

Climate: The comparatively low elevation of the Poconos does not produce a true mountain climate, but temperatures are generally 10 degrees cooler than in the surrounding lowlands. Summers are pleasant, with high temperatures averaging in the 70s and 80s. Winters are cold, with temperatures averaging between 10 and 30 degrees. April, May, and October are gorgeous.

C E N T R A L

The author Robert Louis Stevenson, traveling through central Pennsylvania on a railroad journey in 1868, wrote in his diary:

> I saw one after another, pleasant villages, carts upon the highway and fishers by the stream, and heard cock-crows and cheery voices in the distance....And then when I asked the name of the river from the brakesman, and heard that it was called the Susquehanna, the beauty of the name seemed to be part and parcel of the beauty of the land.

Except for rolling farmland near Gettysburg, central Pennsylvania is a region of wooded ridges and narrow valleys. To the west, rising above all, is the Allegheny Ridge. Fed by dozens of creeks and streams, the wide Susquehanna River is the third-largest river in the state, flowing from Pennsylvania's northern border with New York south through Harrisburg to the Chesapeake Bay. Indigenous Americans called it "Long Reach River."

Because many parts of the Susquehanna are not navigable and its forests were once impenetrable, Seneca and Iroquois Indians lived here largely undisturbed until the late 1700s, when the land was annexed for settlement. Soon, roads following Iroquois trails tied the region to the rest of the state, and dependable land routes allowed goods to reach the Susquehanna's navigable sections. Mining and refining operations exploited the region's coal, iron ore, and limestone deposits, but the chief export was white pine. When these resources were exhausted, the area was abandoned, its ridges stripped bare and its streams polluted from mine drainage. Now the land has begun to heal, and much of the natural beauty has been restored.

■ HARRISBURG

Pennsylvania's capital city sits on the Susquehanna's eastern bank. An important trading post was built here in the 1700s, and later, during the French and Indian War, a fort. The city underwent several growth spurts and transformations in the 19th century, finally becoming an important transportation hub, first as a link on the Main Line Canal from Pittsburgh to Philadelphia and later as a railroad interchange. Harrisburg was chosen as the capital in 1812 because of its central location. In this city of 52,000 people, the primary industry these days is government.

BEAUTIFUL SUSQUEHANNA

The Susquehanna, though more than two hundred miles longer than the Hudson, is born among men. A few yards from the lake it is not quite four feet deep, and there children swim, shadowed sometimes by the high bank across from Riverbrink. Canoes drift here and fishermen, hardly expecting a catch, idle with short lines dangling in water so clear that the fish can see them. In spring and summer, lawn and stream and high bank across meld varying shades of green, making a lush and subtly arranged background for the fading hues of the house, like a landscape by the French painter, Courbet. And, somehow, ever consistent, through other backyards and through coal towns, through deep chasms and wide flat bottoms, the Susquehanna always keeps a relationship to the men on its banks. Sometimes dangerous, sometimes friendly, it ever maintains its unique unchanging quality, minding its own business, a "character" among streams.

—Carl Carmer, "The Susquehanna," 1955,
in *The Way It Was*

A choral group performs in the state capitol's rotunda.

■ **STATE CAPITOL** *map page 178*

When Theodore Roosevelt came to the dedication of this building as the Pennsylvania State Capitol in October 1906, he gazed up at the great dome, which was modeled after St. Peter's Basilica in Rome, and declared it "is the handsomest building I ever saw." Roosevelt wasn't the only one impressed. The six-story building, designed by Joseph Huston to mimic architecture of the Italian Renaissance, has long been admired by architects and architecture buffs.

The capitol cost more than $13 million to construct, a princely sum for its time. The ornate interior includes a grand staircase and murals by Edwin Austin Abbey. The artist's crowning work is *The Apotheosis of Pennsylvania,* which depicts 35 of the state's historic figures, including William Penn, Benjamin Franklin, Robert Morris, Daniel Boone, Gen. George Meade, and Chief Justice Thomas McKean (founder of the Democratic party). In one of the ceiling murals, 24 goddesses representing the passage of the hours float in a celestial heaven. Thirty-minute tours of the Senate chambers, the House of Representatives, the Supreme Court, and the Rotunda are given every half hour from 8:30 A.M. to 4 P.M. on weekdays and at 9, 11, 1, and 3 on weekends. *Third and State Streets; 717-787-6810.*

■ **STATE MUSEUM OF PENNSYLVANIA** *map this page*

The state's official museum, worth a stop, has exhibits that encompass Pennsylvania's history from prehistoric times to the 21st century. The first floor contains a detailed re-creation of a colonial street, with storefronts and furnished rooms from a typical family home. The Civil War gallery has paintings, uniforms, and munitions from the war, and there is a collection of clothing, artifacts, and weaponry used by the state's native peoples. Mammal Hall has dioramas of the first creatures to inhabit Pennsylvania, and in the Hall of Industry and Technology are models and photos of steamboats, trains, gristmills, and automobiles. In the Curiosity Corner, designed for children, young ones can dress up in Indian buckskins and Victorian dresses, explore a full colonial kitchen, and have their picture taken in front of a 20-foot-tall statue of William Penn. *Third Street between North and Forster Streets; 717-787-4980.*

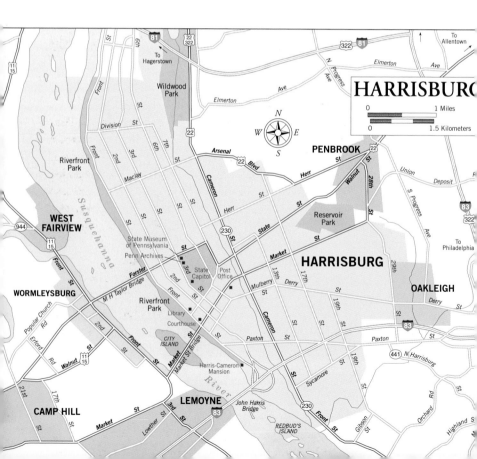

An open house at the Harley-Davidson factory in York.

■ JOHN HARRIS–SIMON CAMERON MANSION *map page 178*

Among the first settlers to arrive in this area was John Harris, sent by the Penn family to mitigate conflicts between settlers and native peoples. Harris established a trading post and a ferry business and began farming the rich soil in the ancient floodplain of the Susquehanna. His son, John Harris Jr., who later earned enduring fame as the founder of Harrisburg in 1784, built himself this splendid mansion overlooking the river in 1766. Simon Cameron, President Lincoln's first Secretary of War, bought the house in 1863, and spent a considerable sum to redecorate it.

The mansion appears today much as it did during Cameron's residency. The house's furnishings include elegant chandeliers that dangle from high ceilings, rooms are copiously decorated with Victorian furniture Cameron purchased from the U.S. Capitol, and the master bedroom has a magnificent bed and a fully appointed bathroom. The house is now the home of the Historical Society of Dauphin County, where photographs, manuscripts, and paintings trace 200 years of local history. *219 South Front Street; 717-233-3462.*

The Millersburg Ferry crosses the Susquehanna about 20 miles upriver from Harrisburg.

■ **MILLERSBURG** *map page 177, D-3*

About 20 miles upriver from Harrisburg is the historic town of Millersburg, on the banks of the Susquehanna. Deeded to one Daniel Miller in 1790, the town is the site of the Millersburg Ferry, which has been crossing the river to a landing about 2 miles south of Liverpool, in Perry County, since the early 18th century. Today, it's the last remaining ferry on the Susquehanna. The ferry operates, weather permitting, from May through October. *717-692-2442.*

■ **THREE MILE ISLAND** *map page 97, A-3*

Ten miles south of Harrisburg lies Three Mile Island. The towers of the nuclear power plant located here betray no hint today of the drama that unfolded deep in the core of one of them on Wednesday, March 28, 1979. At 4 A.M. that day, a minor malfunction in the system that feeds water to the steam generators at the Unit 2 reactor set off a chain of events that led to the worst nuclear accident in U.S. history. Temperatures within the reactor rose precipitously, and the unthinkable, a nuclear meltdown, suddenly seemed possible. Radioactive gases escaped

President Jimmy Carter leaving Three Mile Island nuclear power plant, April 1, 1979. (National Archives)

into the containment vessel and some were released into the atmosphere. For a time, it also seemed that a hydrogen bubble in the reactor might explode.

Confronted with contradictory information from officials at the Nuclear Regulatory Commission and the plant's operator, Metropolitan Edison, Gov. Richard Thornburgh struggled to decide whether or not to evacuate a quarter of a million people from the area. On March 29, local residents were told to stay indoors with their windows closed, and on March 30 evacuation of children and pregnant women living within a 5-mile radius was advised. On April 1, President Jimmy Carter toured the plant to calm fears. Still, by the time the crisis was declared over, on April 9, thousands had fled.

A partial core meltdown did occur. Clean up took a dozen years and cost almost a billion dollars. Officially, no long-term adverse health or environmental effects have been reported, but the accident led to a sharp decline in nuclear construction. The undamaged reactor, TMI-1, shut down for refueling at the time of the accident, was restarted in 1985 and is still in operation. TMI-2 was placed in "post defueling monitored storage" in 1993 and will never be operational again.

■ CIVIL WAR TRAIL

The Cumberland Valley, in Franklin County, saw more military activity during the Civil War than any other region in the North. Four important historical sites can be visited in this area, about an hour's drive from Lancaster. The most important is the site of the Battle of Gettysburg, where the Confederate Army was dealt a devastating blow in July 1863. If you drive here, take back roads, where quiet farms and small towns are the norm. Route 34 is among the most scenic routes into Gettysburg. If you come from Maryland, drive through Waynesboro, which is known for its high-quality antiques shops.

■ GETTYSBURG *map pages 177, D-6, and page 183*

Gettysburg has 6,000 permanent residents and 2,000 students attending Gettysburg College; at least two million tourists visit the area each year. The 6,000-acre Gettysburg National Military Park surrounds the town on all but its west side. Trees and Civil War–era wood-frame homes line the streets, and closer to the town center are older Federal-style brick row houses with white trim.

In the town itself, a central square contains memorials to the battle and is surrounded by historic buildings with bronze plaques explaining their significance. Many of the town's houses and buildings still bear the scars of bullets and cannon shells fired during the three-day campaign.

■ GETTYSBURG NATIONAL MILITARY PARK *map page 183*

The park that commemorates the Battle of Gettysburg consists mostly of rolling hills and groves of oaks and hickory. More than 1,400 markers, memorials, and monuments identify battle points and pay homage to soldiers and regiments from the Confederate and Union armies.

Official army drawings of Union and Confederate cavalry officers.

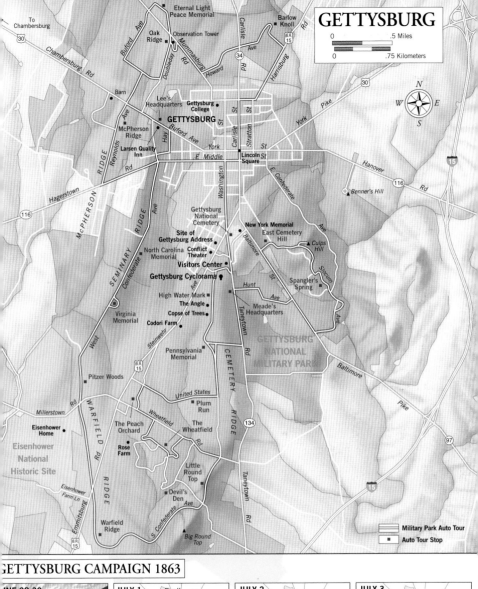

GETTYSBURG CAMPAIGN 1863

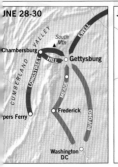

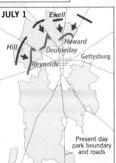

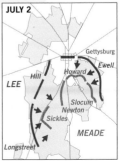

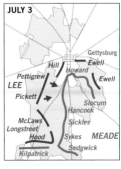

BATTLE OF GETTYSBURG

In the third year of the Civil War, after an important but costly Confederate victory at Chancellorsville, Virginia, Gen. Robert E. Lee urged the Confederate president, Jefferson Davis, to move the war north and strike at Pennsylvania. A victory there, he reasoned, could weaken the North's will to fight, raise Southern morale, and at the same time improve chances for European recognition of the Confederacy. Furthermore, Pennsylvania's farms were supporting the Union army, its factories were supplying weapons, shoes, and clothing, and its railroads were moving troops and supplies with great efficiency. Cutting the flow of supplies from Pennsylvania to Union soldiers could turn the course of the war. In June 1863, nearly 75,000 Southern troops crossed the Mason-Dixon Line, the border between Maryland and Pennsylvania.

DAYS PRECEDING THE BATTLE
The Union army had received reports of the movement but was unsure of Confederate intentions. Lee kept enough troops in Virginia to deceive the Union generals into thinking that Washington, D.C., was his objective. When the newly appointed commander of the Union Army of the Potomac, Gen. George Meade,

heard reports that Confederate troops had occupied Chambersburg, Greenwood, and York in southern Pennsylvania, he ordered 90,000 Union troops north.

Meade moved quickly. The Confederate army was spread out over the rural area around Harrisburg and was planning an assault on it. A unit of Confederate Gen. A. P. Hill's cavalry was just north of Gettysburg when they met with a division of Meade's advance cavalry, commanded by Gen. George Buford. The Confederates drove the Union forces south of Gettysburg, where they entrenched themselves along Cemetery Ridge, determined to fight until Meade's reinforcements arrived.

Day One

On July 1, the Battle of Gettysburg began with Confederate troops attacking Union troops on McPherson Ridge, west of town. Though outnumbered, the Union forces managed to hold until afternoon, when they were overpowered and driven back through town. In the confusion, thousands of Union soldiers were captured before they could rally on Cemetery Hill, south of town. Long into the night, Union troops labored over their defenses while the bulk of Meade's army arrived and took positions.

Day Two

On July 2, battle lines were drawn up in two sweeping arcs. The main portions of both armies were nearly a mile apart on two parallel ridges: Union forces on Cemetery Ridge facing Confederate forces on Seminary Ridge to the west. Lee ordered an attack against both Union flanks. James Longstreet's thrust on the Union left broke through D. E. Sickles's advance lines at the Peach Orchard, left the wheat field strewn with dead and wounded, and turned the base of Little Round Top into a shambles. R. S. Ewell's attack proved futile against the entrenched Union forces on East Cemetery Hill and Culp's Hill.

Day Three

On July 3, Lee's artillery opened a bombardment that for a time engaged the massed guns of both sides, but did little to weaken the Union center on Cemetery Ridge. The climax of the Battle of Gettysburg came when Maj. Gen. George E. Pickett led an infantry assault of 12,000 Confederate troops across the open field toward the Union center on Cemetery Ridge. Raked by artillery and rifle fire, Pickett's men reached but failed to break the Union line, and the battle ended in disaster. In 50 minutes, 7,500 men and 5,000 horses were killed, and the attack—known as Pickett's Charge—became history.

AFTERMATH

With the failure of Pickett's Charge, the battle was over and the Union was saved. There were more than 51,000 total casualties, making Gettysburg the bloodiest battle in American history. On July 4, Lee prepared for an attack that never came, and that night, under cover of a heavy rain, began his withdrawal to Virginia with an army that was physically and spiritually exhausted. Lee would never again attempt an offensive operation of such proportions. Meade, though he was criticized for not immediately pursuing Lee's army, had carried the day in the battle that has become known as the "High Water Mark of the Confederacy." The war was to rage for two more years but would never again be fought north of the Mason-Dixon Line.

On November 19, 1863, President Abraham Lincoln delivered his Gettysburg Address as part of the dedication ceremony for the National Cemetery.

Photographs in this essay were taken during the filming of the Civil War movie Glory.

A monument in Gettysburg National Military Park.

Across from the visitors center is the **Gettysburg Cyclorama,** a 26-foot-high, 360-foot-long, circular oil-on-canvas painting that depicts Pickett's Charge, the final and fateful confrontation of the Battle of Gettysburg. The French artist Paul Philippoteaux labored over the work between 1882 and 1884. Unveiled in Boston, the work, weighing three tons, wasn't brought to Gettysburg until 1913. An audio-tape describes events depicted on the mural. *97 Taneytown Road; 717-334-1124.*

Gettysburg National Cemetery
Two days after the Battle of Gettysburg, Gov. Andrew Curtin of Pennsylvania toured the battlefield, where he viewed the bodies of hundreds of young men—Union and Confederate—buried in shallow graves or decaying in the hot summer sun. By nightfall, the shaken governor had ordered the immediate purchase of burial ground that would be turned over to the federal government to honor those who had given their lives. Four months after the battle, an emotional President Abraham Lincoln came here to dedicate the cemetery. Monuments to regiments, divisions, battles, generals, and soldiers and can be found throughout the park. *97 Taneytown Road; 717-334-1124.*

GETTYSBURG ADDRESS

After the Battle of Gettysburg, a national soldier's cemetery was established in the town. President Abraham Lincoln came to address those gathered at its dedication. Lincoln left Washington, D.C., by train on November 18. Fifteen thousand people were gathered on Cemetery Hill for the ceremonies, listening first to a former Massachusetts senator, Edward Everett, who spoke for two hours. Lincoln then rose to deliver his address. His two-minute dedication ranks among the great speeches of history.

Four score and seven years ago our fathers brought forth on this continent a new nation, conceived in liberty and dedicated to the proposition that all men are created equal.

Now we are engaged in a great civil war, testing whether that nation or any nation so conceived and so dedicated can long endure. We are met on a great battlefield of that war. We have come to dedicate a portion of that field as final resting place for those who here gave their lives that that nation might live. It is altogether fitting and proper that we should do this.

But, in a larger sense, we cannot dedicate—we cannot consecrate—we cannot hallow—this ground. The brave men, living and dead, who struggled here have consecrated it far above our poor power to add or detract. The world will little note nor long remember what we say here, but it can never forget what they did here. It is for us, the living, rather, to be dedicated here to the unfinished work which they who fought here have thus far so nobly advanced.

It is rather for us to be here dedicated to the great task remaining before us—that from these honored dead we take increased devotion to that cause for which they gave the last full measure of devotion; that we here highly resolve that these dead shall not have died in vain; that this nation, under God, shall have a new birth of freedom; and that government of the people, by the people, for the people shall not perish from the earth.

—Abraham Lincoln, 1863

The following day, Senator Everett wrote to Lincoln: "I should be glad if I could flatter myself that I came as near to the central idea of the occasion in two hours as you did in two minutes."

A grave marker in Gettysburg National Cemetery.

General Robert E. Lee Headquarters

The 18th-century stone farmhouse commandeered by Lee as his battlefield headquarters contains displays of Civil War military equipment (including surgical instruments) and biographical materials on Lee that provide insight into his battle strategies. The kitchen is set up with Lee's original table and chairs, and another room contains the saddle of the first general to be killed in the Civil War. *Larsen Quality Inn, 401 Buford Avenue (Route 30 West); 717-334-3141.*

Eisenhower National Historic Site

President Eisenhower and his wife, Mamie, purchased a 189-acre farm in Gettysburg in 1950 and he used the farm as a weekend retreat while president, often hosting national and world leaders. After leaving the White House in 1961, "Ike" and Mamie made this their primary residence. Ike died in 1969, and Mamie lived here until her death in 1979. The following year the property was opened to the public. The house is furnished with antiques, family heirlooms, and gifts from heads of state. Shuttle bus service, the only way to reach the site, departs from the Gettysburg Visitors Center. *250 Eisenhower Farm Lane; 717-338-9114.*

These columns were all that remained of the Bank of Chambersburg after it was burned by Confederate soldiers. (Kittochitinny Historical Society)

■ CHAMBERSBURG *map page 177, B/C-5*

After the crucial victory in September 1862 at the Battle of Antietam, where General Lee's advance on Maryland was stopped, Chambersburg became an important hospital and supply center for the Union army. When 400 wounded soldiers were evacuated from battlefields to the town, residents opened up their homes to them.

The Confederate army occupied Chambersburg several times from 1861 to 1863. A month before the Battle of Gettysburg, Gen. Robert E. Lee and 65,000 troops camped in the area, and Lee and his generals held strategy sessions in the town center. This is where Lee made the fateful decision to lead his troops east, toward Gettysburg, after scouts reported that the Union army was headed in their direction. In 1864, a Confederate force under the command of Gen. John McCausland held Chambersburg ransom and threatened to burn the city if

$100,000 wasn't paid in gold. To dramatize the point, he had a cannon fire into the west wall of the Franklin County courthouse. No gold was brought forward, the general's deadline passed, and the town's buildings were set ablaze. Residents ran for refuge to the Cedar Grove Cemetery, on King Street at the edge of town.

Only a few buildings were spared, including the **Masonic Temple** (74 South Second Street)—supposedly as a gesture of respect from Confederate brother Masons. The building, completed in 1824, is the oldest Masonic institution in the state and among the oldest in the country.

Chambersburg looks very much as it did when laid out by founder Benjamin Chambers in 1788. The main route to the town square follows Route 30 West, off Exit 6 of I-81. Once beyond the budget hotels and fast-food restaurants, Route 30 travels through tree-lined residential neighborhoods made up of tidy 20th-century homes fronted by manicured lawns. The business district begins several blocks beyond a large hospital complex and continues to the town square, beyond the intersection of Route 30 and Route 11.

In the square is a four-tier, cast-iron fountain created in 1878 as a monument to Union soldiers from the area who died serving in the Civil War. In front of the fountain, a full-size sculpture of a Union soldier faces south, the direction from which the invading Confederate army came. Also at the square is a marker memorializing the burning of the town and a piece of the battleship USS *Maine,* a tribute to locals who fought in the Spanish-American War. The town's best residential architecture—restored Civil War–era homes built of local gray limestone and wood—can be seen along Philadelphia Avenue off Route 11 North.

■ **MERCERSBURG** *map page 177, B-6*

The seeds of the Battle of Gettysburg were sown in 1862 with a series of Confederate cavalry raids in the Cumberland Valley. The citizens of Mercersburg supported the Union cause, and the Confederate raids made it a regular target. The **Steiger family house** (120 North Main Street) was taken over by Confederate Gen. J.E.B. Stuart for use at mealtimes. When the tide turned against the Confederacy in 1863, wounded rebel soldiers were captured and placed in makeshift hospitals throughout Mercersburg. Many of the soldiers are interred in the local cemetery. Much less conspicuous than the neatly kept and much honored soldiers' cemetery at Gettysburg is the **Black Cemetery** at the end of Bennet Avenue, where hundreds of USCT (United States Colored Troops) are buried.

More than 40 log homes and shops from all over Pennsylvania were transported to Old Bedford Village, a simulation of a pioneer-era settlement.

Acres of lush farmland and dairy pastures extend in every direction from Mercersburg. Route 16 runs east-west directly through the small downtown, a four-block area with a small green square bordered by large-limbed oaks.

Most people make the trip here to tour the 370-acre campus of **Mercersburg Academy,** an exclusive prep school whose distinctive chapel, dedicated in 1927, was designed by Ralph Adams Cram, a leading proponent of neo-gothic ecclesiastical architecture. In his writings about the chapel, Cram discusses its placement on the campus grounds: "Raised on the highest land of the Academy, with its tower and slender spire lifting high in the air, it is a proclamation in enduring stone, and to the whole community, of the vigour, the aspiration and the . . . power of religion, not only in education but in human society." The school was started as Marshall College in 1836, evolving into Mercersburg Academy by 1893. A few original buildings remain on campus, including the log cabin in which President James Buchanan was born. The late actor Jimmy Stewart is among the school's illustrious alumni. *300 East Seminary Street; 717-328-2151.*

Fishermen try their luck next to a covered bridge.

■ BEDFORD COUNTY BRIDGES AND TRAILS *map page 177, A-5*

Forty miles northwest of Mercersburg is a region of forested hills and valleys known for its covered bridges. The **Bedford County Visitors Bureau** (141 South Juliana Street; 814-623-1771) provides maps of the bridges. You can view them from a car, but seeing them on a bicycle is more rewarding. **Grousland Tours** (467 Robinsonville Road, Clearville; 814-784-5000) arranges tours and rents bikes.

About 20 miles northeast of Shawnee State Park is a trail known as **Maple Run,** a 7-mile trek through forests and past mountain streams with moss-carpeted banks and native plants. To hike the rocky trail, you will need good hiking boots. The southern portion, heading west, follows difficult terrain and requires stamina. *From Bedford, take Route 30 east about 3 miles to the caution signal on the west side of the hospital. Turn left and head to Loysburg. At Loysburg, take Route 36 north for 3 miles and turn right on Hickory Bottom Road (Route 1017). Look for the Shady Trail Riding School sign and follow for 2.3 miles. At Pulpit Road, turn right, look for the second Shady Trail Riding School sign, and go 1.5 miles farther on Pulpit Road to Maple Run Road. Travel 1.3 miles to the trailhead.*

■ **ALTOONA AREA** *map page 177, A-3*

Altoona, the largest town in Blair County and an old-time railroad center, lies at the base of the Allegheny Ridge. In 1850, it was a farm community next to an iron plant, but then the Pennsylvania Railroad made Altoona the site of its maintenance facility. At its peak, the workforce reached 17,000, and railroad life so dominated the city that even tasks as mundane as laundering clothes were governed by railroad schedules. Monday was the citywide day for hanging clothes on backyard lines, because trains were inside maintenance buildings instead of spewing thick clouds of coal dust.

As diesel fuel replaced coal-powered steam, the maintenance operation became obsolete, and Altoona's economy slumped. Then, during the 1990s, the Consolidated Rail Corporation (Conrail), a descendant of the Pennsylvania Railroad, retrofitted the old steam-engine repair complex to accommodate diesel locomotives. Today, more tons of freight travel the Main Line rails through Altoona than at any time in the city's history.

Altoona's railroad boom years are captured in the **Altoona Railroaders Memorial Museum,** a memorial not to the tycoons who ran the corporations, but to the laborers who laid the track, repaired the cars, and worked on the lines. Exhibits are on three floors of the building, which is across from the Amtrak station. Each year in October, the museum conducts excursions to local towns as part of its Railfest celebration. *1300 Ninth Avenue; 814-946-0834.*

Nearby are the villages of **Tyrone,** which has the Victorian homes of yesteryear's railway executives, and Sinking Valley, home to **Fort Roberdeau** (from I-99 take the Bellwood Exit), built in 1778 to protect lead mines in the region. The fort is named after Gen. Daniel Roberdeau, a wealthy merchant, member of Congress, and patriot. The fort is on 45 acres of fields and woods, with nature trails and picnic facilities. Caverns once used by Indians can be toured in **Spruce Creek,** and **Hollidaysburg** and **Duncansville** contain many antiques stores.

■ **HORSESHOE CURVE** *map page 177, A-3*

The Allegheny Ridge, which rises steeply 1,200 feet above Altoona and Hollidaysburg, long presented a major barrier to east-west traffic. One of the most dramatic solutions to this challenge occurred in 1854, with the building of Horseshoe Curve, located just outside Altoona in the foothills of the Allegheny Mountain range. This expanse of track, designed by Pennsylvania Railroad Chief Engineer J. Edgar Thompson, is now a national historic landmark.

A train winds around the famous Horseshoe Curve.

Thompson's plan called for a ravine to be filled between one of the main mountain ridges and a bed to be carved out of the mountainside. Four-hundred-fifty Irish immigrants worked for three years digging and sculpting the new grade. When Horseshoe Curve was completed, the two-day trip by horse from Hollidaysburg to Pittsburgh was slashed to 12 hours by train. During World War II, Horseshoe Curve was considered so strategically important that it was the target of an unsuccessful attempt by Nazis to sabotage it. The saboteurs landed by U-boat on the East Coast, but were almost immediately apprehended in a bar. *Horseshoe Curve Road, about 5 miles northwest of Altoona; 814-946-0834.*

■ **ALLEGHENY PORTAGE RAILROAD HISTORIC SITE** *map page 177, A-4*
In 1834, the Portage Railroad was not a railroad but a link in the Main Line canal system that ran from the Delaware River, near Philadelphia, to the Ohio River in Pittsburgh. Here, passengers, cargo, and canal boats were transported over the summit of Allegheny Mountain between Hollidaysburg and Johnstown. A series of stair-step locks, connected by track, hauled barges from one platform to another, up the mountain, and then down the other side. The trip took five days, covering

A canal boat is pulled up an incline on the Allegheny Portage Railroad. (Pennsylvania Historical and Museum Commission)

36.5 miles over 10 inclines. By 1854, with the more practical Horseshoe Curve and Gallitzin Tunnels in operation, the Portage Railroad became obsolete. On view at the site are models of the horses and vehicles used to operate the system. *U.S. 22, 12 miles west of Altoona; 814-886-6150.*

■ **BLACK MOSHANNON STATE PARK** *map page 177, B-2*

Once the site of a stagecoach way station, this small park lies on the Allegheny Plateau in Centre County about 30 miles northeast of Altoona. During the 1800s, it was the site of an extensive pine lumber operation. Black Moshannon has a well-planned network of trails. More than 20 miles have been groomed for bicycles and there are 16 miles for hiking. The longest and most interesting trail winds around 250-acre Black Moshannon Lake. Trails are well maintained throughout the winter for cross-country skiing, and most of the park is open during hunting season. Lodgings include 13 cabins that can be charitably described as "rustic." *Moshannon State Forest, Route 504 and Julian Pike; 814-342-5960.*

ALLEGHENY PORTAGE RAILROAD

The crowd and bustle attendant upon the arrival of every train—the change to the cars which stood ready for the mountain passage—the immense locomotives provided by the State to draw the trains to the foot of "Plane 10"—the anxious pause there while the clanking of chains indicated to the passengers that their car was being attached to the wire rope which was to draw it up the steep ascent—the halt at the top of the plane while this attachment was severed, and horses or a locomotive hitched on to draw it to the next summit, was continued until the train was made up again and went on its way to Pittsburgh—can never be forgotten by those who participated in the passage. This means of crossing the mountain was used until 1854, when the great tunnel was finished, and the trains then continued on from Altoona, without interruption.

—William B. Sipes, *The Pennsylvania Railroad,* 1875

Lemon Inn on the Portage Railroad *(ca. 1850), by George Storm.*
(State Museum of Pennsylvania)

■ STATE COLLEGE *map page 177, B-2*

In 1855, James Irwin, a Union general and cofounder of Centre Furnace Works, donated 200 acres of woodland as the site for an agricultural technology school for central Pennsylvania farmers. Today, his modest land grant is known as Penn State University. Alongside the university is the town of State College, which performs double duty as university town and flagship municipality of the region.

Downtown State College is a typical college town, with a collection of cafes, bars, bookstores, and shops that range from student budget to alumni expensive. On fall weekends, when the nationally ranked Nittany Lions football team plays at home, returning alumni and fans from across the state overwhelm the downtown area.

■ PENN STATE UNIVERSITY *map page 177, B-2*

This is a campus that has modernized and expanded while preserving its historic buildings and charm. Stroll from the point where town meets gown—the corner of East College Avenue and South Allen Street—along the main walkway across campus to the university libraries, the highest point on campus. On the way, near Schwab Auditorium, you'll pass **Old Main** (Pollock Road; 814-231-1400), the building where top administrators have their offices. Though not the oldest building on campus, it dates from 1862. For many years it provided housing for students and faculty and had a chapel, dining rooms, a library, classrooms, and a museum. Henry Varnum Poor, a noted muralist, painted the frescoes in the grand entrance foyer between 1939 and 1949. They depict the champions of the federal Land Grant Act that created Penn State, and they pay homage to the university's contributions to engineering, mining, and agriculture. *207 Mitchell Boulevard; 814-865-5403.*

The extensive collection of the **Palmer Museum of Art** ranges from the 4th century to the present. Eighth-century pottery from Greece, decorative arts from 17th-century Europe, and 19th-century portraiture generously fill the museum's walls and rooms, and there are contemporary works on paper by Donald Judd, Louise Nevelson, Henry Moore, Sol LeWitt, Willem de Kooning, Robert Motherwell, and many other noteworthy artists. *Curtin Road, Penn State University campus; 814-865-7672.*

(preceding pages) Penn State football games draw massive crowds.

■ BOALSBURG *map page 177, C-2*

Boalsburg, a 10-minute drive east from State College, was settled by Scots-Irish immigrants in the early 1800s. Strolling down Main Street here is like stepping from a time machine into 1830s America. Nineteenth-century homes and shops selling antiques line the clean, tree-shaded streets.

The tradition of Memorial Day is said to have begun at **Boalsburg Cemetery** in October 1864, when Emma Hunter, Sophie Keller, and Elizabeth Meyers decorated the graves of all the war dead in the cemetery. The tradition was quickly adopted by the townspeople. A life-size bronze statue at the cemetery memorializes the three women. Gen. John Logan officially established Memorial Day in 1868, and today 25,000 people or more attend ceremonies here. *U.S. Business Route 322, across from Pennsylvania Military Museum.*

The **Columbus Chapel and Boal Mansion Museum** are Boalsburg's most important sights. The mansion was begun in 1789 by Capt. David Boal, the Irishman who founded Boalsburg and encouraged further Scots-Irish settlement before leaving to fight in the Revolutionary War. Nine generations of Boals have made this their home, and the furniture, treasures, and keepsakes on display speak to the colorful personalities who lived here. (The CEO of the Boal Mansion Museum, a Boal descendant, currently resides in the house.)

One of the Boal wives was the niece of a direct descendant of Christopher Columbus, and because her uncle and aunt died childless, she inherited significant relics from the chapel at Columbus Castle in Asturias, Spain. Contents of the chapel include a desk studded with gilt cockleshells, 16th-century Renaissance paintings, and a silver reliquary containing pieces of what is purported to be the True Cross. They were detached by the Bishop of Leon and presented to the Columbus family in 1817. *300 Old Boalsburg Road, parallel to U.S. Business Route 322; 814-466-6210.*

Army officers from Pennsylvania who served in the south of France at the end of World War I created the **Pennsylvania Military Museum**. One of the soldiers was Col. Theodore Boal, a great-great-grandson of Boalsburg's founder. Each year he organized a group to place memorial plaques on a stone wall bordering Spring Creek to honor those who "gave their lives in defense of freedom." What became known as the Shrine of the 28th Division was purchased by the state in 1931 and became the current location of the museum.

A highlight of a visit here is a tour through a replica of a World War I battlefield trench, with the re-created sounds and light flashes of rifles and artillery. The museum also displays uniforms, weapons, medals, and other materials from the Revolutionary War and Civil War. *U.S. Business Route 322; 814-466-6263.*

■ BELLEFONTE *map page 177, C-2*

About 10 miles northeast of State College lies Bellefonte, home to seven of the state's governors and the Bellefonte Springs. Surveyors who poked around the area in the 1770s found an enormous natural spring that generates, according to current estimates, 11.5 million gallons of water a day. In 1785, William Lamb saw the value of such a resource and purchased 750 acres around the spring. Settlers flocked to the area, which became known as Spring Creek.

The name didn't stick. When the French statesman Charles-Maurice de Talleyrand visited the area in 1795 and sampled the water, he reputedly exclaimed *"Oh, Belle Fontaine!"* Impressed by the Frenchman's elocution, Bellefonte's citizens built a creekside park in his honor. In a nod to French taste, Talleyrand Park has a sculpture park and a gazebo.

Volunteer railroad buffs of the **Bellefonte Historical Railroad Society** operate a two-car diesel train that snakes through several central Pennsylvania counties, into Bald Eagle Valley, and over Mount Nittany. The trip begins at Bellefonte's historic Pennsylvania Railroad Station. Other stops include a picnic trip to Sayers Dam, the tiny, picturesque village of Lemont at the base of Mount Nittany, the Curtin Village Iron Works, and the Keystone Gliderport, where sailplanes have set world records riding Appalachian air currents. The society also schedules fall foliage excursions and dinner train outings. *High and Water Streets; 814-355-0311.*

■ MID-STATE TRAIL

■ BALD EAGLE STATE FOREST *map page 177, C-1*

In Bald Eagle State Forest (not to be confused with Bald Eagle State Park, north of Bellefonte), the leaves of tall oaks form dramatic canopies that allow only slivers of light to reach the ground. The forest covers a vast area to the east and south of State College and is bisected by the Mid-State Trail.

Autumn colors brighten a Boalsburg street.

The beautiful Kishacoquillas Valley in Mifflin County, not too far south of Poe Valley State Park, is typical of the scenery in this part of the state.

One section of the Mid-State Trail descends along the north flank of Thick Mountain, crosses Woodward Gap Road, and leads to a natural spring. Part of the Mid-State Trail hike follows an abandoned Penn Central Railroad grade and trestle that goes under Paddy Mountain by way of a 280-foot-long tunnel. Maps are available at the R.B. Winter State Park Visitors Center, where trails begin and end. *Off Route 150, Howard; 814-625-2775.*

■ **POE VALLEY STATE PARK** *map page 177, C-2*
A 9.6-mile leg of the Mid-State Trail begins in Poe Valley State Park at the blue-blazed hunters path at the park's concession stand. Following is an overview of the hike, but you should get a map if you plan to go. (No one wants to carry a guide-book to all of Pennsylvania on a hike.)

Follow the hunters path to the intersection with the orange-blazed Mid-State Trail (MST) at the top of the ridge. Turn left on Thorpe Trail and follow it along Little Poe Mountain to Little Poe Road Creek. Beyond the creek is Dry Hollow Trail; follow it to the top of Long Mountain. You will pass a section known as

Panther Hollow, which has spectacular views of a hollow flanked by tall oaks. Return via the Dry Hollow Trail to Big Poe Road and then bear right to return to nearby Poe Paddy State Park, named so because of its proximity to both Poe Mountain and Paddy Mountain. For longer hikes, it's best to consult with a park official, or get a copy of *50 Hikes in Central Pennsylvania* by Tom Thwaites. *Poe Valley, off Route 322; 814-349-2460.*

■ CAVES *map page 177, C-2*

Chemical reactions that occurred underground about 20 million years ago have left at least a thousand caves under central Pennsylvania. Most are closed to the public, but two of the biggest and longest caves can be toured.

Penn's Cave was bought in 1773 by a relative of Edgar Allan Poe, and the dark interior would seem a likely setting for one of his horror stories. It's been open for public tours since 1885, when owners Jesse and Samuel Long chipped in money for a boat to take people along the river that runs through the cavity. The cave is filled with bizarre limestone sculptures that seem to take on whatever shape your imagination assigns them. *State Road 192, 5 miles east of Centre Hall; 814-364-1664.*

When Pine Creek was running at full capacity, **Woodward Cave,** 22 miles west of Penn's Cave, was filled with water. But in 1923, engineers turned the creek flow away from the cave and removed tons of clay and river sediment, revealing hundreds of Native American drawings on cave walls and artifacts secreted away in unexplored spaces. In 1926, the cavern was opened to the public.

Passageways lead to chambers crowded with stalactites (ceiling limestone formations) and stalagmites (those anchored to the floor). One space contains the 50-ton Woodward Cave stalagmite, estimated to be two million years old. *Route 45, 22 miles east of State College; 814-349-9800.*

■ SUGAR VALLEY LOOP DRIVE *map page 177, C-2*

North of Woodward is a valley named for its sugar maple trees. In the small enclave called Sugar Valley, Amish can be seen driving horse-drawn buggies. Drivers or fit bicyclists can take a 25-mile-long route that leads past a 19th-century gristmill, a covered bridge, a schoolhouse, and a number of old churches and graveyards. *Take I-80, Exit 27, and head south on State Road 477 toward Loganton. After Loganton, turn right on Route 880 to Carroll-Tylersville Road.*

(above) A reunion of Piper Cub pilots, seen from the air. (opposite) Penn's Cave is one of the few caves in Central Pennsylvania open to the public.

■ LOCK HAVEN *map page 177, C-1*

On the banks of the western branch of the Susquehanna River, 20 miles west of Williamsport, sits the town of Lock Haven. Logging operations during the late 1830s made millionaires out of many native sons in small communities like this one. Stroll down the Water Street block known as Mansion Row to see how the swell folks lived. Some homes have fallen into disrepair, but others have been cleaned up and opened for tours.

Lock Haven is known among aviation aficionados for its **Piper Aviation Museum.** William T. Piper was a natural entrepreneur. An oil prospector and businessman, he teamed up with aeronautics engineer Walter Jamouneau in 1937 to build the first assembly-line-produced private airplane—the J3, or "Piper Cub." For 47 years the company produced small aircraft for leisure flying. The museum, established in 1985, has prototype aircraft, photographs, films, artifacts, and memorabilia relating to the development of the Piper Cub and aircraft it inspired. *William T. Piper Memorial Airport, Hangar One, 1 Piper Way; 570-748-2586 or 570-748-8283.*

■ **WILLIAMSPORT** *map page 177, D-1*

Northeast of Lock Haven on U.S. 220 is Williamsport, the seat of Lycoming County. The town's location along the Susquehanna River's scenic western branch, in the shadow of the Allegheny Mountains, makes it worth a visit. In the 1880s, when it was the center of the timber industry, Williamsport was one of the state's wealthiest towns. Its Millionaires' Row—an opulent stretch of mansions along West Fourth Street—is evidence of Williamsport's flush days.

Many of the old homes are still here, and some can be toured. The fanciful **E. A. Rowley House** (707 West Fourth Street) was the first mansion on the street to have electric lights and a dumbwaiter. Other noteworthy residences include the **Eutermarks-Harrar House** (915 West Fourth Street), an Italianate design, and the **Emery House** (835 West Fourth Street), an impressive example of the Richardson Romanesque style. The **Lycoming County Historical Society** (570-326-3326) has information about house tours.

Exhibits at the **Thomas T. Taber Museum** trace local history from its Native American roots to the present. Highlights include pottery and stone tools of the

Woodland Indians, period rooms filled with Victorian furniture, paintings by 19th-century still-life painter (and 10-year Williamsport resident) Severin Roesen, and a 300-piece toy train collection. *Fourth and Maynard Streets; 570-326-3326.*

Williamsport is also famous for the Little League Baseball World Series, played here each year at Howard J. Lamade Stadium in late August. (Little League was born here in 1939.) Adjacent to the stadium is the **Little League Baseball Museum,** which has photographs of players and teams and displays other memorabilia. *Howard J. Lamade Stadium, Route 15, South Williamsport; 570-326-3607.*

Millionaires' Row mansion.

A game in progress at the Howard J. Lamade Little League Baseball Stadium.

■ TRAVEL BASICS

Interstate 76, the Pennsylvania Turnpike, runs through Harrisburg and then moves south through Bedford County, Shanksville, and Laurel Hill. Route 81, south from Harrisburg, is the most direct route to Chambersburg and provides easy access to Shippensburg, Mercersburg, and Waynesboro. Route 15 south from Harrisburg is the most direct route to Gettysburg. Central Pennsylvania's interior is crisscrossed by back roads that wind through hilly woodlands and small towns, and past family farms with barns made of fieldstone and logs. U.S. Route 322 cuts through the central part of the state, skirting Boalsburg, State College, and Bald Eagle Mountain, before connecting with U.S. 220, which heads south to Altoona.

Climate: Temperatures here run about 10 degrees lower in every season than elsewhere in the state. Summers average from 75 to 85 degrees Fahrenheit with generally low humidity. Fall comes early, with nighttime lows dropping into the low 40s as early as the middle of September. Winters are long, cold, and snowy, with the north-central area receiving as much as 100 inches of snow in a season and daytime temperatures averaging from 15 to 30 degrees.

PITTSBURGH

At the narrow end of an island that seems to float in the Allegheny River, just off Pittsburgh's North Side, a weathered steel bridge reaches across the water to connect well-manicured running and biking trails on both shores. There's no frou-frou design to this bridge, just heavy black metal with a brownish patina from a century of Pittsburgh weather. Passersby include joggers, walkers, bicyclists, in-line skaters, and mothers pushing babes in strollers from one attractive setting to another. Few of them know that the former Herr's Island, now called Washington's Landing, was once home to meat-packing plants whose odors, according to a Pittsburgh resident "were foul enough to make a fellow just about swear off breathing." In fact, even as recently as the late 1980s few Pittsburghers would have imagined the dramatic transformation that took place during the 1990s. But Washington's Landing and the pedestrian bridge stand as symbols of a city that has scraped off the rust of its industrial past, cleansed its three rivers, and built up its skyline, in the process becoming one of the country's most livable cities.

Pittsburgh was founded at the point where the Allegheny and Monongahela Rivers converge to form the mammoth Ohio River. The two rivers unite at Point State Park, a spacious green at the tip of a bustling area known as the Golden Triangle. Synonymous with downtown Pittsburgh, the area is filled with fine restaurants, shops, historic landmarks, and many new commercial enterprises. Beyond the buildings, a ring of forested hills circles the city.

■ HISTORY

■ BRITISH AND FRENCH FIGHT FOR CONTROL

By 1750, the French recognized that control of the land at the confluence of the Monongahela and Allegheny Rivers was the key to the defense of an important inland trade route linking France's colonies in Canada with New Orleans on the Gulf of Mexico. The Ohio River, created by that confluence, led to the Mississippi River and directly to New Orleans.

Pittsburgh's skyline reveals a patchwork of architectural styles, a reflection of a city on the move.

George Washington raises his hat as the British flag is raised over Fort Duquesne in 1758.
(The Granger Collection, New York)

The British also recognized the area's strategic importance and sent George Washington, then a 21-year-old major in Virginia's colonial militia, north with some soldiers. He carried with him a letter from Virginia's Ohio Company, a group of businessmen granted a British charter for 500,000 acres of land in the Ohio Valley, protesting French plans to build forts in the area. "I spent some time in viewing the rivers and the land at the Fork, which I think extremely well situated for a Fort," he wrote in his journal in 1753.

The French officer who commanded Fort Le Boeuf, on French Creek to the north, wined and dined George Washington but replied that the French were in western Pennsylvania to stay. The exchange was a polite preview of the bloody confrontation to come—the French and Indian War.

On this first trip through western Pennsylvania, Washington nearly drowned in the Allegheny River. His version of the story, told to dinner companions in his years as president, was that he saved himself from the river and also fought off an Indian attack. The version offered by a companion on the trip, missionary Christopher Gist, was that he was forced to dive in after the drowning man and haul him to the island now known as Washington's Landing.

Heeding Washington's advice, British forces were dispatched to the area to build a fort and establish a presence. The French, better supplied and manned, encircled the fort, forced the British out, and set about building a larger defense post they named Fort Duquesne. Their fort gave them command of all points of entry.

In 1758, with their naval blockades proving highly effective against the French, the British attacked Fort Duquesne, but the French burned it to the ground rather than see it overrun. The British rebuilt the fort and named it for their prime minister, William Pitt, who had taken over management of the French and Indian War in 1757 and is largely credited with Britain's ultimate success.

■ PITTSBURGH AND THE REVOLUTION

In the fall of 1776, the first of many "Ohio Valley Volunteers" joined George Washington's army to fight in the Revolutionary War. As a reward to veterans, one of Pennsylvania's first official acts was to offer discounted land about a mile north of the confluence of the Allegheny and Monongahela Rivers. By 1786, the area had a fledgling settlement and its own newspaper, the ancestor of the largest newspaper in the city today, the *Pittsburgh Post-Gazette.*

If cheap land lured settlers to the area, rivers provided Pittsburgh with the means to grow and prosper. The nation's first steamboat, the *New Orleans*, was built in 1811 on a bank of the Monongahela near what is now Try Street. The popularity of steamboat travel, combined with the efficiency of barge transportation, made Pittsburgh a premier inland port. During the War of 1812, the city's location facilitated

The New Orleans *was launched in Pittsburgh in 1811. (Historical Society of Western Pennsylvania)*

Emma Gibson's View of the City of Pittsburgh in 1817. *(Historical Society of Western Pennsylvania)*

timely transport of military supplies and was key to America's victory in that conflict. After the war, the city's economic life and the quality of the environment would change forever as Pittsburgh became a major manufacturing center.

■ INDUSTRY AND IMMIGRANTS

By 1816, Pittsburgh was thriving and its citizens numbered 10,000. Word of job opportunities spread literally around the world, and soon immigrants were arriving in droves to work in glass manufacturing, among other enterprises, and to build the city's bridges and roads. Housing for workers sprang up in the shadow of most factories and mills, usually in ethnic enclaves. In 1852, when the first rail line in the region was completed, cutting in half the four-day journey between Pittsburgh and Philadelphia, many immigrants moved to neighborhoods along the tracks.

In the years following the Civil War, Pittsburgh became a magnet for the industrial revolution's most successful magnates: Andrew Carnegie created a steel empire; Henry Clay Frick produced the coke that fired the steel foundries; Alfred E. Hunt and five partners started what later became the Alcoa aluminum company; Henry J. Heinz took processed foods to a new level; and George Westinghouse invented that watershed gadget, the air brake.

Steel refining and manufacturing prospered in Pittsburgh because the city offered abundant low-cost labor, water for processing and transportation, and coke (processed coal), a cost-effective fuel source for heating blast furnaces. Unfortunately, however, coke was a noxious pollutant. As blast furnaces along the rivers multiplied, a thick haze that would last more than a century settled over the city. When mills were chugging along at full capacity, from the late 1910s through the 1940s, it was common practice for business executives to go home on their lunch hours to change their white shirts, which had become soiled during the morning from the coke ash in the air.

Pittsburgh industrialists controlled their labor forces as they saw fit, and working conditions, according to historical accounts, were horrific. Workers received barely enough to live on and there were no provisions for time off, health care, disability payments, or compensation for work-related accidents. In Pittsburgh, the gap between rich and poor was a yawning chasm with few opportunities for mill workers to move up.

Pioneering unions organized to help workers, but their leaders underestimated the ruthlessness and determination of businessmen who fought unions using every tactic available. In 1877, a strike by conductors and porters protesting a wage reduction turned violent, and 25 people were killed.

The Bessemer converter revolutionized steel production so greatly that a factory whose output had measured in tens of tons began producing in the thousands of tons. (Library of Congress)

A pall of smoke from steel factories hangs over Pittsburgh in this 1903 stereograph. (Library of Congress)

The most famous union-management battle came more than a decade later when 3,000 workers at Andrew Carnegie's Homestead Steel Mill walked off their jobs to fight management changes in wages and work hours. Carnegie's chief executive at the mill, Henry Clay Frick, pitted a force of armed Pinkerton guards against the strikers. In the confrontation that followed, several guards and one striker were killed.

The intervention of the National Guard in the conflict played right into Frick's strategy of depicting the strikers as lawless thugs. The largest union movement in the nation at the time—the Amalgamated Association—was shut down, and 20 years would pass before organized labor would reemerge as a strong voice for workers.

■ RUST BELT REALITIES AND MODERN RENEWAL

For almost 150 years, Pittsburgh's scenic splendor was buried under the haze of mill smoke, and its rivers ran with industrial waste. But with the election of Mayor David Lawrence in 1945, the city began an organized effort to clean itself up. The use of coal was either eliminated or severely restricted. Railroad engines were switched to diesel; coal-burning furnaces, the standard heating method for most Pittsburgh homes, were banned and residents had to pay for oil or gas-powered units. As the post–World War II era progressed, southwestern Pennsylvania began

PITTSBURGH NOTABLES

The Pittsburgh area has produced some amazing people. Whether by birth or circumstance, those who have experienced Pittsburgh long enough to call it home know its power to nurture, especially in close-knit neighborhoods like Polish Hill and the Serbian South Side. Working-class blood still pulses in Pittsburgh's veins, and its ethnic enclaves provide daily reminders of the immigrant backs and brawn that made this city work. Still, although Pittsburgh is home to prestigious educational and arts institutions and counts many philanthropists and research scientists, lawyers, and other professionals among its population, the misconception lingers that the town's blue-collar roots are its only ones. A list of famous people associated with Pittsburgh would have to include:

ACTORS ▪ F. Murray Abraham, Sharon Stone, Shirley Jones, Michael Keaton

ARTISTS ▪ Mary Cassatt, Andy Warhol, Philip Pearlstein

AUTHORS ▪ George S. Kaufman, Annie Dillard, Rachel Carson, August Wilson

BASEBALL PLAYERS ▪ Bill Mazeroski and Roberto Clemente

COMPOSERS ▪ Stephen Foster, Henry Mancini, Samuel Barber

CHILDREN'S-SHOW HOST ▪ Fred "Mister" Rogers

DANCERS ▪ Martha Graham, Gene Kelly, and Paul Taylor

ENTREPRENEURS ▪ Andrew Carnegie, Henry Clay Frick, and Henry J. Heinz

INVENTOR ▪ George Westinghouse

MUSICIANS ▪ Erroll Garner, Billy Strayhorn, Earl "Fatha" Hines, George Benson

QUARTERBACKS ▪ Johnny Unitas, Joe Montana, and Dan Marino

SINGERS ▪ Lena Horne, Patty Lupone, and Christina Aguilera

to lose population because of declining steel production—between 1975 and 1990, the area lost nearly 800,000 residents. The mills and their supporting industries withered in the face of competition from factories in countries where labor costs were lower and production techniques more efficient.

Many riverside mill towns near Pittsburgh have never fully recovered from the loss of steel-related jobs, but Pittsburgh's economy has survived because the city has attracted high-tech industries, health care, medical research, financial management, banking, and some light manufacturing. Under the leadership of more recent

In the 1950s, J&L Steel, concerned about the increased use of aluminum and plastic, ran advertising campaigns showing happy consumers glowing with pride over their steel products. (National Museum of American History)

mayors, Richard Caliguiri in the late 1970s and the 1980s and Tom Murphy in the 1990s, the city transformed itself economically and aesthetically. A commitment to wise use of the riverfronts may be the biggest legacy of Murphy, who was elected to his third term in 2002. His administration has emphasized providing public parks and walkways along the rivers, in downtown areas, and in many neighborhoods.

Pittsburgh's renaissance has been focused largely on remaking downtown to include offices, upscale retail space, residential areas, and entertainment options. More than $1 billion in new construction has changed the face of the city in just a few years. Among the more high-profile projects to be undertaken is the $354 million redesign (by Rafael Viñoly, also design architect of Philadelphia's Kimmel Center) and expansion of the David L. Lawrence Convention Center. Named after one of Pittsburgh's most beloved mayors (1946–58), the revamped structure is among the first "green" convention centers in the United States, incorporating, says the Viñoly design team, "natural ventilation and lighting, a water-reclamation system, and use of nontoxic materials."

These new amenities are typical of the city's ongoing rejuvenation. Factor in the low cost of living here and the stellar cultural scene, and it should be no surprise that since 1985 Pittsburgh has been on the Rand McNally *Places Rated Almanac* list of Top 20 Most Livable Cities.

A BEAUTIFUL THREE DECADES

From 1968 to 2001, the late Fred Rogers hosted the PBS kids' show *Mister Rogers' Neighborhood,* produced in Pittsburgh. Rogers, famous for his cardigan sweaters and mild manner, was such a legend here that his picture appeared on billboards and posters, his opinions were sought out by local newspapers, and area baseball teams asked him to throw out the first ball of the season.

Rogers would have been revered in any town, but he was especially loved in Pittsburgh, a city whose close-knit and friendly neighborhoods served as inspiration for the nurturing society at the heart of the show. Recurring characters like friendly Lady Aberlin, Handyman Negri, Mr. McFeely, and Police Officer Clemmons speak to a sense of community and small-town know-how that are as much a reality of everyday Pittsburgh as are the show's "neighborhood trolley," corner bakery, and local library. "Pittsburgh has distinct and unique neighborhoods, and so does the show," said Rogers, who was born in 1928 in Latrobe, 30 miles east of Pittsburgh. "We've always been glad that our neighborhood has always been able to be produced on the soil of the Pittsburgh neighborhood."

The overriding concept Rogers had for *Mister Rogers' Neighborhood* was elegant in its simplicity: "Look at the television camera and present as much love as you possibly could to a person who needs it." The approach resonated—*Neighborhood* is the longest-running program in PBS history. And though the show stopped production in 2001, Rogers didn't hang up his cardigan. He and his regulars are on the Web, and an exhibit based on the Emmy Award–winning program is touring the country. Rogers died in February, 2003. In 2002, he received the Medal of Freedom from President Bush and a star on the Hollywood Walk of Fame.

Children's TV is all about love for Fred Rogers. (Family Communications, Inc.)

■ DOWNTOWN

Condensed into an 11-square-block area and bounded by the Monongahela and
Allegheny Rivers, downtown Pittsburgh is a medley of office towers, government
buildings, hotels, and river bridges that create a dramatic skyline.

■ THE POINT AND FORT PITT *map below, A-2/3*

Nearly every adventure in downtown Pittsburgh begins or ends in **Point State
Park,** where an impressive fountain forms the apex of a geographical triangle
whose base is a series of crosstown ramps and expressways known as I-579. By any
measure, this is a truly beautiful park, with expansive lawns and promenades, the
triangle's dramatically tapered point leading the eye upward to forested green hills.
If greenery and blue skies provide a beautiful setting, the people in the park seem

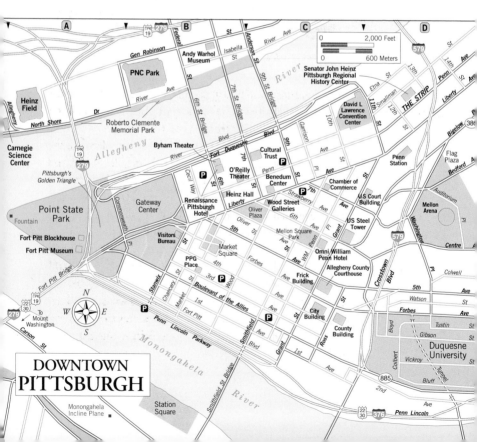

DOWNTOWN
PITTSBURGH

The Point, at the confluence of two rivers, is the site of many civic festivals.

all politeness and vigor, just out for a stroll. Coal barges and pleasure boats ply the nearby waters, and in summer, sunbathers relax in the wide open area around the great fountain whose arched plume leaps 30 feet into the air.

The park is a National Historic Landmark. The Point is the site of old earthworks and the remains of a wall of **Fort Pitt,** where French and British soldiers contested this strategically important sliver of land in the late 1750s. Artifacts and monuments at **Fort Pitt Museum and Blockhouse** (412-281-9284) bestow much of the credit for Britain's eventual victory on Gen. John Forbes. A Scotsman, Forbes was appointed to his post by British prime minister William Pitt in 1757.

Forbes knew that retaking the fort (then called Fort Duquesne) from the French might require a long siege. To win, he would need to outlast the French and would need a dependable route for provisions and weaponry. His response was to turn his soldiers into road builders—chopping down trees, hauling out boulders, and clearing away brush. Soon the road stretched from the Point east across the Allegheny Mountains. The French abandoned Fort Duquesne to the British, but only after burning it to the ground.

"I have used the freedom of giving your name to Fort Duquesne," Forbes wrote Prime Minister Pitt in November 1758 after the French deserted it, "as I hope it was in some measure the being actuated by your spirit that now makes us masters of the place." *Point State Park, main entrance at 101 Commonwealth Place; 412-471-0235.*

■ MARKET SQUARE *map page 220, B-2*

About a third of a mile due east of the Point, between Fourth and Fifth Avenues, is Market Square, the city center in the years just before the Revolutionary War. The square was a civic gathering place—the Declaration of Independence was read aloud here in 1776—and today it is a popular lunchtime hangout for office workers. At a Friday evening entertainment event called First Night, people gather to drink, mingle, and listen to bands on an outdoor stage.

■ HIGH-RISE GRANDEES

Near Market Square rises **PPG Place,** the headquarters of PPG Industries, founded in 1883 as the Pittsburgh Plate Glass Company. The structure is made almost entirely of plate glass (19,750 pieces, to be precise), and at sunset, with orange light bouncing off so many glass panes, the effect is pure magic. The building, designed by Philip Johnson and John Burgee, remains a spectacular example of postmodern corporate architecture. *Boulevard of the Allies and Stanwix Street.*

Pittsburgh's **Allegheny County Courthouse** is a beautiful reminder of the attention paid to detail by architects of another era. Architect Henry Hobson Richardson's 1888 design incorporated Boston-quarried stone, castle-like towers, and an inner courtyard with an impressive circular fountain. The building's rounded arches, rugged stone walls, and Byzantine carvings characterize the architect's style, known as Richardsonian Romanesque. Don't miss the frescoes on the first floor, the grand staircase near the entrance to the old law library, or the "bridge of sighs" connecting the courthouse and former jail (now a court facility). Tours can be arranged through the Pittsburgh History and Landmarks Foundation (412-471-5808). *436 Grant Street.*

The 21-story **Frick Building,** erected in 1901 to a design by D. H. Burnham and Company, is a high-class affair that mixes black-and-white marble and multicolored stained glass. The building, bankrolled by coke-and-steel baron Henry Clay Frick, whose bust is displayed in the lobby, is an exceptional example of the beaux-arts style. *437 Grant Street, across from the County Courthouse.*

High-rise buildings tower over the sturdy Allegheny County Courthouse.

As a former director of U.S. Steel, Frick might just as logically have his bust grace the lobby of the **US Steel Tower,** the 841-foot-high, triangle-shape tower designed by architects Harrison, Abramowitz & Abbe. When completed in 1970, the handsome, rust-color building was the tallest skyscraper outside New York and Chicago. *600 Grant Street.*

Mellon Square Park provides welcome green respite from the marble, stone, and steel of the Golden Triangle. Noontime concerts often take place here, and there are fountains and a waterfall. *William Penn Place and Sixth Avenue.*

Mellon Square Park bumps up against the **Omni William Penn Hotel,** a project begun by Henry Clay Frick to provide Pittsburgh with a hotel up to New York City standards. Built in 1916, the luxury property, ideally situated downtown between the Allegheny and Monongahela Rivers, was designed by Benno Janssen, also responsible for the Pittsburgh Athletic Association building and the Mellon Institute, among other local buildings. The hotel is listed on the National Register of Historic Places, and tours can be arranged through the Pittsburgh History and Landmarks Foundation (412-471-5808). *530 William Penn Place; 412-281-7100.*

Exhibits at the Wood Street Galleries focus on the contemporary arts.

If you're in the mood for more historic-hotel-hopping, head over to the nearby **Renaissance Pittsburgh Hotel,** the 21st-century reincarnation of the Fulton Building, a (pardon the pun) Renaissance Revival–style edifice completed in 1906. Over the years, the Fulton Building housed offices and medical spaces. Among the structure's noteworthy elements is the copper and granite exterior facade, but even more enchanting is what's inside: the grand staircase, mosaic tiles, and marble everywhere. The beautiful cast-iron and glass rotunda dome had been blacked out since World War II but now sheds light over the entire atrium. *107 Sixth Street; 412-562-1200.*

■ **ARTS SPACES** *map page 220, C/2*
One of the city's funkier art spaces, **Wood Street Galleries** is a project of the Cultural Trust, a consortium of arts groups. Conceptual art, multimedia works, and photography are the main attractions, and the long list of notables who have shown work here includes Marina Rosenfeld, Catherine Opie, and Nicole Eisenman. *601 Wood Street; 412-471-5605.*

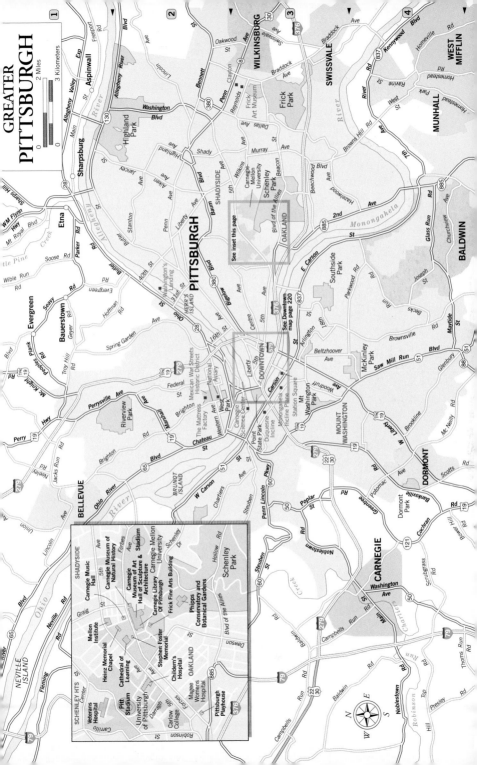

The performing arts are alive and well throughout the city, but downtown is the headquarters of many of the major cultural groups. Among the venues of note are the **O'Reilly Theater** (621 Penn Avenue), where the Pittsburgh Public Theater performs; **Heinz Hall** (600 Penn Avenue), which hosts performances by the Pittsburgh Symphony and visiting orchestras; and **Byham Theater** (101 Sixth Street), a handsomely renovated early-20th-century theater that hosts performances by dance and theater companies. A stone's throw from the Byham Theater is **Benedum Center for the Performing Arts** (Seventh Street at Penn Avenue), a 1928 movie palace that was renovated and expanded in 1987 to accommodate the Pittsburgh Ballet, national dance troupes, and touring Broadway musicals.

■ THE STRIP *map page 220, D-1*

Just outside the Golden Triangle and northeast of downtown, the Strip is a 15-block-long, three-block-wide produce and wholesale district where the air is filled with the scent of gourmet coffees, ginger chicken, fresh fish, pastries, breads, cookies, and other taste sensations. For many years, this area was filled with warehouses and small factories, and the restaurants that lined the streets were geared toward the lunchtime work crowd. In the 1950s, the neighborhood had a down-at-the-heels reputation, but today a cosmopolitan air pervades this outdoor emporium where local entrepreneurs sell clothing, CDs, art, and ethnic food and where people from all social classes and walks of life come together.

Some of Pittsburgh's best wholesalers set up shop along the Strip, like **Wholey's Fish Market** (1711 Penn Avenue; 412-391-3737), where you can find dozens of varieties of fresh fish daily, from scrumptious salmon to jumbo Icelandic cod. **Jimmy and Nino Sunseri's** (1906 Penn Avenue; 412-255-1100), a Strip tradition for decades, has mouthwatering Italian sausages, pasta, cheese, and olives. At **Primanti's** (1150 Smallman Street; 412-263-2142) you can order enormous tuna, cheese combo, or steak sandwiches for under $5. To revive yourself, have a cup of joe at **La Prima Espresso Bar** (205 21st Street; 412-281-1922). Come evening, restaurants and clubs to suit every taste fire up along Penn Avenue and Smallman Street. **Metropol** (1600 Smallman Street), one of the city's trendiest nightspots, frequently hosts concerts by big-name rock artists.

The **Senator John Heinz Pittsburgh Regional History Center,** an impressive redbrick building that looms over Smallman Street, is named after the popular Pennsylvania politician who served in the U.S. Senate from 1977 to 1991. The seven-story building, once owned by the Chautauqua Lake Ice Company, serves today as a center for learning about western Pennsylvania's people, history, and geography. Among the permanent exhibits is *Points in Time: Building a Life in Western Pennsylvania, 1750–Today*, which includes life-size models of dwellings from three historic periods: a log cabin from 1790, an immigrant worker's home from 1910, and a suburban ranch home from the 1950s. Furniture from several centuries, artifacts, costumes, and live theater provide a historic look at the lives of Pennsylvanians. *1212 Smallman Street; 412-454-6000.*

■ OAKLAND *map page 225, D-3*

Oakland is a lively commercial and residential area with art museums, cinemas, shops, prestigious universities, and restaurants serving international cuisine. Lush **Schenley Park** is here, as is the four-block, L-shaped complex of buildings that house the Carnegie Museum of Art, the Carnegie Museum of Natural History, the Carnegie Library of Pittsburgh, and the Carnegie Music Hall.

■ CARNEGIE COMPLEX *map page 225, E-3*

The permanent collections at the **Carnegie Museum of Art** include ancient sculpture, classic Roman statuary, decorative arts, painting, works on paper, and film and video. The painting collection is extensive, stretching from the 1400s to the 1960s and including works by Renaissance artists and European masters Rubens, Goya, van Gogh, and Degas. The museum opens a revealing window on American art with works by Winslow Homer, John Singer Sargent, Edward Hopper, Andy Warhol, Joan Mitchell, and Jackson Pollock, among many others.

John White Alexander's 1907 mural *The Crowning of Labor,* an ode to industrial workers, graces the entryway to the Hall of Sculpture, a room modeled after the Parthenon and built with marble from the same quarries. Behind it is the Hall of Architecture, inspired by the Mausoleum at Halicarnassus. Besides decorative arts objects, these rooms contain Carnegie's collection of 69 plaster casts of Egyptian, Greek, and Roman statues and his collection of 144 plaster casts of architectural masterpieces. Copying fragile art works is frowned on today, but it wasn't in Carnegie's time (or earlier—even the Romans made copies of Greek works), and his collection rivals those at museums in Paris and London. The Heinz Architectural Center contains drawings, photographs, prints, and models, most from the 19th and 20th centuries. *4400 Forbes Avenue; 412-622-3131.*

The Diplodocus carnegie *in the Carnegie Museum of Natural History.*

A walkway connects the art museum to the **Carnegie Museum of Natural History.** Carnegie, a hands-on collector, dispatched one of the earliest teams of paleontologists to unearth fossils and dinosaur bones for reconstruction back in the museum. Aware of the source of their funding, team members named a small dinosaur *Diplodocus carnegie* in his honor. Almost as popular as the dinosaurs are the exhibits on American Indian culture. *4400 Forbes Avenue; 412-622-3131.*

The **Carnegie Library of Pittsburgh** is the mother ship of Andrew Carnegie's network of libraries, which extended first to southwestern Pennsylvania and then to other parts of the country. In all, Carnegie built 2,509 libraries throughout the English-speaking world. Libraries reaped the lion's share of his largesse because of his own experience as an immigrant boy who had benefited from access to a then-rare small library to educate himself. Carnegie believed that in a meritocracy like the United States, where effort and ability, not family background, determined success, libraries could provide everyone with an equal opportunity, and allow immigrants to absorb the principles of American democracy.

This library, opened in 1895 and engraved with the words "Free to the People" over its entrance, is an architectural gem that has undergone significant renovation

CONTRADICTORY CARNEGIE

As a businessman, Andrew Carnegie was ruthless toward competitors and workers, but upon his retirement he gave most of his wealth away, becoming in the process one of America's greatest philanthropists. His charitable works were not just a guilty afterthought to a life of acquisition. Carnegie wrote in a famous article known as the "Gospel of Wealth" that a talented businessman is entitled to great wealth, but he has a duty to live without ostentation, provide modestly for his dependents, and help his "poorer brethren, bringing to their service his superior wisdom, experience, and ability to administer." Carnegie's tone is patronizing in titan-of-industry style, but his works have the better of the argument. The wisest fields for philanthropy, he wrote in 1889, are universities, libraries, hospitals, parks, concert halls, swimming pools, and church buildings. Critics may carp that homes should come before swimming pools, and that the "libraries" were just buildings without books, but many of the 2,509 Carnegie libraries endure, as do Carnegie Mellon University in Pittsburgh, the Carnegie Endowment for International Peace and the Carnegie Institution of Washington in Washington, D.C., New York City's Carnegie Hall, and many other structures and entities financed by his $350 million in gifts.

The illustrator of this 1892 cartoon contrasts Carnegie's lavish philanthropy with the low wages he paid his employees. (Library of Congress)

and repair in recent years, thanks to a regional funding system for cultural projects approved by Allegheny County voters. *4400 Forbes Avenue; 412-622-3116.*

The **Carnegie Music Hall** opened in 1895, the same year as the Carnegie Library, to which it is connected. The hall is famous for exceptional acoustics, an intimate environment (it has 788 seats), and grand foyer. Small ensembles such as the Pittsburgh Chamber Music Society perform here. *4400 Forbes Avenue; 412-622-3131.*

Connected to the museum complex and park are the campuses of Carnegie Mellon University and the University of Pittsburgh. The well-endowed CMU is the result of the merger in 1967 of two institutions, the Carnegie Institute of Technology, founded by Andrew Carnegie in 1900—it was known as Carnegie Technical Schools for its first dozen years—and the Mellon Institute of Industrial Research. The latter had been established in 1911 as a department of the University of Pittsburgh by Andrew W. and Richard B. Mellon, members of another Pittsburgh philanthropic dynasty; it was incorporated in 1928 as an independent research center. Carnegie Mellon today is a premier scientific-technical institution.

Many structures on the University of Pittsburgh campus are historic landmarks. One of the most impressive buildings in the entire city is the **Cathedral of Learning.** Architect Charles Z. Klauder went to town with a Gothic structure, built between 1926 and 1936, that rises 535 feet and is covered with India lime-stone and Gothic ornaments. Even more famous than the building itself are the 26 impressive Nationality Classrooms (for tours: 412-624-6000) on the first and third floors. Realized over a period of many years, the rooms, each one unique in design and ornament, are meant to symbolize the cultural diversity of the immigrant workers who helped build Pittsburgh. *4200 Fifth Avenue; 412-624-4141.*

Across the main plaza and in the shadow of the secular "cathedral" is the French Gothic–style **Heinz Memorial Chapel,** whose ornate spires and detailed stone carvings contrast wonderfully with the smooth lines and mass of the Cathedral of Learning. The building, with its 73-foot-high stained-glass transept windows, was commissioned by the Heinz family as a memorial to the family patriarch, Henry John, and to his mother, Anna Margareta. The chapel is often a busy place on weekends because Pitt students, employees, and extended families have wedding privileges there. *Heinz Memorial Chapel; 412-624-4157.*

The Cathedral of Learning towers over all on the campus of the University of Pittsburgh.

The **Stephen Foster Memorial** celebrates the life of Pittsburgh native Stephen Foster (1826–64), who composed tunes that have become American classics. "Oh Susanna," "Old Folks at Home," "Jeannie with the Light Brown Hair," and "Camptown Races" are all familiar tunes from the Foster canon. At the memorial are a museum and a research library with letters, books, articles, and compositions by Foster, in all 30,000 documents and artifacts connected to Foster. *4301 Forbes Avenue; 412-624-4100.*

The **Frick Fine Arts Building,** across Schenley Drive from the Carnegie Library of Pittsburgh, houses the University of Pittsburgh's History of Art and Architecture Department and the Frick Fine Arts Library. Commissioned by Helen Clay Frick as a memorial to her father, the building draws on the architecture of the Italian Renaissance for inspiration. Its many impressive features include elegant fruitwood paneling in the library and an inner courtyard in an Italian cloister style. The inner walls of the cloister bear replicas of 15th-century Florentine works of art by Russian painter Nicholas Lochoff, who had been commissioned by the Moscow Museum of Fine Arts in 1911 to go to Italy and make copies of Italian masterpieces. Miss Frick, who apparently inherited her father's talent for negotiating deals, bought 22 of Lochoff's works for $40,000.

Helen Clay Frick offered to endow a larger museum, but the university refused to accept her conditions for the bequest: that the museum contain no contemporary art, and that no one of German extraction work on the staff. *Schenley Drive; 412-648-2400.*

■ CLAYTON AND FRICK ART MUSEUM *map page 225, F-3*
When University of Pittsburgh officials declined to accept Helen Clay Frick's conditions for building a campus museum, she took her millions back home to the city's Point Breeze neighborhood and set about commissioning a museum of her own.

The result, the **Frick Art Museum,** built in 1969, is a showcase for her collection of paintings, drawings, and decorative arts. The painting collection focuses mostly on Italian Renaissance and 18th-century French works. Highlights include works from the 14th and 15th centuries by Sassetta, Duccio, and Giovanni di Paolo, and a portrait by Peter Paul Rubens. The museum is laid out according to the scion's wishes that works be displayed in an atmosphere of intimacy. Thus, paintings hang next to porcelains, bronzes, and rare examples of 17th- and 18th-century furniture.

The Frick Art Museum sits on the same manicured 5.5-acre stretch of lawn and gardens as the restored family home, **Clayton.** It was an 11-room house when

Early auto models in the Car and Carriage Museum. (Frick Art & Historical Center)

Henry Clay Frick and his wife, Adelaide Howard Childs, bought it in 1882, but by the end of the century the industrialist had transformed it into a 23-room mansion. In 1905, the family moved to New York, but Helen Clay Frick returned to Clayton in 1981 and lived there until her death in 1984. Since 1990, the house has been open to the public, and its furnishings—more than 90 percent of them original—include several of Henry Clay Frick's earliest acquisitions. Also on the property is the Car and Carriage Museum, where his 1914 Rolls Royce Silver Ghost touring car is among the conveyances on display. A visit to Clayton sheds light on the lifestyles of Pittsburgh's multimillionaires as they stood firm against the unions that were trying to better the lives of their workers. *7227 Reynolds Street, at Homewood Avenue, Point Breeze; 412-371-0600.*

■ PUBLIC PARKS AND BYWAYS *map page 225, E-3*

Much of the city's East End is covered by a network of gorgeous public parks, but the premier green space is **Schenley Park,** a gift of Mary Schenley, a wealthy expatriate who lived in England. Edward Bigelow, Pittsburgh's director of public works, secured the land for the park, and William Falconer designed it. Schenley Park has

Many varieties of tropical plants thrive at Phipps Conservatory and Botanical Gardens.

456 acres of rolling hills, woods, and trails. The facilities here include a large botanical conservatory, a swimming pool, tennis courts, a nature center, and an ice-skating rink. *Schenley Park Drive (follow signs from I-376, Exit 5).*

Phipps Conservatory and Botanical Gardens, which opened in 1893, is a stellar example of Victorian "glasshouse" architecture. Under the glass canopy are a dozen rooms containing lush tropical plants—fantastically tall palms, dizzyingly aromatic orchids, and many varieties of exotic flowers. Nearly 3 acres of outdoor gardens surround the complex, including the Japanese Courtyard Garden and its show-stopping bonsai collection. From late April through mid-October, the conservatory's Stove Room becomes a butterfly forest filled with nature's winged wonders. *1 Schenley Park; 412-622-6914.*

■ NORTH SIDE *map page 225*

The architecture of Pittsburgh's North Side includes Victorian-era and Craftsman-style row houses along tree-lined streets. The residential sector is separated from the commercial sector, where an H. J. Heinz plant employs thousands of workers adjacent to lush, 50-acre West Park.

Repetitive Vision, *an installation by Yayoi Kusama at the Mattress Factory.*

■ ANDY WARHOL MUSEUM AND MATTRESS FACTORY
map pages 220, B-1, and page 225, C-2

As soon as Andy Warhol, son of Carpatho-Russian immigrants, graduated from the Carnegie Institute of Technology (now Carnegie Mellon University), the Pittsburgh native headed to New York City to pursue fame and fortune. The quixotic artist-celebrity may have fled Pittsburgh as a youth, but these days the prodigal son is posthumously the toast of the town.

The **Andy Warhol Museum,** the ultramodern shrine to the artist, inside an old warehouse, includes thousands of works in many media: painting, drawing, silkscreen prints, photographs, sculpture, film, and video. An enormous collection of source materials—audiotape interviews with friends and associates, thousands of photographs, books, magazines, and other curiosa—sheds light on the artist, the man, and his legacy. One of the museum's most intriguing exhibits presents the earliest commercial graphics work Warhol did for New York City advertising agencies. Seen together, these endeavors create a portrait of an artist trying to break out of a forced discipline. Don't miss the bulletin boards crammed with gossip and celebrity memorabilia—the sort of stuff Andy loved. *117 Sandusky Street; 412-237-8300.*

The **Mattress Factory** is a museum with a reputation for presenting challenging shows of contemporary art—mostly installations and environmental and multimedia works. The space gets its name from its location, a former Stearns & Foster mattress factory warehouse. The rock garden outside, designed by Winifred Lutz, is breathtaking. All is tranquility here, with passageways, uniquely shaped rock structures, and a small stream. *500 Sampsonia Way; 412-231-3169.*

■ **CENTERS AND STADIUMS** *map pages 220, A/B-1, and page 225, C-2*
The **National Aviary** is an important center for the breeding and study of exotic and endangered birds. More than 450 birds representing 225 species live here, some in cages, but many in tree-filled aviaries visitors can walk through. The main building is part of a glass-enclosed former plant conservatory. *Allegheny Commons Park, Arch Street between West North and West Ohio Streets; 412-323-7235.*

The Pittsburgh Pirates baseball team and the Pittsburgh Steelers football team used to play in Three Rivers Stadium, which stood just north of the Allegheny River. In 2001, it was knocked down and replaced by the 38,000-seat **PNC Park** (Federal Street, General Robinson Street, and Mazeroski Way), where the Pirates now play, and the 64,475-seat **Heinz Field** (100 Art Rooney Avenue), where the Steelers now hold forth.

Near the stadiums is the **Carnegie Science Center,** which aims to make science entertaining as well as educational. The center has a planetarium and observatory, a theater that shows mostly science films, and a huge railroad exhibit that reflects the state's landscape from 1890 to 1930. *1 Allegheny Avenue; 412-237-3400.*

■ **RESIDENTIAL AREAS OF NOTE** *map page 225, C/D-2*
The eight-block **Mexican War Streets** residential district, lined with trees and narrow red brick houses, was developed in the 1850s. One of the more important residents of the neighborhood was Gen. William Robinson Jr., a mover and shaker in Pittsburgh politics who had served in the Mexican War. Later, as mayor of Allegheny, he named many of the streets in this district after well-known battles and generals of that struggle.

(preceding pages) Andy Warhol's silkscreen Ladies and Gentlemen *(1975) is part of a series of portraits the artist made of underground drag performers. (opposite) The Point as seen from Mount Washington.*

PNC Stadium frames dramatic views of downtown Pittsburgh.

Beginning in the 1920s, the neighborhood slipped into decline. As the middle class started to buy automobiles, residents began to flee the city for the suburbs. By the 1950s things had deteriorated so badly that city planners talked about razing the neighborhood altogether. But in the 1960s, many homes here—some of them built for craftsmen, others built for people of means—became the focus of intense renovation. Today, the Mexican War Streets area is something of an architectural wonderland, with design styles ranging from Queen Anne to Richardsonian Romanesque to Greek Revival. The modest homes, with their pretty doors and front porches, contribute to an intimate, harmonious environment.

The name of the formerly odiferous **Washington's Landing** commemorates the day a youthful George Washington scrambled ashore here in the mid-1700s after his boat capsized in the Allegheny River. His landfall today, a residential area with commanding bridge and river views and a jogging trail that follows the shoreline, has become the focus of intense redevelopment, with plans for upscale housing and a business park. *Reached by River Road on the North Side and by the 31st Street Bridge in the Strip District.*

■ MOUNT WASHINGTON *map page 225, C-3*

Directly across the Monongahela River from downtown is 367-foot-high Mount Washington, the best place to go for a fine view of Pittsburgh and its rivers. At the foot of Mount Washington, adjacent to the Sheraton Hotel and on the Allegheny riverfront, is **Station Square,** a development of shops and restaurants. The draw here is the Pittsburgh and Lake Erie Railroad terminal, which became the **Grand Concourse Restaurant** (1 Station Square; 412-261-1717) in 1978. The restaurant's interior—brass, wood, marble, and a glass ceiling—is as pleasurable as the kitchen's often inventive cuisine.

You can get to the top of Mount Washington by taking one of two "inclines," the **Monongahela Incline** (412-488-3102) or the **Duquesne Incline** (412-381-1665). Both date from the 1870s and run every few minutes from either the base, along West Carson Street, or the top, along Grandview Avenue. Along the Monongahela River, you'll see the South Side neighborhood, filled with the homes and churches of Ukrainian, Serbian, and Lithuanian immigrants. Surrounding this are wooded hills, and the overall effect is one of space and beauty. The Duquesne Incline, slightly younger than the Monongahela, still has its original cars, with cherry and maple interiors.

■ TRAVEL BASICS

Getting Around: I-79 and I-279 are the main roads downtown from the north or south. From the east, take the Pennsylvania Turnpike (I-76), then I-376 to the Grant Street exit. From the west, take I-76 to I-79 south, then follow I-279 to downtown. Pittsburgh can be easily explored on foot and by car, though some streets zigzag and climb hills so steep that the sidewalks are stepped, changing names as they go. Major highways disappear into tunnels that run all over the city. Something is always under construction here, diverting traffic into a maze of detours.

Climate: Pittsburgh has more cloudy days than Seattle, but when the sun shines, it is glorious. High temperatures in the summer average in the low 80s; high humidity in June, July, and August is common. By the end of September, daytime highs reach only the low 60s. By November, highs are in the low 40s and rain is frequent. Winter snowfall averages about 40 inches. From December to mid-March, monthly temperatures average in the mid- to upper 30s.

S O U T H W E S T

Much of southwestern Pennsylvania consists of farm country or rolling forested hills. People here live simply, on isolated produce and dairy farms or in small towns with mom-and-pop businesses. On the grittier side, some parts of this region still lie in the shadows of abandoned steel mills. East of Pittsburgh, beginning at Greensburg, rise the majestic Laurel Highlands where, in September or early October, hardwood forests turn brilliant red, orange, and all shades of brown and yellow. By December, snow has cloaked these mountains in white, and until early March, skiers flock here for downhill and cross-country skiing. During the spring and summer, the countryside north of Pittsburgh is an explosion of buttercups, violets, and white hemlock.

■ LANDSCAPE

Amish farms prosper near New Castle and Harmony, where wide valleys are ringed by hills and forests. In the south, ridges gather into mid-size mountains and subside into canyons of lush vegetation fed by creeks and streams. During spring and summer, the scent of spruce and white pine fills the air. In the hilly counties near West Virginia, shrubs mix with hardwood forests of oak, maple, and hickory. The Laurel Highlands region, at the southernmost end of the Allegheny Mountains, is a dramatic mass of ridges that fold out in wide pleats like an accordion.

Water is everywhere in the southwest——it cascades down sheer cliffs at McConnell's Mill State Park in the west; it churns and roils in the rapids of the Youghiogheny [YAWK-ah-gain-y] River in the east; it tumbles wildly in hillside streams up north; and it meanders through creeks and streams into the Monongahela River in the south.

■ NORTH OF PITTSBURGH

High-end suburbs and wide-open farmland testify to the competing forces at work north of Pittsburgh. In the far northwestern tier, communities remain rural. Amish farms can be found in and around New Wilmington and New Castle in Lawrence County. In Harmony and Zelienople, the architecture and local crafts reveal the towns' German immigrant roots, and in Ellwood, Italian immigrants have put

On the Monongahela (*1860*), *by William Coventry Wall. (Westmoreland Museum of American Art)*

their own stamp on things. Interstate 79 runs north from Pittsburgh, passing suburbs, open country, scrub forest, and scattered farms. Crossing the interstate about
65 miles north of Pittsburgh is Route 208, a winding backcountry road that tra-
verses the heart of western Pennsylvania's Amish farm country. Driving along this
road, you may catch glimpses of Old Order Amish farmers in wide-brimmed hats
tilling their fields with horse-pulled plows.

■ **NEW WILMINGTON** *map page 245, A-1*
The peaceful borough of New Wilmington, a Main Street U.S.A. community, is
known to many in Lawrence County for Westminster College, whose ivy-covered
stone walls date back to 1852. Graceful homes and maple trees line the residential
streets, and the downtown is busy, with an assortment of shops, many of them selling furniture and goods made by Amish families. Most of the Amish who live in
the area ride into town in horse-drawn buggies. Amish women come here to shop
for sewing supplies, which are used to make quilts that are sold at auctions held
around town throughout the year.

In the mid-1800s, what is now the **Tavern on the Square** was a refuge for escaped slaves following the Underground Railroad. In 1933, two graduates of Westminster College bought the house and converted it into a restaurant that today is known for creamed chicken on a biscuit, grilled pork chops, ham steaks, and delicious sticky buns. *108 North Market Street; 724-946-2020.*

Though small today, **Volant,** 4 miles east of New Wilmington on Route 208, was a mini-metropolis in the late 19th century, when it was a stop on the New Castle–Franklin Railroad. People flocked here to use the gristmill or to shop in the many stores near the train station. A stone quarry developed around 1900 contributed to Volant's prosperity, but the Great Depression ended the town's run of luck. By the time the train stopped coming in the 1970s, Volant was nearly a ghost town. In recent years, though, things have improved. **Volant Mills** (550 Main Street; 724-533-5611), in the old gristmill, sells antiques, and stores, boutiques, B&Bs, and restaurants along Main Street have begun to attract tourists and locals.

■ HARMONY *map page 245, A/B-2*
Halfway between Volant and Pittsburgh in Butler County is Harmony, settled in 1804 by Harmonists, a group of pietists. Followers of George Rapp, a German preacher who came to America in 1803, Harmonists believed that the Second Coming of Christ was imminent and that the integrity of their lifestyle—they were celibate, did not indulge in tobacco or drink, and believed in hard work—might warrant a visit and a blessing.

The Harmonists planted orchards and vineyards, built a brewery, a tannery, a general store, a schoolhouse, and an inn. Industrious, they were admired for their furniture and the simplicity of their quilts. The range of their talents can be sampled at the **Harmony Museum,** which exhibits handmade clothing, furniture, antiques, and other artifacts. The museum's Log House contains early-American chairs and tables and equipment used for spinning, weaving and rope-making. *218 Mercer Street; 724-452-7341.*

When the climate proved too harsh for the Harmonists, they moved to Indiana, but they returned to western Pennsylvania in 1824 to found the town of Economy, on the Ohio River in what is now Ambridge. The **Old Economy Village** is a 6-acre site with 17 buildings from the 19th century. On guided tours you can view the buildings and gardens that sustained this unique community. *Church and 14th Streets, Ambridge; 724-266-4500.*

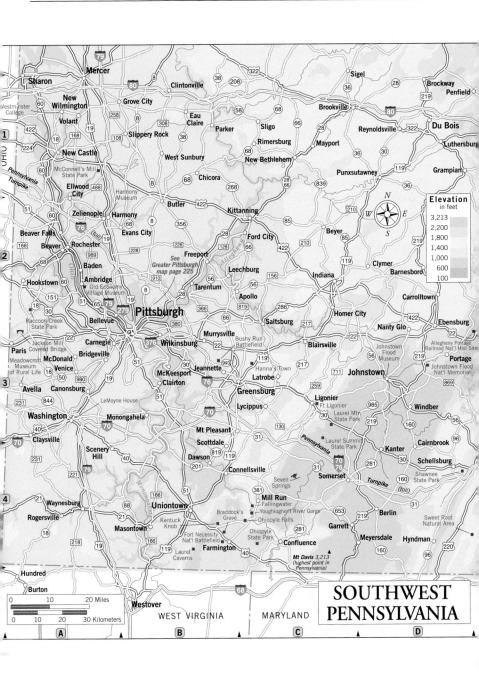

SOUTHWEST PENNSYLVANIA

McConnell's Mill was built in 1852 beside Slippery Rock Creek.

■ **McCONNELL'S MILL STATE PARK** *map page 245, A-1*

A hidden gem, McConnell's Mill State Park is set in the deep gorge of Slippery Rock Creek. Within this spectacular 400-foot-deep chasm are house-size boulders, waterfalls, and a restored gristmill. The first mill on this site was built in 1852 from hand-hewn oak timbers on a foundation of stone blocks. Fire destroyed the first mill, but it was rebuilt in 1868. The best place to view it and the creek is on the opposite bank, accessible via an old covered bridge.

The park's 7 miles of rugged trails touch only a small portion of its 2,512 acres. Hell's Hollow Trail winds through an area where spectacular wildflowers bloom in spring. Patches of violet and light blue merge into blazing yellows against soft green leaves and tiny white flowers of hemlock.

With its multi-story rock formations, cascading waterfalls, and abundant wildlife, the park is a magnet for rock climbers, anglers, rafters, and nature lovers. Canoeing, kayaking, and picnicking are permitted. *Route 422 off I-79, 40 miles north of Pittsburgh; 724-368-8091.*

Beaver Falls, Pennsylvania *(1854), by Emil Bott. (Westmoreland Museum of American Art)*

■ WEST OF PITTSBURGH: BEAVER COUNTY

In the 19th and early 20th centuries, the titans of heavy industry built huge mills and factories along the Ohio River in Beaver County. When steel production came to a halt in the late 1970s, many company towns hit on hard times. Since then, some towns have been successful in creating new economic bases and forging new identities. In the borough of New Brighton, for instance, weekenders come to shop and dine. Other communities, though, are still struggling.

Beaver County's population and its aging industrial facilities are concentrated mostly along rivers and creeks, among them Connoquenessing Creek, Slippery Rock Creek, Wolf Creek, and the Ohio River. What's left is mostly rural countryside, with few roads and even fewer signs of life.

■ RACCOON CREEK STATE PARK *map page 245, A-2*

Twenty-five miles west of Pittsburgh on U.S. 30 is Raccoon Creek State Park, which has a lake, bridle and hiking trails, and the remains of a historic mineral spring. The exceptional wildflower reserve, on the park's eastern edge, holds 5

St. Nicholas Chapel in Beaver County.

miles of trails that lead through woods containing hickory, elm, black cherry, and a few huge sycamore trees. The peak blooming period for wildflowers is late April through mid-May, when sprays of yellow, white, pink, and purple poke out of the meadow. Information about when different wildflowers bloom is available at the nature center. *Wildflower information: 724-899-3611.*

In the 1800s, the park's **Frankfort Mineral Springs** were part of a well-known health spa. The remains of the spa are visible amid lilies and ancient oak trees, and the nearby footbridge offers an unforgettable view of a waterfall pouring over a broken ledge into a rocky grotto. *3000 Route 18, Hookstown; 724-899-2200.*

■ **MEADOWCROFT MUSEUM OF RURAL LIFE** *map page 245, A-3*
Meadowcroft Village, in Avella, is a 200-acre outdoor museum that recreates aspects of 19th-century village life. In the 1960s, Albert and Delvin Miller, two Pennsylvania brothers with an interest in history, located structures around the state that were 100 years or older and moved them to the family farm. The complex includes a log house built by the brothers' great-great-grandfather in 1795, a small schoolhouse, a blacksmith's shop, and a covered bridge.

An ongoing archaeological dig at Meadowcroft Village has uncovered remains dating back 17,000 years, to what may be the earliest human occupation of the Western Hemisphere. The dig area is not open to the public, but an exhibit details the work. *Route 50, Avella, 35 miles southwest of Pittsburgh; 724-587-3412.*

■ **REBELLIOUS WASHINGTON COUNTY**

South of Pittsburgh, the countryside gives way to suburbs sprinkled with upscale homes, the by-product of a burgeoning high-tech industry. Farther south, the landscape alternates between flat farmlands and hills sprinkled with country villages. The pace of life here is mellow.

Historically, people in Washington County have distrusted government, an attitude that can be traced back to the years after the Revolutionary War, when the area figured prominently in the Whiskey Rebellion, a violent campaign to thwart the federal government in its first attempt to tax its citizenry. In 1791, Congress raised excise taxes to help pay off the remaining debts of the Revolutionary War. It instituted a tax of seven cents per gallon on whiskey—which the farmers expected would decrease the amount of whiskey sold and weaken demand for their main cash crop, rye. Farmers who tried to obey the law were ridiculed and threatened, and tax collectors were tarred and feathered.

George Washington, acting on the advice of the Federalist Alexander Hamilton, decided to make an example of the rebels and rode personally into Pittsburgh with 13,000 troops commanded by Gen. Harry "Lighthorse" Lee. Political differences could be tolerated, but open lawlessness could not, and the rebellion was quelled.

■ **WASHINGTON** *map page 245, A-3*

Washington, a 30-minute drive from Pittsburgh, maintains much of the spirited independence that bubbled to the surface during the Whiskey Rebellion. A mid-size city, it has a mixed economy built around light manufacturing, service industries, and education.

Just outside of Washington proper is the **LeMoyne House,** the residence of Dr. John Julius LeMoyne, one of the most courageous visionaries of 19th-century Pennsylvania. He preached the idea of equality between the sexes and races and, as a result, was treated as a pariah in his community. LeMoyne practiced what he preached, helping 25 slaves to freedom on the Underground Railroad. He also started colleges for African-Americans. *49 East Maiden Street; 724-225-6740.*

The **David Bradford House** was the residence of one of the behind-the-scenes leaders of the Whiskey Rebellion. By 1786, when he was 26, David Bradford had married, had been appointed deputy attorney general of the state, and had made a fortune from his gristmill and sawmills. With the profits from the mills, he built this house, which became the unofficial headquarters for the plotters of various seditious acts. Though he was never directly linked to them, there was enough evidence against him for George Washington to sign a warrant for his arrest. Soldiers were dispatched to search for him, and they nearly caught their man, but while they were heading toward his estate, Bradford was escaping from the bedroom window to his saddled horse below. He eventually made his way down to the Louisiana Territory, where he resettled and prospered. President John Adams pardoned David Bradford in 1799; he died in 1810.

General David Bradford's House, *ca. 1794, drawn by J. Howard Iams. (Westmoreland Museum of American Art)*

By the late 1880s, trolleys had enabled the growth of Pennsylvania's suburbs. (Historical Society of Western Pennsylvania)

Artifacts from the Whiskey Rebellion are displayed in Bradford's house, which at $4,500 was the most expensive and talked-about home in the region. Its mahogany staircases and marble fireplace mantels themselves are reason to visit. *175 South Main Street, Washington; 724-222-3604.*

Several southwestern Pennsylvania communities still have trolleys, but few of these vehicles carry as much nostalgia as those on display at the **Pennsylvania Trolley Museum.** The 9,000-square-foot museum contains about four dozen trolley cars, including several prize examples from 1920s-era Philadelphia and a relic that survived the Johnstown flood of 1936—after the big one of 1889, the second-deadliest flood to hit that city. The museum also has archival photos and a film about Pennsylvania's trolley era, which lasted from 1890 to the late 1940s. Price of admission includes trolley rides. *1 Museum Road, Washington; 724-228-9256.*

The **Century Inn** dates back to the Whiskey Rebellion. Tradition has long had it that instigators of the insurrection met here to drink and plot their next moves, which explains why a rare flag used by the insurgents was discovered hidden in the basement during a recent renovation. The flag now hangs on a wall in the bar. A National Historic Landmark, the inn is the oldest continuously operating hostelry along the National Road, the first linking of the East Coast to the western frontier. The stone structure has five dining rooms and nine bedrooms with authentic furniture. *Route 40, Scenery Hill; 724-945-5180.*

■ **BRIDGES OF WASHINGTON COUNTY** *map page 245, A-3*

Spread out across Washington County on backcountry roads are 23 covered bridges, sometimes called "kissing" bridges because they were reputedly the places where young swains took their would-be brides for a covert smooch. That, however, is not the reason why the bridges are covered. Covering them protected the wood from the harsh Pennsylvania elements. To explore this area, pick up a map at the **Washington County Historical Society** (LeMoyne House, 49 East Maiden Street, Washington; 724-225-6740).

One of the more popular routes begins on U.S. 22 and is a bit more than 12 miles long. Proceed west from Pittsburgh International Airport, turning right on Route 18-N, and continuing along Route 18 through the intersection with County Route 4004 (Pennsylvania Avenue). One-tenth of a mile in, on the left—heading west—is King's Creek Road, which takes you along a 7-mile stretch to Jackson Mill, a covered bridge. King's Creek Road eventually loops back to the village of Paris, which has a small restaurant and a store.

■ EAST OF PITTSBURGH: WESTMORELAND COUNTY

East of Pittsburgh rise the Laurel Highlands, where towns have remained unchanged despite fast and furious resort and condominium development in surrounding communities. Many people who live here are employed in factories, including Sony's large television assembly center near New Stanton. Increasingly, though, outdoor recreation and tourism drive the economy. For a good tour of the region, take any of the smaller roads off I-70 east, most of which wind around small towns and farms.

■ **BUSHY RUN BATTLEFIELD STATE PARK** *map page 245, B-3*

In 1763, British general Henry Bouquet was sent to assist the soldiers of Fort Pitt, who'd been under siege by a war party led by Chief Pontiac. The Indians were angry about continued European encroachment on their lands, despite promises made in several treaties. On his trek to the fort, Bouquet camped at what is now Bushy Run State Park, where he was caught in a surprise attack. In retaliation, Bouquet sent half his surviving forces to loop around when the Indians regrouped for a second attack. The maneuver was devastating and Indians retreated. These days, the setting is idyllic, perfect, weather permitting, for picnicking and hiking. *Route 993, 3 miles west of intersection with Route 66, Jeanette; 724-527-5584.*

■ **HANNA'S TOWN** *map page 245, C-3*

Hanna's Town was the seat of Westmoreland County government, but when Indians set it ablaze at the behest of the British in 1782, it lost that honor to nearby Greensburg. The site has a reconstructed courthouse and a log fort. *Forbes Road between Routes 119 and 819, North Greensburg; 724-836-1800.*

■ **GREENSBURG** *map page 245, B/C-3*

Greensburg, the oldest county seat west of the Alleghenies, is a hilly, midsize town with a beauty of a courthouse and the **Westmoreland Museum of American Art,** which exhibits works by artists such as Norman Rockwell, William Michael Harnett, Paul Manship, Winslow Homer, and John Singer Sargent. The museum also displays early-19th-century furniture, and during the Christmas holidays you can view a 2,000-piece toy exhibit. *221 North Main Street; 724-837-1500.*

■ **LAUREL HIGHLANDS** *map page 245, C-3/4*

East of Greensburg, gentle slopes rise toward the arching foothills of Laurel Ridge and the beginning of the Allegheny Mountains. The Pennsylvania Turnpike (I-76) and secondary roads cross forests of oak and hemlock and trout-filled mountain streams. This is the Laurel Highlands region, a place of spectacular valleys and ridges and the 1,700-foot-deep Youghiogheny River Gorge. The highlands area has been a magnet for city dwellers from Pittsburgh and surrounding communities since the early 1900s. Today, vacation homes, ski resorts, condo communities, and rustic backwoods hideaways can all be found here. One of the biggest ski resorts is **Seven Springs** (777 Waterwheel Drive, Champion; 814-352-7777), which has downhill and cross-country skiing and plenty of accommodations.

■ **LIGONIER** *map page 245, C-3*

The main route to the Laurel Mountains extends east from Greensburg to Ligonier. This area was the last outpost of the British in Pennsylvania during the French and Indian War. Fort Ligonier, one of the main tourist attractions here, was created when British Gen. John Forbes, ordered to take Fort Duquesne from the French, needed a staging area for his forces. In 1758, he built "Loyalhanna," later renamed Ligonier. Though attacked numerous times, the fort was never taken by an enemy. It became inactive in 1766.

(following pages) A truss bridge spans the Monongahela River in Brownsville.

Fort Ligonier was rebuilt in the 1950s and turned into a museum. Exhibits include weapons, uniforms, munitions, documents, dioramas, audio-visual presentations, and several noteworthy paintings, including one by society portraitist Sir Joshua Reynolds. *Route 30 West, Ligonier; 724-238-9701.*

Ligonier is an attractive town, the playground of the old-money crowd from Pittsburgh, some of whom keep horse farms nearby. Country clubs and bridle trails can be found throughout the region.

In 1878, Ligonier Valley Railroad magnate Judge Thomas Mellon donated 350 acres of his own estate as a park. There was one stipulation to the creation of **Idlewild Amusement Park,** however: no trees or other plants could be disturbed. Ranked among the state's most beguiling parks, Idlewild's attractions include a carousel, a steam train, a roller coaster, water rides, and the Mister Rogers' Neighborhood of Make-Believe, based on the children's television show. *Route 30, off Route 711; 724-238-3666.*

■ JOHNSTOWN *map page 245, D-3*

Johnstown is surrounded by high hills that once contained a precious resource: coal. It was a prosperous industrial town in the 19th century, with jobs aplenty in steelmaking, river transport, and mining—which attracted immigrants from nearly every country of Europe.

The event that will forever haunt Johnstown is its Memorial Day flood of 1889. Bad luck, the wrath of nature, and scandalous indifference to safety on the part of public officials and mill owners combined to make the calamity that hit the city one of the worst preventable disasters in American history.

Johnstown's historic district, a three-block-long stretch that survived the flood, is interesting to explore on foot. The **Johnstown Flood National Memorial** (Lake Road off Route 869; 814-495-4643) overlooks the ruins of the dam, whose failure caused the death of more than 2,000 people. The **Johnstown Flood Museum** (304 Washington Street; 814-539-1889) reveals the tragedy through vivid archival photographs and a 26-minute Academy Award–winning documentary, *The Johnstown Flood,* which identifies the culprits and causes of the disaster. For an untrammeled view of the town and the route the floodwaters took through the valley, travel up Yoder Hill via the **Johnstown Incline** (711 Edgehill Drive; 814-536-1816). A kiosk on the observation deck traces the town's history and recounts the flood.

JOHNSTOWN FLOOD DISASTER

High above the town of Johnstown, at the head of the Little Conemaugh River, stood the South Fork Fishing and Hunting Club, known locally as "The Bosses Club" because its membership included Andrew Carnegie, Andrew Mellon, and Henry Clay Frick, all residents of Pittsburgh. The club owned a reservoir encircled by summer mansions. The 72-foot-high South Fork Dam had been built in 1853 to create a reservoir for the Pennsylvania Main Line Canal. But the canal system had been abandoned by the time the dam was completed and the dam went through several other owners before being purchased by the sporting club in 1879.

When the dam showed signs of age, club officers ordered it repaired but failed to authorize an engineer to oversee the work. To prevent the loss of the black bass that had been stocked in the lake, a screen was placed across the spillway. Meanwhile, the hillsides around Johnstown had been stripped of timber to supply housing and land for a growing population, creating the potential for a dangerous erosion problem.

Years of complaints about the decrepit condition of the South Fork Dam, 14 miles upriver from Johnstown, fell on deaf ears. On Memorial Day 1889, a storm dropped 7 inches of rain on the area, and the runoff rushed down the denuded hillsides and filled

the reservoir. The fish screen quickly became clogged, preventing the water from escaping. The dam burst with a thunderous roar. More than 20 million tons of water raced through the narrow valley, creating a wall of water 35 to 75 feet high. The force, powerful enough to carry houses, train locomotives, and boulders, destroyed Johnstown and killed 2,209 people in what remains America's deadliest flood. The disaster initiated the first relief effort organized by Clara Barton's American Red Cross.

The Johnstown Flood Museum, formerly the Johnstown Library, was built with funds supplied by Andrew Carnegie. In the background is the Johnstown Incline. (Johnstown Area Heritage Association)

Of the many homes Frank Lloyd Wright designed, Fallingwater is generally considered his masterpiece.

■ **FALLINGWATER** *map page 245, C-4*
Fallingwater, a private residence improbably suspended over a waterfall, is unquestionably a masterpiece of one of America's most important architects.

In 1936, Edgar J. Kaufmann, who had made a fortune as owner of Kaufmann's, Pittsburgh's premier department store, hired Frank Lloyd Wright to design a weekend retreat for his family on a piece of land in Mill Run. Wright's design incorporated much of what was already on the site, including rocks, trees, and a rushing creek. Battles of will between Kaufmann and Wright over the details of the design became legendary. Wright wanted to cover the concrete parapets of the house with gold leaf; Kaufmann didn't. Kaufmann wanted a swimming pool on one of the balconies; Wright didn't. Despite their many differences, though, they produced a grand house.

Tours of the house are essential not just for what you see but for the stories you hear. *Take the Pennsylvania Turnpike to Donegal Exit, then take Route 31 east to Route 381 south and look for signs; 724-329-8501.*

FAITH IN OBJECTS: FALLINGWATER

There are many who say that Frank Lloyd Wright's Fallingwater was his crowning achievement. I am inclined to agree. If I am anywhere within a hundred miles of this historic house, I will always try to schedule a visit. A trip to Fallingwater is good for the soul. Well, it's good for my soul anyway. I can spend a few hours wandering from room to room on a brisk Fall afternoon and my faith in objects is restored.

Fallingwater is an absolutely wonderful object. I wish I could say the same for its architect, for Frank Lloyd Wright was an egotistical, petty tyrant. . . .

If you've been inside many Frank Lloyd Wright houses, you'll quickly notice that the ceilings are exceedingly low. Wright was a short man, but he firmly believed that his own height was the ideal human stature and designed his buildings accordingly. When Wright's taller brother accompanied him to Fallingwater, Wright asked him to remain seated while he was talking to the Kaufmanns because he was "spoiling the scale of the architecture."

Wright and the Kaufmann family are all dead now. Their many eccentricities and character flaws seem trivial when compared to the building itself. The building lives on. It has become objectified. After 50 years of study by architecture students around the world, Fallingwater has been transformed into an icon of truth and beauty. . . .

—John Sealander, "Object Lessons," an essay from *The Road to Nowhere*, 1995

■ **KENTUCK KNOB** *map page 245, B-4*

A few miles southwest of Fallingwater is another, though far less famous, Frank Lloyd Wright home, Kentuck Knob. Impressed by Wright's Fallingwater, Pittsburgh businessman Isaac Newton Hagan hired the architect in 1953 to design a more modest home for his family. Typical of the Usonian style Wright favored between 1930 and his death in 1959, the design for Kentuck Knob emphasizes openness with a single-floor plan without basement or attic. A strict triangular grid pattern makes the home's rooms appear bigger than they really are.

The exterior of the house, like Fallingwater, was designed to blend in with its natural setting. To this end, Wright used native sandstone, and the wood is Tidewater red cypress. The copper roof mimics colors of nearby brush. Tours for up to 15 people are conducted year-round, weather permitting. It's wise to call ahead. *Chalk Hill/Ohiopyle Road, off Route 381; 724-329-1901.*

■ **OHIOPYLE STATE PARK** *map page 245, C-4*
In 1754, George Washington had high hopes that the Youghiogheny River would provide a quick route for his 300-man Virginia militia in its quest to oust the French from Fort Duquesne. Standing at the edge of Ohiopyle Falls, however, he was sobered at the sight of its 20-foot drop, and decided to detour his troops through Great Meadows, near Farmington.

Nearly 19,000 acres surrounding one section of the **Youghiogheny River Gorge** have been preserved as Ohiopyle State Park. A testament to the restorative powers of nature, the Yough, or the "Yawk," as natives know it, was for years considered a dead waterway after being polluted by a century of pit and strip mining. A concerted clean-up effort in the 1980s, however, has restored the ecosystem. Several white-water rafting companies operate in the area and the park is popular with mountain bikers, swimmers, and hikers. *Ohiopyle State Park, Route 381, 6 miles north of U.S. 40; 724-329-8591.*

■ **FORT NECESSITY NATIONAL BATTLEFIELD** *map page 245, B-4*
Young George Washington's first military campaign—one of the events that sparked the French and Indian War—took place here in 1754, when the 22-year-old lieutenant colonel was sent by Virginia's governor to force the French out of the Ohio Valley. After Washington and about 300 Virginia volunteers stumbled across 33 French soldiers, Washington ordered a surprise attack at dawn and 10 French soldiers were killed, including the commander, Ensign Jumonville. Within 10 minutes the survivors had surrendered, but one soldier escaped and made his way to Fort Duquesne in what is now Pittsburgh.

Flush with his first victory, Washington camped at Great Meadows to regroup and ordered his men to build a slap-dash fort "of necessity" to protect them from a possible French counterattack. In July 1754, a French force, led by the brother of the fallen Jumonville, did return—and, outnumbered, Washington surrendered after an eight-hour siege. In return for being allowed to march from the fort with swords and weapons, George Washington signed a document of surrender written in French. Either deliberately or inadvertently, the English translation omitted a line in which Washington acknowledged that Jumonville's death was the result of an assassination instead of legitimate combat. The signed French document wreaked havoc in diplomatic circles in Europe.

Demoralized, Washington was forced to resign his commission. He returned to Virginia, but redeemed himself the following year and led a company of soldiers back into southwestern Pennsylvania. British Gen. Edward Braddock followed the road Washington's men had cut through the woods and headed toward Pittsburgh. When Braddock was fatally wounded in the Battle of the Monongahela in July 1755, Washington risked his own life to help remove the still-conscious general from the battlefield. A gravestone to Braddock stands not far from the fort.

The renovated fort also contains the **Mount Washington Tavern,** a rebuilt stagecoach stop from the early 1800s. *U.S. 40, 11 miles southeast of Uniontown; 724-329-5512.*

■ TRAVEL BASICS

Getting Around: From Philadelphia, the most direct route to Pittsburgh and other points southwest is I-76 (the Pennsylvania Turnpike), which travels through Harrisburg and Bedford County, skirting Shanksville and Somerset before moving north to Monroeville and the I-376 connector to Pittsburgh. Route 381 south, off I-76, leads to Mill Run and Fallingwater, Ohiopyle State Park, Braddock's Grave, and Fort Necessity National Battlefield. Interstate 79, starting in Washington, travels north, brushing the outskirts of Pittsburgh and traveling near Harmony, Zelienople, and McConnell's Mill State Park. Route 208, off I-79, offers direct access to Volant and New Wilmington. Route 50 east, off I-79, leads through tranquil countryside to Hickory and Avella, where you'll find the Meadowcroft Museum of Rural Life.

Climate: Temperatures in the warm-weather months range from the high 60s Fahrenheit in mid-April to the 80s in summer. Cloud cover is common. The wettest months are in spring and late fall. Cool, crisp fall temperatures begin in late September, with highs in the low 60s and nighttime temperatures as low as 35. By November, daytime highs are in the low 40s and rain is frequent. In deep winter, temperatures range from the high 30s to single-digit lows. Annual snowfall averages 40 to 45 inches.

N O R T H W E S T

Northwestern Pennsylvania is the least-visited corner of the state, but in many ways this is what gives it its unique character. The largest city in this region is Erie. East of Erie lies an agriculture and wine region, and farther east is the Allegheny Forest, a sparsely settled, remote area where people canoe, hike, camp, and fish along creeks and lakes.

■ EARLY HISTORY

Erie—the city, the county, and the lake—was named for the Erie Indians, whose history became obscured following their conquest and assimilation in the early 1600s by the Senecas, one of the powerful five nations of the Iroquois Confederacy. (The others were the Mohawks, Oneidas, Onondagas, and Cayugas.) French explorers and trappers working their way down from Canada were the first Europeans to set foot on Seneca land. The French, however, were allied with the Huron and Algonquin nations, archenemies of the Iroquois, and fierce battles were waged until 1696, when the French finally prevailed.

In the early 1700s, the French sought to control a direct route via the Ohio River south to the Mississippi River and the French colonies in Louisiana. When English settlers began flooding into Iroquois land, the Iroquois turned on them. Capitalizing on their anger, the French recruited the Iroquois to help fight the British, initiating what came to be known as the French and Indian War. The French built defensive forts on Presque Isle and other key lakeside points, abandoning and burning them after a wave of British attacks forced them to retreat.

Fort Presque Isle and Fort Le Boeuf were rebuilt by the British, but lost again to the Indians, led by Chief Pontiac. The forts were in Indian hands for several years until the 1768 treaty of Fort Stanwix returned the northwestern Pennsylvania territory to British control. The treaty also opened Indian land to settlement, and by the end of the decade, immigrants were moving westward. The second treaty of Fort Stanwix, in 1784, effectively ended the reign of the Iroquois Confederacy.

Throughout the 19th century, Lake Erie was of tremendous economic importance to the fledgling United States, as freight crossed from the interior into the port of Erie. During the War of 1812, Commodore Oliver Hazard Perry, aboard

When it was built in 1882, Kinzua Bridge was the highest railroad bridge in the world.

the brig US *Niagara*, defeated the British at the Battle of Lake Erie, thus securing American control of that trade route. It wasn't until after the Civil War that cities like Erie began to expand, and smaller outlying communities sprang up to link the port city to other areas of the state and to New York City. In 1859, an area on the outskirts of Titusville became the site of the nation's first oil well, and for a time the region rode the prosperity of an oil boom.

■ MODERN TIMES

While the economy across the United States boomed during the 1990s, the north-western region continued to lose population and industry at a slow but steady rate. Many factories have moved south, and farms have ceased production. The shrinkage of manufacturing here has allowed nature to reclaim land that was originally part of the vast Eastern forest: great herds of elk and other animals that used to roam the region have been reintroduced, birds of prey have returned, and formerly distressed habitats now thrive with living creatures.

■ WOODED HILLS, SMALL TOWNS

There is no mistaking the towns of northwestern Pennsylvania for the suburbs of Pittsburgh. Places like Mercer and Franklin are the kind of communities Americans envision when they talk about wanting to have a simpler life. These are Norman Rockwell–type hamlets, often with a town square and a bandstand, a majestic courthouse, big Victorian homes, and broad, tree-lined streets.

■ MERCER *map page 265, A-4*

With a population of 2,440, Mercer is typical of the picturesque small towns in this area. Its courthouse is built on the highest elevation in the county and can be seen for miles around. There are many stately old homes here and the locals are friendly. The town puts on a Victorian festival (724-662-4185) on the last weekend in July. Sponsored by the Chamber of Commerce, the event includes walking tours of old mansions, concerts, food, fireworks, and a parade.

Mercer is 7 miles from the **Grove City Shops** complex, an outlet mall with both familiar chain stores and local establishments. You'll find everything from handmade clothing to colossal pretzels to gourmet coffees and cheese. *I-79 and Route 208, Grove City; 888-545-7221.*

■ PYMATUNING STATE PARK *map page 265, A-3*

To control flooding and reclaim swampland, the Pymatuning Dam was completed in 1934, creating in the process Pymatuning Lake, one of the largest man-made lakes in the eastern United States (it's 17 miles long, with 70 miles of shoreline). The area was occupied by the Iroquois in the 18th century and may have been settled first by the Lenni Lenape tribe before them. It is now one of Pennsylvania's largest state parks.

The name Pymatuning is derived from the Seneca phrase meaning "crooked mouthed man's dwelling place"—a reference to the Erie tribe that lived here, and to its queen, known to the Senecas for her crooked dealings. The lake provides ample opportunities for swimming, boating, and camping. Fishing from the causeway is forbidden, but there are plenty of other places to cast a line. The park is open year-round but is especially pleasant in summer, when cool breezes take the edge off the summer heat, and in fall when the pine, maple, and birch trees are splashed in autumn's colors. *2660 Williamsfield Road, Jamestown; 724-932-3141.*

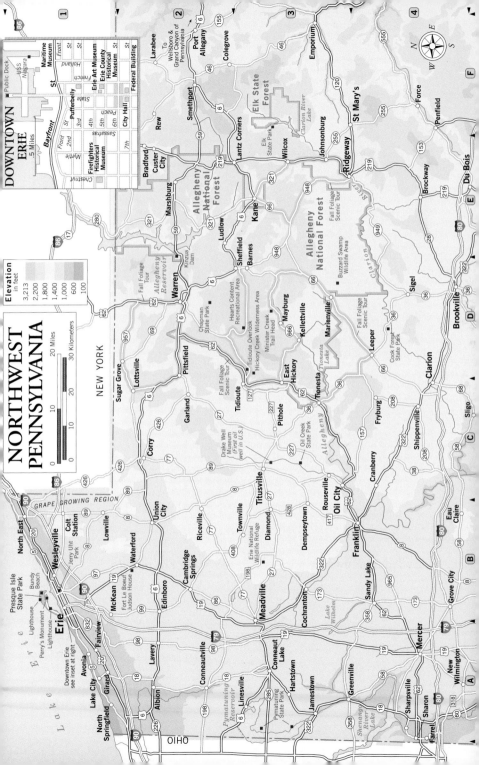

A farm in Nauvoo, in Tioga County.

■ **LAKE ERIE** *map page 265, A/B-1*

The Great Lakes, including Lake Erie, were formed by the final expansions and contractions of the Wisconsin Glacier about 15,000 years ago. Much of the land was scraped to bedrock by glaciers, and in some cases gouged into deep craters. When the ice melted, water filled the craters and the Great Lakes were formed.

In the early 1800s, Erie became one of the busiest inland ports in the United States. The great sailing ships eventually gave way to steam-powered vessels, and by 1850 Lake Erie and the other Great Lakes were bustling with hundreds of 300-foot-long steamers, popular with travelers because of their speed and comfort. (Interestingly, the once-polluted lake has become cleaner in recent years, and the clearer water is revealing hundreds of sunken ships, the exploration of which has spawned a booming new business in scuba diving.)

Transport businesses continued to search for a more efficient way to move goods from vessels docking in Erie to inland Pennsylvania. They found it in the Erie Extension Canal, a man-made waterway from Erie to Pittsburgh. An eastern route stretched to the Allegheny River, with stops at Conneaut Lake, Franklin, and

Meadville. A western extension covered New Castle and points along the Beaver River. As the chorus from a popular song described it:

Oh, the Erie was a'risin
The gin was a'gettin low
I didn't think we'd get a drink
Till we got to Buffalo-ho-ho
Till we got to Buffalo

By 1853, water transportation was supplanted by the railroad lines connecting Erie to Pittsburgh and Pittsburgh to the East Coast. The town of Erie survived the resulting economic U-turn by specializing in ship repair and fishing, but its boom era was drawing to a close.

The lake continues to be a popular year-round tourist attraction. In summer, the waters of Lake Erie temper the heat, making this a great place for swimming and water-skiing. Winter can be very cold, though, and some restaurants and tourist attractions operate "in season" only. From November through January, intense snow squalls often blow off the lake, making travel hazardous.

■ CITY OF ERIE *map page 265, B-1*

Downtown Erie is level and major streets are unusually wide, having been designed for horse- and ox-drawn wagons to make wide turns. State Street, which bisects the area, has plenty of excellent coffee shops and boutiques. Finding your way around town is easy because the cross-streets are numbered, starting at the lake. The higher the number, the farther from the lake you are. Whether you walk or drive, check out West Sixth Street, once known as Millionaire's Row, where many restored Victorian mansions still stand.

At the foot of State Street, on the city's bayfront, stands the 187-foot-high **Bicentennial Tower** (Dobbins Landing; 814-455-6055), built in 1995 to celebrate Erie's 200th birthday. The tower's two observation decks provide spectacular lake views. To take a ride on Lake Erie, catch a water taxi (814-881-2502) at Dobbins Landing, Liberty Park, or the East Avenue Boat Launch.

Farther up on State Street is the **Warner Theater,** a restored 1930s movie palace with art deco details and a gold-leaf grand lobby recalling the glamour of bygone days. The theater presents touring Broadway shows and performances of the Erie Philharmonic. *811 State Street; 814-452-4857.*

■ ERIE SIGHTS

The **Erie County History Center** has a vast array of historical documents and a superb photographic archive whose images trace Erie history from the late 1800s through the early 1900s. This is also where you can pick up excellent driving-tour maps of the area's many back roads. A walkway in the building leads directly to the Cashier's House, an 1839 Greek Revival town house that served as the residence of Peter Benson, chief executive of the Erie branch of the U.S. Bank of Pennsylvania. The house, typical of those built by Erie's wealthier citizens in the mid- and late 1800s, was designed by the noted Philadelphia architect William Kelly. It has a no-nonsense exterior hiding an ornate interior of wood carvings and marble fireplace mantels. *417 State Street, off the Bayfront Parkway; 814-454-1813.*

The showpiece of the **Erie Maritime Museum** is a reconstruction of the US *Niagara,* which figured prominently in the War of 1812 when, under the command of Commodore Oliver Hazard Perry, it won the Battle of Lake Erie. On September 10, 1813, Perry's flagship, the *Lawrence,* had endured two hours of cannon fire from the British, which crippled the vessel and either killed or wounded more than 80 percent of his crew. Reestablishing himself aboard the nearby US *Niagara* and bearing his signature flag with the words "Don't Give Up the Ship," Perry daringly re-engaged the enemy and emerged victorious. Following his conquest, he sent the famous message: "We have met the enemy and he is ours."

Perry's victory won the War of 1812, but in 1820, the US *Niagara* was "scuttled" by the navy—a practice in which boats were sunk and then scavenged for useful material. In 1913, the ship was resurrected and restored as part of the centennial celebration of the 1813 battle. Though restored again in the 1930s, the ship was in a dismal state by the 1980s. This time, the Erie County Historical Society came to the rescue, building a new boat from original plans (and including 100 pieces of the original vessel). The reconstructed craft is berthed on the bayfront. The museum also has exhibits about the War of 1812 and other famous warships and sea battles. *150 East Front Street; 814-871-4596.*

Erie County history is movingly told through paintings, documents, and artifacts at the **Watson-Curtze Mansion and Planetarium.** Built in 1891, the mansion suggests the good life enjoyed by some residents of Millionaire's Row in the late 19th century. Handsome friezes, stained-glass windows, paintings, and antiques dazzle the eye. The planetarium, in the carriage house, has regular slide shows and lectures. *356 West Sixth Street; 814-871-5790.*

This print shows Commodore Oliver Hazard Perry being rowed to the US Niagara *after the* Lawrence *was sunk.*

The imposing Old Custom House, a Greek Revival structure built in 1839, houses the **Erie Art Museum.** Ceramics, Japanese prints, Indian bronzes, Chinese porcelains, and Tibetan art objects are among the thousands of objects on display. *411 State Street; 814-459-5477.*

The **Firefighters' Historical Museum,** which occupies a once busy Erie fire-house, has hundreds of fire-fighting artifacts, including a horse-pulled water wagon, fire call-boxes, uniforms, a hand-pulled pumper, a horse-drawn fire engine, and a vintage fire truck from the 1920s. The enthusiastic guides, who are all con-nected to firefighting in some way or another, know the stories behind every object on display. *428 Chestnut Street; 814-456-5969.*

Pufferbelly, an unusual eatery on French Street, also recalls the old days of the Erie Fire Department. The restaurant is in the former Fire House No. 1, built in 1907, and on the walls are old fire-fighting equipment and pictures from the late 1800s, when firefighters used steam pumpers and engines (or "pufferbellies") to put out fires. Firehouse chili is a house specialty. *414 French Street; 814-454-1557.*

■ PRESQUE ISLE STATE PARK *map page 265, B-1*

Presque Isle is treasured by nearby residents, who flock here for water sports, kite-flying, picnics, bird-watching (migratory birds of all sorts pass through here), or to enjoy the serene views of the open water.

More a peninsula than an island, Presque Isle is fringed by sandy beaches and favored by several varieties of sandpipers. Wetland areas on the southern-facing inner shore are a breeding ground for blue herons, which strut majestically through the reeds. The song of a whippoorwill sometimes provides background music for an afternoon stroll. A National Natural Landmark, Presque Isle is one of the world's premier venues for the study of the ecological succession of plants. More than 500 plant species grow here, in habitats that reflect the progression of development from dune stage to pond stage to final forest stage. *Birder's World* magazine calls Presque Isle one of the top birding spots in the country, with more than 320 species spotted. Forty-seven species of mammals live here as well.

(above) Sunfish on Lake Erie, off the coast of Presque Isle.
(opposite) The Presque Isle Lighthouse was built in 1872.

Presque Isle can be visited at any time of year, although it's awfully cold in winter. An 1872 lighthouse overlooks the lakeshore and a 14-mile loop road provides excellent opportunities to view autumn foliage or winter ice dunes. Misery Bay is where the US *Niagara* was scuttled in 1820. A monument to Oliver Hazard Perry can be found at Crystal Point. *Presque Isle State Park: Take I-90, Exit 5 and follow Route 832 North to Sterrettania Road, which becomes Peninsula Drive and leads into the park; 814-833-7424.*

Before the entrance to Presque Isle State Park you'll come upon **Waldameer Park & Water World,** a family park with some of the longest and steepest water slides in the country. The park's giant Ferris wheel twirls riders 100 feet in the air. *220 Peninsula Drive; 814-838-3591.*

■ **GRAPE-GROWING REGION** *map page 265, B/C-1*

About 15 miles east of Erie is grape-growing country. Most of the grapes in this region are of the sweet Concord variety, and likely to end up in jams and jellies, but some are wine varietals. All the wineries listed below are in the town of North East. To bicycle through the area, drop by **Lake Country Bike** (21 East Main Street, North East; 814-725-1338) for maps and rentals.

Wineries

Run by six generations of the Bostwick family, **Heritage Wine Cellars** has the largest tasting room in the area and an astonishing variety of Pennsylvania reds, whites, and sparkling wines. All 55 varieties can be sampled for free. *12160 East Main Road (U.S. 20), North East; 814-725-8015.*

Mazza Vineyards, on a hilly estate overlooking Lake Erie, has sweet dessert wines, champagnes, and chardonnays in addition to a merlot, a cabernet sauvignon, and a French hybrid, vidal blanc. *11815 East Lake Road, North East (Route 5); 814-725-8695.*

Its wine- and cheese-tasting parties have made **Penn Shore Vineyards** a popular destination. Kir, a dessert wine made from black currants, is the specialty, but the winery has a full range of whites, reds, and French hybrids. *10225 East Lake Road (Route 5), North East; 814-725-8688.*

The merlots and cabernets at **Presque Isle Wine Cellars** are celebrated, as are the late-harvest vignoles. The winery is located alongside scenic Twelve Mile Creek. *9440 West Main Road (U.S. 20), North East; 814-725-1314.*

■ **SOUTH FROM ERIE** *map page 265, B-1/2*
South from Erie, U.S. 19 quickly leaves the strip malls behind and enters rolling farm country sparsely dotted with farm equipment dealers, modest homes on endless lawns, and the occasional tackle shop.

■ **WATERFORD** *map page 265, B-2*
Picturesque Waterford can take you quite by surprise. Looming over most of the town is the **Eagle Hotel**, which is no longer a hotel but a historical exhibit operated by the Fort Le Boeuf Museum. The upper floors, open to the public, are jammed with interesting bric-a-brac and period furniture. The first floor is a lively restaurant, Kellie's Sugar and Spice, which, at lunchtime, swarms with local businesspeople and grandmothers, but few tourists. Although Waterford offers little in the way of shops, the taxidermy studio keeps its door open, and the proprietors are friendly. Don't be surprised if you smell a strange aroma in the place—the head of a bear or some other animal part might be boiling on the stove in the back room. *32 High Street; 814-796-0060.*

Next to the Eagle Hotel is a famous statue of George Washington. It's close to the site of the now-gone fort where, in 1753, Washington presented Britain's demands that the French leave the territory. Washington was received cordially, but the consequence of his visit was the French and Indian War.

■ **CAMBRIDGE SPRINGS** *map page 265, B-2*
In the late 19th century, Cambridge Springs hosted 10,000 people at a time. Most came to enjoy the supposed healing properties of the mineral waters that flowed from local springs.

Most of the magnificent old hotels that once lined the streets here are long gone, but the 73-room **Riverside Inn** (1 Fountain Avenue; 800-964-5173) still stands. This white clapboard structure, built in 1885, is surrounded by luxurious gardens. A block from the Riverside Inn on U.S. 19 is an octagonal house—a popular, if now rare, style of early-American house design. Among the advocates of eight-sided dwellings was phrenologist Orson Squire Fowler, whose book *The Octagon House: A Home for All* argued that octagonal houses were easier to heat than conventional ones, remained cooler in the summer, and received more natural light.

Many of the springs in this region are fed by French Creek, a major waterway for Indians and French fur traders. It remained the primary access to the area until the emergence of the railway. The bed of French Creek is especially deep near Cambridge Springs. You can rent canoes from **French Creek Canoe & Kayak** (U.S. 6 and U.S. 19, 4 miles south of Waterford; 814-796-3366). The proprietors will drop you off and pick you up at any of 13 or more access points along French Creek and its tributaries.

■ OIL COUNTRY *map page 265*

Pennsylvania's Oil Heritage Region is not as bleak as visitors from other oil regions might expect. This is a hilly, wooded area south and west of the Allegheny National Forest, sprinkled with small towns and surrounded by areas of great natural beauty. You can access the region from U.S. 6, the Commonwealth's longest highway and one of the nation's most scenic routes.

The country's first oil well was drilled near Titusville in 1859, and the region was soon pockmarked with "black gold" wells. Scores of small businessmen from towns such as Franklin, Oil City, and Pithole became millionaires overnight. The boom continued until the early 1900s, when more efficient extraction methods made backyard oil wells obsolete.

Small-town charm mixes with history in far northern Custer City, near Bradford (along Route 219). Exhibits at the town's **Penn-Brad Oil Museum** showcase the tools of the oil trade and shed light on the "miracle molecule." Professionals who have had first-hand experience working on oil rigs lead guided tours of the oil fields, where you'll see a 72-foot-tall drilling rig left over from the oil-rich 1880s. *Open Memorial Day to Labor Day. 50 Parkway Lane; 814-362-1955.*

■ THE DRAKE WELL MUSEUM *map page 265, C-3*

The museum, south of Titusville, provides a detailed history of the late 19th century, when oil was Pennsylvania's most valuable commodity. Exhibits tell the story of New York lawyer and entrepreneur George Bissell, who was fascinated by petroleum, then viewed as a messy substitute for kerosene. Working with a Yale University chemistry professor, Bissell developed uses for the product—but in order to get his petroleum products to market, he had to get it out of the ground in a way that would assure sufficient quantities to cover his extraction costs.

The person who worked out the details was a retired railroad conductor, Edwin Drake, who built the first successful oil well in the United States on Bissell's country estate near Titusville. A month after Drake perfected the oil well machinery, a

(above) Drake Well Museum, south of Titusville. (below) During Pennsylvania's oil boom, derricks were a common sight. (Pennsylvania Historical & Museum Commission)

The late-19th-century oil boom in this area made possible the mansions lining the streets of even the very small towns in Oil Country.

New York Times reporter wrote about the "excitement attendant on the discovery of this vast source of oil." Soon, well operations were chugging throughout the region and the refined petroleum was selling well. Some oil products that came from the region were rather dubious, though. One example: "Rock Oil," a medicine that promised "wonderful curative powers." *East Bless Street (Route 8), south of Titusville; 814-827-2797.*

■ **OIL CREEK STATE PARK** *map page 265, C-3*
Paralleling both sides of Oil Creek, between the Drake Well Museum to the north and the main park entrance at Petroleum Center, a 37-mile loop has both a walking and a biking trail, with a 500-foot elevation change along the Westside trail. In the 1860s, oil wells, hamlets, and refineries lined this 13-mile stretch of the creek. Directions and maps are available at the park entrance. There are 12 shelters, with water and toilet facilities, for overnight camping. Reservations are required. *Off Route 8 (follow signs)1 mile north of Rouseville in Oil City; 814-676-5915.*

■ **FRANKLIN** *map page 265, B-3/4*

Few of the prospectors who came to this area in search of oil realized their dreams, but many who rode the oil wave successfully came from the little town of Franklin, which became a trading and management center for the oil industry in the years after Drake's discovery.

A small town in the heart of Venango County, Franklin has an imposing, white-topped courthouse, plenty of wide, tree-lined streets, and many stately homes. Buildings in the downtown business area have red brick exteriors with white stone lintels, and sidewalks are graced with elegant cast-iron street lamps. Two parks downtown are adjacent to each other, one with a three-tier cast-iron fountain, the other containing memorials to local movers and shakers.

Franklin played a key role during the French and Indian War. In 1753, prior to the war, the French claimed the surrounding territory and erected Fort Machault. From here, French forces hoped to amass enough might to stage an attack on Fort Pitt, in what is today Pittsburgh.

Downtown Franklin.

Clusters of handsome mansions can be found in the Liberty, Miller Park, and Adelaide neighborhoods. Most were built between 1860 and 1890—the styles range from Queen Anne to Victorian to Arts and Crafts. Many are private residences, but one is open to the public: the **Venango County Historical Society House Museum,** which contains period furniture, paintings, antiques, and other finery of the era. *301 South Park Street; 814-437-2275.*

St. John's Episcopal Church has 30 stained-glass windows from the studios of Louis Comfort Tiffany. The most beautiful of these, the Rose Window, is made of *favrile* glass, a favorite medium of the decorator-designer. Call ahead for hours. *1145 Buffalo Street; 814-432-5161.*

■ U.S. 62 ABOVE OIL CITY *map page 265, C/D-2/3*

Above Oil City, U.S. 62 meanders through rolling hills covered with aged trees that bear magnificent colors in fall. All is quiet here, and you can hear yourself think. As you near McPhearson Road and the Allegheny General Store (814-676-5769) you'll see signs along the road advertising old-fashioned ring bologna, slab bacon, and Amish baked goods. Step inside the store for a sandwich, or sample the excellent cookies, breads, jams, and maple syrup.

As you continue north, the hardwood forest is replaced by conifers. By Tionesta Lake, the Allegheny River is wide and beautiful.

■ ALLEGHENY RIVER *map page 265, C/D-2/3*

From Oil City north to Kinzua Dam, the Allegheny River has been designated a Recreational Waterway under the federal Wild and Scenic Rivers Act.

Along U.S. 62 from Franklin to Tionesta and north past Warren, the Allegheny River is slow-moving and tranquil. Many people go north to Warren and canoe down the Allegheny, camping on islands along the way. Canoe outfitters advertise their services here, and there are several places downstream to rest or be picked up and brought back to your car. Among the outfitters are **Eagle Rock** (814-755-4444) and **Outback Adventures** (814-589-7359), both near Tionesta; **Allegheny Outfitters** (814-723-1203), in Warren; and **Indian Waters** (814-484-3252), north of Tionesta in Tidioute.

Rates begin at $25 a day per canoe, for people planning their own pickup and transportation, to more expensive weekend trips, starting at $75 per person, that

The Grand Canyon of Pennsylvania.

include shuttle service, guides, meals, and tents. Experience isn't necessary, according to river guides, although it's probably safe to say that most people would benefit from at least some instruction. Floating down the river, you'll marvel at the beautiful green water and overhanging trees; some report seeing bald eagles, snapping turtles, great blue herons, and Canada geese.

■ **ALLEGHENY NATIONAL FOREST** *map page 265, E-2/3*

The Allegheny National Forest is known for its rugged beauty and status as one of the few remnants of the ancient forest that used to cover most of the eastern United States. There is something primordial about the forest. Track marks in the dirt tell you where wild critters have searched for food, the animal kingdom here including white-tail deer, raccoons, skunks, wolves, and plenty of bears. Elk roam free and the bald eagle is a frequent guest. This is among the most majestic spots in Pennsylvania, a place of still-unspoiled natural beauty. Between mid-September and mid-October, back roads throughout the Alleghenies are ablaze with color. *Allegheny National Forest Headquarters, 222 Liberty Street, Warren; 814-723-5150.*

■ **HEART'S CONTENT RECREATION AREA** *map page 265, D-3*
Spectacular groves of Eastern hemlock can be found here, alongside black cherry, sugar maple, and white pine, some of them hundreds of years old. The trail from Heart's Content to Minister Creek passes through some of these stands, which often have a dense undergrowth of large ferns. If you climb some of the boulders along the way, you'll be rewarded with astonishing views of ridge upon forested ridge extending into the distance. This trail makes a good backpacking trip, and camp-sites can be found along the way. A second, west-running 12-mile loop trail tra-verses the valleys and hills of nearby **Hickory Creek Wilderness Area,** which contains meadows, hardwood forest, and narrow Jack's Run Creek. *15 miles south-west of Warren; 814-723-5150.*

■ **COUNTRY ROUTE 666** *map page 265, D-3*
Don't be in a hurry if you want to travel Route 666, which heads east from the Allegheny River to the town of Barnes. The road has many sharp twists and turns, with only a few straight-ahead stretches. The views are spectacular as the route cuts through wooded valleys, past small farms with red barns and silos, and past many small white houses backed by forest. Route 666 starts in East Hickory and moves east through Kelletville and Porkey, before ending in Barnes. It's easy to get lost on side roads, but that's one of the pleasures of traveling through this serene territory.

■ **COOK FOREST STATE PARK** *map page 265, D-4*
South of the Allegheny National Forest is Cook Forest State Park, established by a private landowner who wanted to save 6,668 acres of forest land from logging. The old-growth forests here are among the most beautiful forests in the state. Some of the trees are more than 300 years old and more than 200 feet tall. Climb the old fire tower for the view, and take time to relax by the Clarion River and contem-plate its deep green waters. *Route 66 or Route 36, north from I-80. 814-744-8407.*

■ **ELK COUNTY** *map page 265, F-3/4*
East of the Allegheny National Forest in Elk County is **Elk State Forest** (Route 120) where elk have been reintroduced to the region. The plan is controversial, however: it introduced elk from western states to encourage the development of local herds, but because the imported elk were larger than the indigenous variety, the cross-breeding produced a strain of voracious eaters with enormous antlers. To

placate local farmers, crops have been planted especially for the elk. **St. Mary's,** west of Elk State Forest on Route 120, is the largest town in Elk County and a good place to seek advice on where the elk with the largest racks might be hanging out.

■ GRAND CANYON OF PENNSYLVANIA *map page 265, F-2*
Nestled in 158,000 acres of Tioga State Forest is the Grand Canyon of Pennsylvania, a 45-mile gorge that runs a zig-zag course through one of the most densely forested regions of the state. In some places, the cliffs of the gorge rise well over 1,300 feet above fast-flowing Pine Creek, giving way to jaw-droppingly gorgeous views of Tioga County. Canoeists, kayakers, and white-water rafters all come here to enjoy their sports, and there's a "rail trail" that follows the east bank of Pine Creek into the Grand Canyon (the trailhead is found 7 miles southwest of Wellsboro). Along the way you can fish for trout and small-mouth bass. In spring, wildflowers are abundant, and in fall the hills are bright with the color of autumn leaves. Bird-watching is popular here, as bald eagles, osprey, and hawks frequent the skies over the gorge. The northern end of the Grand Canyon is reached by Route 6, the southern end by Route 414. *For maps and information, contact the Tioga State Forest District Office at 1 Nessnuk Lane, Wellsboro; 570-724-2868. For canoe and kayak rentals, contact Pine Creek Outfitters, Wellsboro; 570-724-3003.*

■ TRAVEL BASICS

Getting Around: The quickest route north to Erie from Pittsburgh is I-273 to I-79, which skirts Harmony, Zelienople, Volant, and Meadville on its way to Lake Erie. From the northeast, scenic U.S. 6 shows the region to its best advantage, passing through Warren, Youngsville, Columbus, and Albion before ending at I-90 near the Ohio border. From southeastern Pennsylvania, the quickest route to the northwest is I-80, connecting from Route 476 if you're coming from Philadelphia, and connecting from Route 81 from Harrisburg.

Climate: Daytime temperatures range generally from 15 to 35 degrees Fahrenheit in winter and from 75 to 85 degrees in summer. Spring arrives late, in May, and fall turns into winter well before December 21. Precipitation is evenly spread throughout the year and averages 35 inches. Heavy snow squalls blowing off Lake Erie between November and February can create hazardous driving conditions.

PRACTICAL INFORMATION

■ AREA CODES AND TIME ZONE

The area code for Erie is 814; use 412 and 724 for Pittsburgh and western Pennsylvania; 717 for Harrisburg; 570 for northeastern and north-central Pennsylvania; 610 and 484 for Allentown, Reading, and some areas to the southeast; and 267 and 215 for Philadelphia and its environs. Pennsylvania is in the Eastern time zone.

■ METRIC CONVERSIONS

1 foot = .305 meters   1 mile = 1.6 kilometers   1 pound = .45 kilograms
Centigrade = Fahrenheit temperature minus 32, divided by 1.8

■ CLIMATE

Cloudy days are common in Pittsburgh and western Pennsylvania throughout the year. Spring starts in late March and early April in most of Pennsylvania (May in the northern regions), and fall comes gradually in October, with temperatures dropping dramatically all around the state by the end of the month. Ski areas in the mountain ranges generally have snow from December through March. Winter in Erie and throughout most of northwestern Pennsylvania can be forbiddingly cold, with heavy snow squalls between November and February.

■ GETTING THERE AND AROUND

■ BY AIR

Philadelphia International Airport (PHL) is served by most major air carriers. The airport is 7 miles from downtown Philadelphia and is accessible from I-76, I-95, and I-476. SEPTA trains run between the airport and downtown, *8800 Essington Avenue; 215-937-6937; www.phl.org.*

Pittsburgh International Airport (PIT), served by most major carriers, is the northeastern hub for US Airways. The airport is accessible to downtown via Route 60 and I-279 South. *1000 Airport Boulevard; 412-472-3525; www.pitairport.com.*

■ BY CAR

The main driving routes through Pennsylvania are I-79, running between West Virginia and Erie in the western portion of the state; and I-80, running between the Ohio border and New Jersey. The Pennsylvania Turnpike (I-76) runs between New Jersey and Ohio, passing through some of the state's most beautiful territory.

■ BY TRAIN

Amtrak. Philadelphia is one of the cities on Amtrak's Northeast Corridor route; trains arrive here from New York, Boston, Baltimore, Washington, D.C., and other cities. Amtrak also provides service to Pittsburgh, Harrisburg, and other cities in central and western Pennsylvania. *800-872-7245; www.amtrak.com.*

■ BY BUS

Greyhound has the greatest number of scheduled bus routes in the state and has long-distance service to New York, Boston, Washington, D.C., and beyond. *800-231-2222; www.greyhound.com.*

PATransit. Port Authority Transit has bus routes throughout the Allegheny County region, many beginning in Pittsburgh. *412-566-5500; www.portauthority.org.*

■ FOOD

Pittsburgh and Philadelphia have many Italian restaurants. Philadelphia is famous for cheesesteaks, and Pittsburgh is famous for its Primanti Brothers sandwiches (cheesesteaks and others), which come with fries and cole slaw inside—yes, inside— the bun. In Pennsylvania Dutch country, you can savor chicken rivel soup (rivel being tiny dumplings, much like spaetzle). Slavic dishes like sauerkraut and kielbasa are popular in western Pennsylvania, as are the two-fisted sandwiches known as hoagies (called submarines elsewhere), a holdover from the days when steel workers toted these in lunch pails.

Hershey, the nation's biggest chocolate producer is in the southeast, as are Benzel's (Altoona) and Julius Sturgis (Lititz) pretzel makers and Herr's Snack Food Factory (Nottingham), which manufactures potato chips and other treats. The state's breweries include Rolling Rock (Latrobe), Yuengling (Pottsville), and Stoudt (Adamstown). Most Pennsylvania wineries are in the Lake Erie region, but there are also vineyards in the Brandywine and Lehigh valleys and even near Gettysburg.

■ LODGING

Hotels and motels throughout the state, both chain properties and independents, range from plain and ordinary to four- or five-star affairs. The most luxurious accommodations are in Pittsburgh and Philadelphia, but almost anywhere you can find Victorian-era mansions or country estates that have been converted into bed-and-breakfast inns. Many of these lodgings are quite affordable, and in most cases proprietors will go out of their way to guarantee a pleasant stay, offering hearty breakfasts and afternoon tea in addition to lunch and dinner menus that please even the most discriminating gourmands.

Country clubs, with spas, gyms, hiking trails, and tennis or golf facilities, are common in the southeast and northeast. Many of these lodgings can be expensive, but there are bargains all over, so it pays to search for a deal. Some country clubs do not have an on-site restaurant, so make sure to ask about dining options before committing to a stay.

You can book rooms and find out about inns all over the state on the **Pennsylvania Bed and Breakfasts** (www.bnbfinder.com) Web site.

■ HOTEL AND MOTEL CHAINS
Best Western. *800-528-1234; www.bestwestern.com.*
Choice Hotels. *800-424-6423; www.choicehotels.com*
Days Inn. *800-325-2525; www.daysinn.com.*
Doubletree. *800-222-8733; www.hilton.com.*
Embassy Suites. *800-362-2779; www.embassysuites.com.*
Four Seasons Hotels and Resorts. *800-819-5053; www.fourseasons.com.*
Hampton Inn. *800-426-7866; www.hamptoninn.com*
Hilton Hotels. *800-445-8667; www.hilton.com.*
Holiday Inn. *800-465-4329; www.6c.com.*
Hyatt Hotels. *800-233-1234; www.hyatt.com.*
La Quinta. *800-531-5900; www.laquinta.com.*
Marriott. *800-228-9290; www.marriott.com.*
Quality Inns. *800-228-5151; www.qualityinn.com.*
Radisson. *800-333-3333; www.radisson.com.*
Ramada Inns. *800-272-6232; www.ramada.com.*
Sheraton. *800-325-3535; www.sheraton.com.*
Westin Hotels. *800-228-3000; www.westin.com.*

An Amish hat shop.

■ CAMPING

From the beaches of Lake Erie to the Amish farmlands and the scenic Pocono
Mountains, Pennsylvania is one of America's great back-to-nature destinations.
Many campgrounds are open year-round and most have cabin and boat rentals,
picnic shelters, and electrical outlets. For more information about camping in
Pennsylvania, visit www.pacamping.com or contact the **Pennsylvania Campground
Owners Association** (610-767-5026).

■ OFFICIAL TOURISM INFORMATION

Allegheny Mountains. *800-842-5866; www.alleghenymountains.com.*
Armstrong County. *800-265-9954; www.armstrongcounty.com.*
Beaver County. *800-342-8192; www.beaver.pa.us.*
Brandywine. *800-343-3983; www.brandywinecvb.org.*
Butler County. *800-741-6772; www.butlercountychamber.com.*
Erie Area. *800-542-3743; www.eriepa.com.*
Gettysburg. *800-337-5015; www.gettysburg.com.*

Laurel Highlands. *800-925-7669; www.laurelhighlands.org.*
Lehigh Valley. *800-747-0561; www.lehighvalleypa.org.*
Mercer County. *800-637-2370; www.mercercountypa.org.*
Penn State Country. *800-358-5466; www.visitpennstate.org.*
Pennsylvania Dutch. *800-723-8824; www.padutchcountry.com.*
Pennsylvania Tourism. *800-847-4872; www.experiencepa.com.*
Philadelphia. *800-575-7676; www.pcvb.org.*
Pittsburgh. *800-366-0093; www.visitpittsburgh.com.*
Pocono Mountains. *800-762-6667; www.800poconos.com.*
Washington County. *800-531-4114; www.washpatourism.org.*

■ USEFUL WEB SITES

City Papers. Philadelphia and Pittsburgh weeklies have news, features, and events listings. *www.pghcitypaper.com and www.citypaper.net.*

Factory Tours in Pennsylvania. Learn about fun and interesting factories and how to visit them. *www.factorytoursinpa.com.*

Pennsylvania Hunting & Fishing. Places to go, plus resources and links. *www.pahuntandfish.com.*

Philadelphia. Glossy mag's online site has great "Best of" lists. *www.phillymag.com*

Philadelphia History. Informative site highlights city history with stories about people, neighborhoods, and events. *www.ushistory.org/philadelphia.*

Philadelphia Inquirer. Site of city's biggest daily newspaper. *www.philly.com.*

Pittsburgh. Monthly magazine has features about the town, plus arts, dining, and other listings. *www.wqed.org/magazine*

Pittsburgh Post-Gazette. Daily newspaper's site. *www.post-gazette.com.*

Pittsburgh Regional History Center. History and culture of western Pennsylvania. *www.pghhistory.org.*

Western Pennsylvania Museum Council. Learn about unique museums throughout the state. *www.westernpamuseums.org.*

■ FESTIVALS AND EVENTS

■ JANUARY
Mummers Parade, Philadelphia. The festive Mummers strut their stuff through Center City on New Year's Day. *215-336-3050.*

■ FEBRUARY
Groundhog Day Celebration, Gobbler's Knob, Punxsutawney. *800-752-7445.*

■ MARCH
Charter Day. Commemorate the granting of Pennsylvania's charter to William Penn: Ambridge (724-266-4500); Fort Washington (215-591-5250).

Pennsylvania National Arts and Crafts Show, Harrisburg. Juried show of ceramics, fine art, jewelry, baskets, clothing, and furniture. *717-761-3116.*

Philadelphia Flower Show. Floral displays and contests. *215-988-8888.*

■ APRIL
New Wilmington Quilt Auction. Wilmington Grange. *724-946-2425.*

Philadelphia Furniture and Furnishings Show. The Pennsylvania Convention Center hosts juried showcases for handcrafted furniture and crafts. *215-440-0718.*

World International Beer Festival, Lake Harmony. *570-722-9111.*

■ MAY
City of Pittsburgh Marathon. Point State Park. *412-647-7866.*

Pennsylvania Arts & Crafts Country Festival, Fayette County Fairgrounds. Memorial Day weekend. *724-863-4577.*

■ JUNE
Kutztown Festival. Arts, crafts, and Pennsylvania Dutch cooking. *888-674-6136.*

Manayunk Arts Festival. Outdoor arts and crafts. *215-842-9565.*

Three Rivers Arts Festival, Pittsburgh. Arts, music, dance, food. *412-281-8723.*

Welcome America, Philadelphia. Celebrate America's birthday in America's birthplace. *800-770-5883.*

■ JULY

Fourth of July at the Point, Pittsburgh. Fireworks and concert. *412-255-2493.*

July 4 in Washington Crossing Historic Park, Philadelphia. Military re-creations, a mock trial of a British spy, open-hearth cooking. *215-493-4076.*

■ AUGUST

Gettysburg Bluegrass Festival. Four days of concerts. *717-642-8749.*

Johnstown Folkfest, Cambria County. Burgers and bluegrass. *814-539-1889.*

■ SEPTEMBER

Covered Bridge Festival, Washington County. Country-style foods, arts and crafts. *724-228-5520.*

Eisenhower World War II Weekend, Eisenhower National Historic Site, Gettysburg. See Allied tanks and hear war veterans' stories. *717-338-9114.*

Mushroom Festival, Kennett Square. Music, arts, and mushrooms. *888-440-9920.*

North East Wine Fest, Erie County. Wine tastings. *814-725-4262.*

Water Works Arts and Crafts Festival, Philadelphia. Arts and crafts booths, live music, a merry-go-round. *www.parkalacarte.com.*

■ OCTOBER

Fort Ligonier Days, Ligonier. Commemorates the battle at the fort. *724-238-4200.*

Great Pumpkin Event, Chadds Ford. Artists carve pumpkins. *610-388-7376.*

■ NOVEMBER

Clayton Holiday Tours, Pittsburgh. Frick house tours. *412-371-0600.*

Overly's Country Christmas, Westmoreland Fairgrounds. See 800,000 lights blaze away at this drive-through display. *800-968-3759.*

■ DECEMBER

Christmas at Old Economy Village, Ambridge. The Beaver County home of the Harmonists holds a two-day event in early December. *724-266-1803.*

Reenactment of Washington's Crossing, Washington Crossing. *215-493-4076.*

I N D E X

COMPASS AMERICAN GUIDES

Alaska	Las Vegas	San Francisco
American Southwest	Maine	Santa Fe
Arizona	Manhattan	South Carolina
Boston	Michigan	South Dakota
Chicago	Minnesota	Southern New England
Coastal California	Montana	Tennessee
Colorado	Nevada	Texas
Florida	New Hampshire	Utah
Georgia	New Mexico	Vermont
Gulf South: Louisiana, Alabama, Mississippi	New Orleans	Virginia
	North Carolina	Wine Country
Hawaii	Oregon	Wisconsin
Idaho	Pacific Northwest	Wyoming
Kentucky	Pennsylvania	

Compass American Guides are available at special discounts for bulk purchases for sales promotions or premiums. Special editions, including personalized covers, excerpts of existing guides, and corporate imprints, can be created in large quantities for special needs. For more information, contact your local bookseller or write to Special Markets, Fodor's Travel Publications, 1745 Broadway, New York, NY 10019. Inquiries from Canada should be directed to your local Canadian bookseller or sent to Random House of Canada, Ltd., Marketing Department, 2775 Matheson Boulevard East, Mississauga, Ontario L4W 4P7. Inquiries from the United Kingdom should be sent to Fodor's Travel Publications, 20 Vauxhall Bridge Road, London, England SW1V 2SA.

ACKNOWLEDGMENTS

■ AUTHOR'S ACKNOWLEDGMENTS

Every book-writing journey begins in a wilderness where the author is lost and wandering. I was fortunate to have found the wise and patient editor of the first edition, Kit Duane, who saw promise in my Pennsylvania experience and set me on a path toward a worthwhile book. The father of a dear friend, Ronald Tardio of Lansdale, also helped me along the way. A Pittsburgher transplanted to Philadelphia, he knows the eastern part of this state in the same way he knows his family—with his heart.

Dozens of times in the researching of this book I found my bearings with the help of local librarians, university historians, and historical society volunteers. A few went out of their way to assist me in bringing tall tales down to truthful size. Among them: the staffs of the Easton and Lancaster libraries. I also gratefully acknowledge the assistance of the National Park Service rangers of Independence Hall National Historical Park, who allowed access to buildings undergoing renovation. I also want to recognize the assistance of workers in the Pennsylvania Department of Community and Economic Development and Barbara C. Chaffee, executive director of the Pennsylvania Center for Travel, Tourism, and Film. I am grateful to other Visitors and Convention Bureau workers across the state but especially to Lucinda Hampton of the Pennsylvania Dutch Convention and Visitors Bureau who brought a lifetime's experience living among the Amish to bear on my writing.

And many thanks to my father, my seven brothers and sisters, and my friends, who graciously accepted my work on this book as an excuse for missed phone calls and late arrivals.

■ PUBLISHER'S ACKNOWLEDGMENTS

Compass American Guides would like to thank Randall H. Cooley and the Allegheny Heritage Development Corporation for making this project possible. Special thanks are also due to Mark Biddle and Stephen Elkins of the Independence Hall Association for their help. We would also like to thank Marc Kravitz and Loriann Hoff Oberlin for updating the text of this edition, Richard Lowe, Allen Kuharski, Georgia Breza, and Pauline Mangin for additional editorial contributions, Rachel Elson for copyediting the manuscript, and Ellen Klages for proofreading it.

All photographs in this book are by Jerry Irwin unless noted below. Compass American Guides would like to thank the following individuals or institutions (from Pennsylvania unless noted otherwise) for the use of their illustrations or photographs:

Compass American Guides would like to thank the following institutions and individuals for the use of their photographs, illustrations, or both: **Abby Aldrich Rockefeller Folk Art Center,** p. 100; **Allegheny Forest National Vacation Bureau,** p. 263; **Atwater Kent Museum of Philadelphia, Historical Society of Pennsylvania Collection,** 21; **Justina C. Barrett,** p. 172; **Bucks County Visitors Bureau,** p. 117; **Carnegie Library of Pittsburgh,** p. 36; **Cumberland County Historical Society, Carlisle,** p. 169; **Family Communications, Inc.,** p. 219 (photo by Walter Seng); **Fonthill Library,** p. 111 (Barry Halkin); **Free Library of Philadelphia Rare Book Department,** p. 23; **Frick Art and Historical Center,** p. 233 (Ken Love); **Granger Collection, New York,** p. 212; **Greater Philadelphia Tourism Marketing Corporation,** pp. 50, 71, 79, and 88 (Bob Krist); **Heritage Center Museum, Lancaster,** pp. 128, 129, 134; **Hershey Entertainment and Resorts,** p. 141; **Historical Society of Western Pennsylvania, Library and Archives Division, Pittsburgh,** pp. 213, 214, 251; **Independence Seaport Museum,** p. 69 (John F. Williams); **Johnstown Area Heritage Association,** p. 257; **Kimmel Center for the Performing Arts,** pp. 52–53 (Jeff Goldberg), 76 and 78 (Roman Viñoly); **Kittochitinny Historical Society,** p. 190; **Library of Congress,** pp. 31, 35, 89, 215, 216, 229; **Library of Congress, Geography and Map Division,** pp. 43, 45; **Library of Congress, Prints and Photographs Division,** p. 28 (LC-USZ62–112159); **Library of Congress Prints and Photographs Division, Farm Security Administration–Office of War Information Photograph Collection,** p. 25 (LC-USF34-082411E); **Library of Congress Rare Book and Special Collections Division,** p. 164; **Laurence Loewy,** p. 164; **Daniel Mangin,** p. 60; **Mattress Factory,** p. 235; **National Archives,** p. 181 (220-TMI-42-2785-29); **National Center for the American Revolution/Valley Forge Historical Society,** p. 30; **National Museum of American History,** p. 218; **New York Public Library,** pp. 26, 49; **Old Print Shop, New York,** p. 269; **Penn's Cave,** p. 206; **Pennsylvania Dutch Convention and Visitors Bureau,** pp. 123, 127, 137 (Keith Baum); **Pennsylvania Historical and Museum Commission,** p. 196; **Pennsylvania Historical and Museum Commission, Drake Well Museum, Titusville,** p. 275; **Philadelphia Convention and Visitors Bureau,** pp. 14 (Edward Savaria Jr.), 61 (Nick Kelsh), 75 (Jim McWilliams); **Philadelphia Museum of Art,** pp. 16 (collection of Edgar William and Bernice Chrysler Garbisch), 44, 131; **Phipps Conservatory and Botanical Gardens,** p. 234; **Pocono Mountains Vacation Bureau,** p. 159 (Bob Krist); **Shelburne Museum,** p. 18; **State Museum of Pennsylvania,** pp. 108, 197; **Valley Forge National Historic Park,** p. 92; **Wood Street Galleries,** p. 224 (William D. Wade); **Westmoreland Museum of American Art,** pp. 243 (gift of Robert J. Hudson), 247 (gift of Thomas Lynch Fund), 250 (gift of J. Howard Iams).

■ ABOUT THE AUTHOR

A graduate of Pennsylvania State University, Douglas Root has written for several newspapers, including *The Pittsburgh Press*. He received an Alicia Patterson Foundation fellowship for documentary journalism, and he has written for *Time*, the *Washington Post*, *Washingtonian*, the *Philadelphia Inquirer*, and *Mother Jones*. He lives in Pittsburgh.

■ ABOUT THE PHOTOGRAPHER

A Lancaster County resident, Jerry Irwin is a nationally recognized photographer known especially for his images of the Amish. His photo essays have appeared in *National Geographic*, *Life*, *Country Journal*, German and French *GEO*, and numerous other publications. A former locomotive engineer with the old Pennsylvania Railroad, Irwin has also been an active skydiver for three decades.